BECKETT, MODERNISM AN
IMAGINATIC

Steven Connor, one of the most influential critics of twentieth-century literature and culture working today, has spent much of his career writing and thinking about Samuel Beckett. This book presents Connor's finest published work on Beckett, with fresh essays that explore how Beckett has shaped major themes in modernism and twentieth-century literature. Through discussions of sport, nausea, slowness, flies, the radio switch, tape, religion and academic life, Connor shows how Beckett's writing is characteristic of a distinctively mundane or worldly modernism, arguing that it is well attuned to our current concern with the stressed relations between the human and natural worlds. Through Connor's analysis, Beckett's prose, poetry and dramatic works animate a modernism profoundly concerned with life, worldly existence and the idea of the world as such. Lucid, provocative, wide ranging and richly informed by critical and cultural theory, this new book from Steven Connor is required reading for anyone teaching or studying Beckett, modernism and twentieth-century literary studies.

STEVEN CONNOR is Grace 2 Professor of English and Fellow of Peterhouse, University of Cambridge. He is the author of many books in the fields of literature, philosophy and culture, including *Samuel Beckett: Repetition, Theory and Text* (1988, 2nd edn. 1993), which remains one of the most influential titles in Beckett studies.

BECKETT, MODERNISM AND THE MATERIAL IMAGINATION

STEVEN CONNOR

University of Cambridge

CAMBRIDGE
UNIVERSITY PRESS

CAMBRIDGE
UNIVERSITY PRESS

32 Avenue of the Americas, New York, NY 10013-2473, USA

Cambridge University Press is part of the University of Cambridge.

It furthers the University's mission by disseminating knowledge in the pursuit of
education, learning and research at the highest international levels of excellence.

www.cambridge.org
Information on this title: www.cambridge.org/9781107629110

© Steven Connor 2014

First published 2014

A catalog record for this publication is available from the British Library.

Library of Congress Cataloging in Publication Data
Connor, Steven, 1955–
Beckett, modernism and the material imagination / Steven Connor,
University of Cambridge.
pages cm
Includes bibliographical references.
ISBN 978-1-107-05922-1 (hardback)
1. Beckett, Samuel, 1906–1989 – Criticism and interpretation.
2. Modernism (Literature) I. Title.
PR6003.E282Z62115 2014
848'.91409–dc23 2014002498

ISBN 978-1-107-05922-1 Hardback
ISBN 978-1-107-62911-0 Paperback

Contents

CHAPTER I

Introduction: Beckett's Finitude

For many writers, Samuel Beckett becomes a kind of life sentence. There are art historians who spend their lives studying Michelangelo and musicologists who devote themselves similarly to Donizetti, but it seems to me that in no other discipline is there quite the same kind of relationship of lifelong indenture to an artistic subject as there is in literary criticism. Perhaps it has something to do with the sharing of the medium between writer and critic, the twinning and braiding of their sentences. If one feels Beckett's sentence forms inveigling themselves into one's own, then one is in good company. J. M. Coetzee and John Banville had the same experience. I once heard Banville explain that he needed to get clean by not reading Beckett for several weeks before starting to write, lest Beckett's cadences insinuate themselves – I have to tell him that it has never worked. It is really like an addiction, a making over of and through the words one uses to speak of these words.

Authors who shape your lifeworld in this way can start to take on the shape of the world as such, becoming a kind of mythos or forming fantasy. Like W. H. Auden's Edward Lear, Beckett 'became a land' to which we 'swarm like settlers' (Auden 1976: 149). There are certain other authors who attain to this status, who, by bequeathing a world, became it – William Shakespeare is one, Jane Austen another and Charles Dickens another still.

My relationship with the mythical world of Beckett has always been a difficult one. It has always been easier for me to try to break away from the fantasy than to bury myself in it, but the rhythm of relapse and resumption in Beckett's work itself seems to predict and proscribe my return to his work. After I published *Samuel Beckett: Repetition, Theory and Text* in 1988, I thought I could show myself that I could get away from Beckett by writing a series of books that didn't seem to have much to do with him, with indexes in which he was scarcely mentioned. But the fact that readers wondered where the Beckett chapter was in a book I wrote on ventriloquism (2000), or another on the skin (2003) or another on the intimate life of things

(2011a) seems to be an indication that for me the longest way around has always been the shortest way home. I even found myself having limbered up for writing books on things like air (2010) and sport (2011b) by writing about these topics in Beckett's work. Where I had not done this, I found myself retrospectively rectifying the anomaly, with an essay on flies in Beckett's work as a pendant to a little book on the fly (2006b). I have on many occasions tried to leave the house of Mr Beckett, thinking that, having arrived on the bottom floor and scrubbed and skivvied my way to the top, the time would come to close the door behind me and head out onto the road. But my journey has always seemed to wind back to the back door of Mr Beckett's house; Beckett – that again. So it goes, it seems, in and out of the world of Beckett studies. It is probably apt, then, that the essays I have brought together here should actually have, as one of their unifying concerns, the question of worlds, worlding and worldliness.

What is to be done with Beckett? At one time, the answer to this question might have been, to borrow the title of Simon Critchley's book (mostly) on Beckett, 'very little, almost nothing' (1997). When I began thinking and writing about Beckett in the late 1980s, his work seemed like an anomalous or residual thing. It was plain that he had something to do with modernism. His close association with James Joyce and with some of the leading forms of literary avant-gardism – for example with the magazine *transition* – and his relentless efforts to reinvent the forms of literary expression seemed to make him an exemplary modernist. And yet, in his strange, obsessive introversion and in the difficulty of generalising his innovations, Beckett seemed also to be awkwardly indigestible to modernism.

And then, for a while during the 1980s and 1990s, it seemed to make more sense for critics to use Beckett's works to make the case for some kind of break within modernism, moving beyond the forms of order and authority represented by high and classic modernism into a world of unlimited contingency. Indeed, for a time, Beckett became the exemplary postmodernist, according to the following formula: where modernism turned from the world in the effort to create a second-order world of art, postmodernism pluralised this act of world-making. Under postmodernism, neither the historical world nor the world of art could stand entire; there could only be multiple ways of world-making, in Nelson Goodman's influential phrase (1978). Slowly, but decisively, the answer to the question of what was to be done with Beckett changed: now, it seemed, the answer was 'almost anything'. But there has always been something strained about the attempt to associate the straitened means and subjects of Beckett's work with the opulent pluralising and opening out of sensibility that was held to be characteristic of postmodernism. Fissure and indeterminacy may be at the heart of Beckett's writing, but then so are impediment and aporia. The lessness of Beckett's work always seemed to sit askew with the openness of what postmodernism was thought to be.

Nowadays, this kind of claim is heard much less often, no doubt an effect of the generalised decompression of the very idea of the postmodern. One expression of the deposing of Beckett from the position of exemplary postmodernist is the place accorded to him in the work of Alain Badiou, as part of his assault upon many of the leading principles of postmodernism, though usually without caring to name them as such. Really, this amounts to an effort to rescue Beckett from association with the sort of liberal pluralism characteristic of the post-Marxist politics of postmodernism. The Beckett of whom we read in Badiou's work is no longer playful but militantly earnest, no longer agitated by contingency but intent and unswerving in his devotion to the most austere of philosophical projects. In one sense, this returns Beckett to a kind of modernism, while at the same time reconstituting the idea of the modern in the form represented by Beckett – now shown to be bent on the aim, close to Badiou's own, of asserting the condition of pure Being. It is in the very strength of Badiou's reading – in its capacity to find in Beckett a sort of philosophical potency – that its weakness, in my view, is to be seen. By contrast, the forms of strong weakness in Beckett's work animate and preoccupy the essays in this volume.

Badiou's philosophy makes two principal and somewhat oddly ill-assorted claims. The first is the argument for a mathematical ontology based around the principle of the infinite. The second is the idea of the event. Badiou believes that mathematics has been shunted away from its position as the determining power of philosophy by what he calls Romanticism, by which he really means the 'temporalization of the concept' introduced by Hegel (Badiou 2010: 40), the idea that philosophical concepts may be embedded in and emerge from historical circumstances, rather than bestriding or standing haughtily aside from them. Unlike many others, Badiou does not identify Romanticism with the principle of expansion beyond every limit; instead, he identifies it with the 'theme of finitude' (Badiou 2010: 39) – perhaps since to identify a particular concept or argument with the contingencies of a historical situation, one must always put a limit on its validity and application. More broadly, Badiou identifies Romanticism with the 'commandeering of being by the one' (Badiou 2010: 42), by which he means the tendency to regard reality as multiple in its appearances but single in its essence. Another, more familiar name for this is Platonism, rather than Romanticism, and it is a little puzzling to find

Badiou bracketing Romanticism and Platonism through their shared commitment to finitude, since the finitude in question seems to be different in each case. Romanticism may be identified with historical finitude, expressed through the historicist reduction of thinking to thinking for the time being and 'the sophistical tyranny of language' (Badiou 2010: 40). Badiou offers a complicated argument that the mourning generated by historical finitude, or 'co-extensiveness with time' (Badiou 2010: 28), produces a pathos which continues to hold open the place of God: 'As long as finitude remains the ultimate determination of existence, God abides. He abides as that which continues to hold sway over us, in the form of the abandonment, the dereliction, or the leaving-behind of Being' (Badiou 2010: 28).

If Romanticism is to be identified with historical finitude, then Platonism may be identified with metaphysical finitude, expressed through the reduction of the thinking of Being to an idea of the One. Romanticism and a certain reading of Platonism converge for Badiou, because of his commitment to the principle that being is intrinsically multiple and never without violence or cowardly acquiescence to be reduced to oneness. Badiou pledges his whole philosophy on the contemporary form of Platonic truth found, he maintains, in mathematics and, in particular, the mathematics of set theory and the centrality in it of the secular reality of the infinite. For Badiou, mathematics is emphatically the warrant of the Platonic claim that 'it is the same to think and to be' (Badiou 2010: 52). As a Platonist, Badiou stands in the mainstream of modern mathematics and against the pragmatic and relativising tendencies of both Continental philosophy and Anglo-American pragmatism.

However, it is not his mathematical Platonism that seems to give Badiou's philosophy traction among readers who seemingly only yesterday were convinced of the unarguable validity of historicism, the constitutive role of language in thought and the violent reductiveness of Platonic metaphysics; rather, it is Badiou's idea of the event. Convinced of the necessity of infinite thought, Badiou is committed to what he calls 'truth', though it is clear that he means by this something like 'force', and not Habermas's 'unforced force of the better argument' (Habermas 1996: 306) but the enforced force of that which refuses to be reduced to the condition of a mere argument. This kind of truth can be guaranteed, Badiou thinks, not by any kind of correspondence with the way things are, but rather by the most radical kind of break with it, because the way things are is always equivalent to *doxa* for Badiou, or its maximisation in the form of what he calls 'the State', by which he means not only every kind of existing political dispensation, but also all stable states of affairs and opinions whatsoever. The name of truth can be given only to a fidelity to whatever breaks absolutely with such states of affairs. So this is not a Platonism that can be embodied in a Republic built around the eternal Ideas, rather, it is formed from a force of radical fission, which resists being reduced to any such finite embodiment. The distinctive character of Badiou's philosophy is to be found in this extraordinary blending of an absolute and authoritarian Platonic metaphysics with its apparent commitment to radical revolution.

Badiou's reading of Beckett no doubt derives much of its force from his recruitment of Beckett to this glamorous and exciting politics of absolute break, revelatory and revolutionary all at once. I suggest in Chapter 9, 'Beckett's Low Church', that, for all Badiou's insistence on the atheism of his position, it draws powerfully and hungrily on the more voluptuously austere forms of religious cathexis. The Beckett who pledges himself to the event is a Beckett of pure and charismatic radicalism. But those who are attracted to Badiou's radicalism, in some cases, one suspects, on the rebound from the very different radicalism of Jean-François Lyotard, Jacques Derrida and Gilles Deleuze, may be inclined to minimise or overlook the authoritarian absolutism and the drastically unworldly, even otherworldly, abstraction to which his anti-liberalism seems to tend.

The most embarrassingly incoherent part of Badiou's argument is the way in which his infinitist metaphysics is supposed to underpin his politics. For all his opposition to the One, Badiou depends upon a wildly implausible reduction of states of affairs to oneness – to that capitalised, rounded-up condition that he is wont to call the State – for his idea of the radical break represented by the event to work. Indeed, Badiou's demanding dream of the absolute exceptionality of events logically depends upon the prior constitution as absolutely homogeneous of the states of affairs from which events diverge, because only this secures the possibility that events could be *absolutely* divergent from them. If Badiou's ontology is opposed to 'the power of a count, a counting-as-one' (Badiou 2010: 41), the cult of the event absolutely requires the egregious counting-as-one constituted in the idea of the State. If the pre-existing situation were in fact the kind of undetermined multiplicity that Badiou's mathematical ontology requires, given that 'situations are nothing more, in their being, than pure indifferent multiplicities' (Badiou 2007: xi), and so could not be counted as one, then there could be no kind of event that could be guaranteed to be discontinuous with every possible element of that unaccounted-for multiplicity or to be, in Badiou's terms, 'an exception to any preconstituted predicate of the situation in which that truth is deployed' (Badiou 2007: xiii). Something cannot come absolutely out of the blue, unless you are sure that it is the blue that it has come out of. If there are constituents of the blue of which you have not taken account, which must be the case with a situation that is purely multiple and irreducible to any kind of entity, then they might very well turn out to be smoothly continuous with, and even determining of, what seems to have broken out spontaneously in the form of the event.

What is more, given that any emergent historical condition that breaks with a prior condition itself adds something to what it breaks from – in the way, for example, the idea of the Victorian is in some sense defined by the modernism that defines itself in its departure from Victorianism or the way modernism itself is given a certain definition by the hypothesis of the postmodern – we might say that the Badiouan event can never in fact be entirely unrelated to that from which it departs, since it must always form a relation by its very divergence. An absolute break could never be a break *from* anything at all. In the casual-hysterical reduction of the complex, interlocking circumstances of world economics and politics to that ultimate count-as-one of the Romantic Left, 'Capital', Badiou's fanatical infinitism comes close to infantilism (one does not need to deny the existence of any of the myriad components of what is called capitalism to be reasonably dubious that they are all the expression of a unified and self-directing world system). There are many, many things in the world that are in need of remedy, but they are, alas, not reducible to a One, from which a once-and-for-all and absolute break might be made.

Badiou's argument is that Beckett's work 'goes from a programme of the One – obstinate trajectory or interminable soliloquy – to the pregnant theme of the Two, which opens out onto infinity' (Badiou 2003a: 17). The 'event' in Beckett's work takes the form of a breaking open of the linguistically centred solipsism of his work up to *Texts for Nothing* by the force of a kind of love, defined as the 'interval in which a sort of inquiry about the world is pursued to infinity' (Badiou 2003a: 67). What is here sentimentality modulates elsewhere into a kind of forcing on to Beckett's writing of a sort of transfiguration, for example, in these remarks about *Watt*:

> At this juncture, thought awakens to something completely different than the vain grasp of its own predestination – not to mention the torture elicited by the imperative of the word. By means of hypotheses and variations, thought will therefore seek to bring its knowledge of the 'indeterminable purport' of incidents to the height of their 'formal brilliance'. This formal brilliance designates the unique and circumscribed character, the eventual clarity, the pure and delectable 'emergence' of the incidents in question. (Badiou 2003a: 56–7)

All this completeness, uniqueness and purity, the libido of absoluteness that constantly erupts through Badiou's religiose readings of Beckett, seems to me to be utterly at odds with the stubbornly sustained approximating of Beckett's writing. I hope that the tendency of the essays gathered here, even if it was not their conscious aim, is to make less compelling all the forms of infinitism – whether represented by Badiou or found in the lexicon of the illimitable governing forms of postmodernist theory to which Beckett's work has given comfort – and to make a case for Beckett's radical finitude. This involves the recognition that Beckett's work must always come up short of a philosophical assertion and certainly must recoil from anything like the constitution of an ontology, a statement of the nature of being, that can add up to a full and remainderless saying of being, or being of saying, or saying of the being of saying. I call Beckett's finitude radical, not because it takes absolute or ultimate forms, but because it imposes a limit on radicalism itself, even and especially on the kind of bracing, yet comforting absoluteness represented by Badiou and his followers.

'What kind of imagination is this so reason-ridden?' the narrating voice of *Company* asks itself, of itself, and promptly, resignedly, gives itself the reply: 'A kind of its own' (Beckett 1989: 27). The phrase translates the Latin slogan *sui generis*. Put in set-theoretical terms, it identifies the singleton set, the set with only one member. But of course, such a set will always form part of the set of such singular sets, the general category of ungeneralisable categories. The general condition is a condition in which no generality is possible, or at least knowable.

Thinking about the nature of finitude in Beckett's work often centres on the faculty he calls the 'imagination', which alternates between the visionary inheritance of Romanticism and a much more limited, often almost mechanical, faculty conceived as the power of forming images. For Beckett, imagination is not a spontaneously indwelling and upwelling power, but a strenuous and exhausting labour that comes close to the ideas of staging, seeing through or putting into practice. 'A voice comes to one in the dark. Imagine' begins *Company*, inaugurating the stern imperative maintained through the text of making possibility actual, of rendering things finite. Although often credited in the Romantic tradition as the power that promises transcendence of the merely finite world, Beckett's imagination is typically described as defective and itself in need of being imagined. This task is strangely insistent. Even when imagination seems to have expired altogether, it represents just another task of imagining: 'Imagination Dead Imagine', an imagination that is completely dead and done for, just imagine what that could be like. 'Imagination at wit's end spreads its sad wings', we read in *Ill Seen Ill Said* (Beckett 1989: 65). Knowing that the imagination in question is an unusually, even grotesquely, reason-ridden affair may help to explain how imagination, traditionally the antagonist or enlarger of wit, might be said to be at its own wit's end, but this does not provide much help in understanding the kinds of wings it might seek to rise on. Indeed, we are told only that the wings are spread, not that they assist in any kind of elevation – which could well be the source of their sadness. And, of course, imagination can have or take wing only by an act of imagining, as it has here in fact in the hobbled form of a rather fatigued and lumbering cliché, even if it is the conspicuous leadenness of the phrase which deploys it that gives it its sardonic lift. The imagination in Beckett's work is always a material imagination, always on the alert against its own tendency to levitate or refine itself out of existence, while Beckett is himself strongly attuned to the gaseous correlates of the mental faculties (Connor 2006a).

Repeatedly, I have found in Beckett's work resources for thinking about a specifically material or finite kind of imagination, an imagination that performs the traditional duty of taking us beyond the merely given or present at hand but does so in ways that seem designed to keep us on terms with its materiality, even as that materiality is itself something still to be imagined. If, for example, radio seems to offer to Beckett the attractions of a purely abstract, purely imaginary kind of art, it nevertheless remains specifically and unignorably material. Radio embodies the condition of situation without site. Chapter 5, 'I Switch Off', explores the importance in Beckett's work of radio apparatus and the corresponding intuition that radio itself constitutes a kind of apparatus that is neither fully specifiable nor dispensable, neither quite there nor not there. Chapter 6, 'Looping the Loop', explores the ways in which the semi-phantasmal matter of tape is similarly entangled in time and dream-eaten desire.

I aim through these readings of the different forms the material imagination takes in Beckett's work – the athletic imagination of effort, the imagination of slowness and speed, the imagination of the body grown literally sick of itself and the imagination of and through the technical and material apparatus of hearing and speaking – to intimate an alternative state or strain of the modern, which stresses its commitment to a kind of being in the world that must nevertheless eschew any sense of that world's, or that being's, simple inherence.

Modernism has two very different characters. There is, first of all, the modernism of expansion and experiment, a modernism that abolished the old and started out anew. This is a modernism characterised by an undoing and abandonment of what had seemed given in the past. It is a modernism that seems at times to operate in thin air, making itself and its world up as it goes along. Alongside the injunction to make it new, we might read the injunction to make it more.

Secondly, there is a modernism characterised by what Peter Sloterdijk has called 'explicitation', which I take to be closely related to my understanding of finitude. For Sloterdijk, explicitation means the process of bringing to conscious awareness and deliberate, overseen operation everything that might previously have been unconscious or part of the given in existence (Sloterdijk 2004: 87). In that this principle involves the rejection of reliance upon what is taken for granted and the desire to make articulate principles of functioning that had previously been taken for granted, it participates in the expansive, self-enlarging project of modernism. Whereas the principle of expansion detaches us from the world, the principle of explicitation returns us to it, for it depends upon the making manifest of forms of situation and limit. With the explicitation of climate, ecological functioning, genetics, neurology and the operations of language and information comes freedom, but also the anxiety of responsibility, as we come to 'depend on what depends on us', in Michel Serres's phrase (Serres 2009b: 36). As Serres has suggested, modernity has gone out into the world and has met itself on the other side (2009a: 5–14). Taking leave of the world, modernism has returned us and itself to it. I find in Beckett's work an exemplary case of this modernism in which excursion curves round into finitude. It is for this reason that the studies of different aspects of Beckett's writing assembled here recur in different ways in regard to the question of worldliness and to the question of the kind of world that Beckett's works constitute.

This kind of worldly modernism looks forward to the new, paradoxical kind of finitude we are encountering and learning to inhabit, in which we are forced as a kind of necessity to exercise what limited mastery we can, not only over the previously exterior world of nature, but also over ourselves, as the engine of a second nature that is both continuous and discontinuous with the first. Our finitude comes not only from our frailty or powerlessness but also from our powerlessness simply to wish away our power. Though Beckett of course offers no blueprint for the kind of extension of knowledge and technical capacity that is likely to continue to be both redemption and predicament, he does go further than most in setting out the extreme immanence required to live in this in-between condition – never at home in the world, but unable to be anywhere else than in the world we will henceforth, but as always, be constrained to make out for ourselves.

Beckett's writing encourages us to see a worldly modernism not just because it is itself worldly in the minor sense, taken up with the unredeemed bric-à-brac of existence – bodies, objects, habits, obsessions, oddities and impediments, along with what Badiou in his lordly way calls 'everything that makes us scurry about blindly on the desolate surface of the earth' (Badiou 2010: 71) – but also because it is so attuned to a larger vocation of making out a, or even the, world. Beckett is more faithful to what Beci Dobbin calls 'granular modernism' (2014) than to the supreme fictions of the heroic kind of modernism represented by William Butler Yeats, Wallace Stevens, Virginia Woolf, Ezra Pound and James Joyce. These essays suggest that Beckett's work will never sanction a letting go of the world. One of the forms of finitising with which Beckett has had no choice but to become entangled, as I try to show in Chapter 10, 'The Loutishness of Learning', is the grounding of modernism's grandeurs in the administering operations of academic life. For this kind of modernism, the world impends upon us as something to be materially imagined, not in the form of alternative worlds, but in terms of 'the world', experienced as a kind of demand for predication as yet without predicative content, as in the climactic moment of Harold Pinter's *The Birthday Party* when Goldberg attempts to explain his philosophy of life to his associate McCann: 'Never write down a thing. And don't go too near the water. And you'll find that what I say is true. Because I believe that the world . . . (*Vacant*) . . . . Because I believe that the world . . . (*Desperate*) . . . . BECAUSE I BELIEVE THAT THE WORLD . . . (*Lost*)' (Pinter 1991: 71–2).

A finitive modernism would be a modernism condemned to exert and – in the Sartrean sense I discuss in Chapter 3, 'The Nauseous Character of All Flesh' – transitively *exist* its freedom from God, from any kind of historical destiny or absolute guarantee, as a limit, coercion or compulsion. We are free, with a kind of carceral liberty, not because we are absolutely free to choose, but because the choice that we have no choice to make is free of absolute determination, in the sense that it lacks it. We are 'finitively' rather than definitively free because we are under a necessity of choosing things which we will never absolutely have had to choose.

If the assertion of a given historical essence or identity is one kind of evasion of this finite (because indefinite) freedom from determination, the identification with an absolute freedom, or illimitability, is another. The first hangs back from the finitude of freedom, hugging its dream of a determining past, in the hope that it can be relied upon to yield the inestimable boon of having no choice; the second accelerates past it into the fantasy of an entirely undetermined future. Finitude means the peculiar and painful mixture of freedom and coercion involved in accepting that we have no choice about our freedom, that our freedom is itself a limit on our fantasies of absolute determination, which leaves us wholly free of the burden of choice and absolute freedom, which leaves us wholly free of any limit. We cannot make what we like of the world; we can only make what *we* like of the world, without our knowing for sure what that is, while also suspecting that what we do will infallibly serve to make up our minds for us.

So, in the account of finitude developed and depended on in these essays, freedom and impediment are chiastically related. Rather than standing opposite each other, in a single, consistent plane, they produce and potentiate each other, such that we can never be sure whether they are continuous or discontinuous with each other. Finitude is not just a limit on our freedom, it is the limit *of* our freedom, the limit (on affirming our self-evident nature, destiny or being) represented by our incalculable freedom. The voice in Beckett's *The Unnamable* articulates modernism's relation to its past and its world. I am free to free myself from myself, but condemned to recognise that freedom as my very self, from which I will never be free. Modernism is the human freedom to make itself anew, against every given, in nature or history, twinned with the recognition that this self-making will have been its nature and history. Modernism means the necessity of making an insufficiently determined choice, using the knowledge that the world is not coextensive with knowledge.

Badiou makes out in Beckett's last substantial text, *Worstward Ho*, a kind of capsule metaphysics, assuring us that 'it is entirely possible to take *Worstward Ho* as a short philosophical treatise, as a treatment in shorthand of the question of being' (Badiou 2003a: 80). He continues: '[W]e can approach *Worstward Ho* conceptually without thereby betraying it. Since it allows us to put together a table of contents for the entirety of Beckett's work, it is entirely apposite to treat this text as if it were, above all, a network of thought or a shorthand of the question of being' (Badiou 2003a: 81). I suggest in these essays, by contrast, that for Beckett the condition of being is such that Being as such can never be. The question of being is everywhere being put, for this is being itself, 'Being' being the issueless issue for being. But being is never graspable by an ontology, least of all by an ontology of Dasein, or 'being-there', precisely because there is never quite a 'there' in Beckett's work – any more than there is ever a nowhere, or nicely immaculate null-and-void. One might perhaps say there is only 'here', wherever that here may happen to be, in a pure deixis without content or coordinates, that is equivalent to Goldberg's uncompleted predication 'that the world . . .'. As I suggest in Chapter 12, 'On Such and Such a Day . . . In Such a World', Beckett's radical finitude finds its form in the tip-of-the-tongue experience of the text 'What Is the Word', in which the word 'this' articulates the thisness of an intensely present sense of abeyance, an aching failure to appear that cannot by any shift be simply ignored or wished away. There is no way to evade the particularity of a being that never fully resides, and so is no kind of specifiable being-there, but rather a being-here, where the 'here' can never be any more than the 'this-here' – but never any less than it either. Beckett does not give us *Dasein*, but *Dies-sein*, not *being-there*, but *being-this*. Beckett's ontology is one that cannot speak its name, since ontology would betray the beingness of being into Being. However imperative it may be, being remains a low-down, low-church, lower-case matter for Beckett.

Beckett's work may be regarded as a finitising of philosophy, from a position that, if not inside it exactly, is not exactly exterior to it either. If Beckett's work is unmistakably philosophical, then it is in its philosophical disinclination to add up to, or amount to no more than, a philosophy. And if the question is asked, what kind of philosophy is it then, that will preserve, prolong or perfect us, for surely there must be such a thing?, the answer harboured by Beckett's work would be, no philosophy at all. This is not because we are under no circumstances to be preserved, prolonged or perfected, but only because it seems so sadly implausible to expect philosophy, of all things, to do that for us. (And no kind of art either, while we are about it, however detaining, astonishing or compelling it may be.) There could be no greater betrayal of the kind of worldly and worlding art that, in these pages, I take Beckett's to be, than to mistake it for the world, or to take it to be on its own formative of a world. I mean, for heaven's sake, or for the sake of the world that persists in not yet being there, there are limits.

PART I

Bodies

CHAPTER 2

'My Fortieth Year Had Come and Gone and I Still Throwing the Javelin': Beckett's Athletics

Strides of Physical Culture

Writers and artists, especially those who are called modernists, are not supposed to be jocks or hearties, and the locker-room and library are normally thought of, without it being thought about very much at all, as mutually exclusive.

Throughout his life, Beckett was an unexpectedly enthusiastic player and spectator of games and sports. Of course, the most well known aspect of his athleticism is his cricketing ability. He played for the school cricket XI at Earlsfort House prep school, playing some of his matches on the Lansdowne Road ground, which is now the setting for Irish international rugby. He found a place in the cricket team of Portora Royal School almost immediately upon his arrival at the age of thirteen, where he opened the batting with Geoffrey Thompson (Thompson was later to be instrumental in arranging Beckett's psychoanalysis). His place in Wisden was secured by the two tours of England he undertook with the Trinity College cricket team, as well as the first-class matches they played against Northampton. He cycled, even played cycle polo and also played a great deal of tennis up to the age of fourteen, frequently entering and winning tournaments at the Carrickmines Tennis and Croquet Club. He shared his father's love of golf and spent much of his early life playing Carrickmines golf course. He was a strong, competitive swimmer and even competed in motorcycle trials on the 2.75 horsepower AJS motorbike his father bought him (Knowlson 1996: 62–3).

There is little difficulty in digesting the ludic side of all this to Beckett's work as a whole – Beckett the player of bridge and chess, with partners like Marcel Duchamp and Alberto Giacometti – but Beckett's interest in the more athletic or corporeal side of gameplay has been much harder to make sense of more than anecdotally. Or perhaps, we should say, there has seemed no need to make sense of it. Beckett's interest in sport is just part of the accidental texture of his life, which, unlike nearly every other accidental feature of that life – his relation to his mother, his Protestantism, his piano playing, his politics, his turbulent epidermis – seems to have no serious relation to his work.

There have been some attempts to establish a strong relationship between modernism and sport. Harold B. Segel's *Body Ascendant* tries to chart the links between modernism and what he calls the 'body imperative', which swept across Europe in the early years of the twentieth century. 'Popular culture embraced the world of sport and the athlete with astonishing exuberance', writes Segel. 'But high culture was not to be found wanting. Artists delighted in the new subject matter and responded appropriately' (Segel 1998, 5). The story that Segel tells is of the modernist embrace of the sensuous and the vigorously living, which runs from Friedrich Nietzsche through D. H. Lawrence and beyond and even washes into Leavisian critical language, in the admiration of qualities like sinew and highly toned supple-ness (F. R. Leavis himself was a runner and was often to be seen loping to lectures across Cambridge courts). Still, the examples chosen by Segel seem to indicate that the cult of life and physical expression was, for most mod-ernists, a sort of sport in the head, or mind game. Theodore Roosevelt, Ernest Hemingway, Henry de Montherlant and Antoine de Saint-Exupéry would not be many people's idea of representative modernists.

In fact, it turns out that the celebration of the body in modernism is a very different thing from the celebration of the body to be found on the pitch or on the track. The modernist body is celebrated for its sensi-tivity, sensuality or (usually sexual) appetites rather than its strength, skill or endurance and even the brawniest Nietzscheans – Yeats, Lawrence, Georges Bataille – tend in their own lives to be a bunch of fops, weeds and touchline-hugging wheezers. Sport was for the petit bourgeois or the middlebrow also-ran. The distance between the artist and the citizen is measured in *Ulysses* by the inconceivability of Stephen Dedalus sharing Leopold Bloom's middle-aged worries about keeping up with his Eugen Sandow fitness regime. The huge expansion of competitive sport in the twentieth century brings about a new form of the stand-off between scrawn and brawn. On the one hand there is the modernist body: frail, tremulous, hysterical but infinitely sensitive. On the other hand there is hiking, mountaineering, the Olympic ideal and the cult of the Aryan superman. On the *Lord of the Flies* castaway island of twentieth-century culture, mod-ernists are the Piggys or the Simons, rather than the rough-handed Ralphs or Jacks. The ludicrous muscularity of counter-examples like Hemingway, a writer who so vulgarly failed to keep his sport in the head, is telling enough.

It used to be a commonplace of Beckett criticism to assert that his work retreats progressively from embodiment. More recent criticism has tended to stress the stubborn irreducibility of the body in Beckett's work, even though we scarcely need reminding how aged, unlovely, constrained and comically impotent his bodies are. Cerebration, when a character like Lucky in *Waiting for Godot* manages to pull it off, addresses itself to a body whose destiny is to fail, which is the very opposite of 'physical culture':

> man ... wastes and pines ... in spite of the strides of physical culture the practice of sports such as tennis football running cycling swimming flying floating riding gliding conating camogie skating tennis of all kinds dying flying sports of all kinds autumn summer winter winter tennis of all kinds, hockey of all sorts ... and ... simultaneously for reasons unknown to shrink and dwindle in spite of the tennis I resume flying gliding golf over nine and eighteen holes tennis of all sorts. (Beckett 1986: 41)

The short fizzle from which this chapter takes its title, 'Horn Came Always', incriminates athletics in actually hastening the process of decline:

> What ruined me at bottom was athletics. With all that jumping and running when I was young, and even long after in the case of certain events, I wore out the machine before its time. My fortieth year had come and gone and I still throwing the javelin. (Beckett 1984: 194)

The French version adds boxing and wrestling to the list: 'D'avoir tant sauté et couru, boxé et lutté, dans ma jeunesse, et bien au-delà pour certaines spécialités, j'ai usé la machine avant l'heure' (Beckett 1976: 44). So Beckett's world is one of debility, disability, impairment and suffering, in which sport is not so much ludic as ludicrous. If sport means prowess, then what part can it possibly play in the consummate art of the 'non-can-er'?

One source for this strain of revulsion against sport in Beckett might be supplied by the political culture of athleticism in which he grew up. The game of camogie, which Lucky mentions, is the female version of hurling, one of the games energetically promoted by the Gaelic Athletic Association during the early part of the twentieth century, and its inclusion throws into relief the distinctively Anglo-Irish cast of many of Beckett's sporting affinities. The games of cricket, rugby and tennis at which he excelled would have seemed to many in Ireland to typify the outlook of the English public school in exile. The years in which Beckett was learning his golf, cricket and tennis were years in which the influence of the Gaelic Athletic Association was strong. The GAA had its beginning in December 1882, when the burly Michael Cusack, the original of the Citizen in Joyce's *Ulysses*, founded the Dublin Hurling Club. The Caledonian Games, which took place two years later, attracted 20,000 spectators. Cusack had been a good rugby player, but now he turned emphatically against this imperial game, writing that it was a 'denationalising plague [carrying] on through winter the work of ruin that cricket was doing through the summer' (quoted in Mandle 1987: 5). The following rhyme appeared in the *Gaelic Athlete* magazine for 3 February 1912:

> Each foreign game, we now disdain
> Golf, cricket, and ping pong
> Rugby and soccer in our midst
> Have flourished far too long   (quoted in Mandle 1987: 129)

Almost from the beginning, the GAA had strong political associations with the Irish Republican Brotherhood (IRB), prompting, for example, an 1887 police report to characterise the GAA as a Fenian faction intent on 'combining the muscular youth of the country into an organization drilled and disciplined to form a physical power capable of overawing and coercing the Home Rule Government of the future' (quoted in Mandle 1987: 9). The parallels between the sturdiness of Irish culture and the cult of power and prowess that later swept across Europe may have been striking to Beckett.

Stayers

Lucky evokes a number of surprising sports. One wonders, for example, what the rules of 'floating' and 'dying' might be. But perhaps the oddest word in his panicky roster is 'conating', which is not itself usually thought of as a sport, though it is that element without which most sports would be unthinkable. 'Conation' is defined as one of the three principal components of mind; where cognition covers thinking and knowing, and affect refers to feeling and emotional value, conation concerns motivation and striving towards goals. Although conation is not treated with much affection or respect in Beckett's work, it does in fact run all the way through it. More than the work of any other writer of the twentieth century, Beckett's works are concerned with and generated from ordeal, test, trial, striving and struggle, which often seem to predominate over the other two dimensions of mental activity. The ego in Beckett's work is never an abstractly self-reflecting ego, nor is floating a sport at which it excels. His is what Bachelard, following Maine de Biran, calls a 'cogito of striving' (Bachelard 1948: 78), a cogito that comes into being and sustains itself in the struggle to overcome obstacle, limit and resistance, even, or perhaps especially, when they are internal. And, more than any other writer, Beckett sees the work of writing as fundamentally bound up with competition as well as formed by the possibilities of winning and losing. The agon of Beckett's work is as much athletic as aesthetic.

Much of the action in Beckett's work involves meeting the arbitrary obligations of what seem like games or sports: 'Me – to play', are Hamm's opening words in *Endgame* (Beckett 1986: 93). One assumes the priority of chess, but Hamm can also be thought of as lining up his first service. 'Come on, Gogo, return the ball, can't you, once in a way?' says Vladimir to Estragon in *Waiting for Godot*, as the latter's attention flags during his explication of the problem of the two thieves (Beckett 1986: 13). Beckett's couples are game-playing couples, in whom antagonism is linked with dependence: 'Keep going, can't you, keep going!' shouts Hamm angrily, as though to someone who is incapable of returning serve (Beckett 1986: 121).

Beckett's world is one of endless exertion without the possibility of overcoming or outcome: of pervasive fatigue that never approaches the consummation of exhaustion, or full-time. But it is not always a world of depleted energy. Some of Beckett's characters are given to angry paroxysms, or deploy physical means to maintain composure:

> The best thing I found was to start running. Perhaps I should mention here that I was a very slow walker. I didn't dally or loiter in any way, just walked very slowly, little short steps and the feet very slow through the air. On the other hand I must have been quite one of the fastest runners the world has ever seen, over a short distance, five or ten yards, in a second I was there. But I could not go on at that speed, not for breathlessness, it was mental, all is mental, figments. Now the jog trot on the other hand, I could no more do that than I could fly. No, with me all was slow, and then these flashes, or gushes, vent the pent, that was one of those things I used to say, over and over, as I went along, vent the pent, vent the pent. (Beckett 1984: 131)

Oddly enough, Beckett himself was more of a stayer in his own running: at Earlsfort House, he won races at middle to long distances, though the fags seem to have taken their toll by the time he was playing rugby in Paris, during his period at the Ecole Normale. One of his team-mates, Camille Marcoux, says he was an explosive centre for the first twenty minutes or so of the game, after which 'il s'écroulait dans les pâquerettes' ('he collapsed among the daisies') (Knowlson 1996: 93). The value of endurance to Beckett is also suggested in 'The Cartesian Centaur', Hugh Kenner's essay on cycles and cycling in Beckett, in the teasing hint Beckett tossed Kenner concerning 'a veteran racing cyclist, bald, a "stayer," recurrent placeman in town-to-town and national championships, Christian name elusive, surname Godeau, pronounced, of course, no differently from Godot' (Kenner 1961: 124).

Another story, here reported in Matt Seaton's review of Tim Hilton's memoir of cycling, has been going the rounds for quite a long time:

> One Roger Godeau was a track ace at Paris's Vélodrome d'hiver after the war – this when the Vél d'hiv was still haunted by the fact that it had been used as a transit camp for 12,000 Jews, shamefully rounded up during the occupation by the French police. From that detention, they were transported to Drancy and thence to Auschwitz. In the late 40s, some of the boys who hung around the stadium for a sight of their cycling heroes told Beckett one day: 'On attend Godeau.' So Beckett perhaps had this melancholy setting, not to mention the shadow of the Holocaust, in mind when he was scripting the lines of Vladimir and Estragon. (Seaton 2004)

Roger Godeau cannot be the same Godeau, since he was only just making his career in the 1940s, and even in 1951 could not yet be regarded as a 'veteran'. Though his arrival was indeed hailed by Raymond Hutier in the *Miroir des Sports* in 1944 as 'la révélation d'un vrai stayer' ('Roger Godeau') – Godeau was not for the most part a touring cyclist.

All-Rounders

When Joyce has Stephen Dedalus set aesthetic values against 'kinetic' ones, he was setting aside not just the body, but also more specifically the body in movement. Beckett's corporeality is kinetic, in the way that one should expect of an athlete or dancer. One of the striking features of Beckett's writing is its attentiveness to questions of weight, balance, position, orientation and speed, whether in its precise notation of Watt's way of walking, or its composition of the constricted figures of *Ping* and *All Strange Away*, or the precise characterisations of stance, gesture and movement when Beckett directed his plays. These are only superficially geometrical: for where geometry dispenses with embodied perspective, Beckett's choreographies are coenesthetically focussed in a body, with coordinates of top and bottom, left and right. Beckett pays precise attention to posture, gesture, gait and modes of locomotion, not because this reduces the body to an object of calculation or contemplation, but because it places the body in a field of action and reaction.

One of the curious aspects of Beckett's cricket was that he batted left-handed, apparently because that was how he had been taught by his brother, but bowled his medium-pace off-breaks right-handed. I think we can see this 'all-roundedness' – the term that Joyce used of the unathletic Bloom (Joyce 1986: 193) – at work through Beckett's concern with doubles and couples, and more particularly the attentiveness throughout his work to handedness. Perhaps we may draw on Michel Serres's account of the universal principle of orientation:

> Only some living things have the pleasure of a sex, whereas everything, in the world, whether animate or inanimate, is provided with a direction . . .
>   The stars turn and advance, oriented, like particles around the nucleus of an atom. Crystals and molecules are lateralized, with highly refined symmetries and asymmetries. Direction or orientation comes neither from men nor from their preferences, from their inclinations, but from the inanimate world that precedes the living, and from the living that precedes culture. Things lean to one side: force fields, boreal auroras, twisting turbulences, cyclones, spots on the planet Jupiter . . . the universal was born, it is said, from spontaneous symmetry breaking. (Serres 1997: 14)

For Serres, the handedness of the universe creates distortion and imbalance. The majority of human beings exist in a 'stupid pathology of division' between left and right (Serres 1997: 4).

> How can a right-handed person be described? As a severed organism, suffering from severe hemiplegia. The pen, the knife, the hammer, and the racket are gathered together in one hand, while the other carries nothing. Hot and supple, one side of the body and its extension lives, trailing behind it a sort of cadaverous twin, stiff and cold, contemptible and impotent – in short, unconscious. (Serres 1997: 3)

There is a symmetry between the asymmetry of the right-hander and that of the left-hander, since '[e]ach, divorced, is composed of two twins, of which only one, whichever side you choose, has the right to life, the second never having been born' (Serres 1997: 3–4). Everywhere, Beckett's pseudo-couples enact this oddity, this disorientation, this off-handedness: Mercier/Camier (in *Mercier and Camier*); Molloy/Moran (in *Molloy*); French/English. Beckett's spatiality is powerfully lateralized, or handed. This universal inclination or obliquity creates both agony and opportunity for Beckett, just as it does on the wicket or the billiard table. It marks the inescapability of irreversible time, for time too seems right-handed.

And yet, one might also say that there is a powerful drive running through all these couples to find a point of balance, the sweet spot of equipoise, where neither left nor right dominates. Such a point would be out of time, though Serres finds in sport an image for this dwelling in possibility, which he calls a state of the 'future participle':

> Have you ever kept goal for your team, while an adversary hurries to take a clean, close shot? Relaxed, as if free, the body mimes the future participle, fully ready to unwind: toward the highest point, at ground level, or halfway

up, in both directions, left and right; toward the centre of the solar plexus, a starry plateau launches its virtual branches in all directions at once, like a bouquet of axons ... Run to the net, ready to volley: once again, a future participle, the racket aims for all shots at once, as if the body, unbalanced from all sides, were knotting a ball of time, a sphere of directions, and were releasing a starfish from its thorax ... It fills its space equally, high as much as low, right as much as left, it abandons preferences and determinations. (Serres 1997: 9, 24; translation adjusted)

Jean-Paul Sartre also found in sport an illustration of the projectiveness of subjective space, which is never the inert 'being there' of *Dasein* but always beside or out in front of itself, in the place where it must urgently, imminently reach in order to get to the drop-shot, parry the blow or tip the ball over the bar. But Serres imagines the possibility of projection in all directions, an attention that is an attenuation: 'Let us call soul the kind of space and time that can be expanded from its natal position towards all exposures' (Serres 1997: 31).

There are hints of this unbodying, or ecstasy, in Beckett's experience. Let us recall, for example, that he was a fearless diver, having learned the art from the rocks of the Forty-Foot at Sandycove. *Company* evokes the young boy's hesitation standing at the top, encouraged by his father:

You stand at the tip of the high board. High above the sea. In it your father's upturned face. Upturned to you. You look down to the loved trusted face. He calls you to jump. He calls, be a brave boy. The red round face. The thick moustache. The greying hair. The swell sways it under and sways it up again. The far call again. Be a brave boy. Many eyes upon you. From the water and from the bathing place. (Beckett 1989: 14)

One could be forgiven for reading this as a memory of a terrified holding back from the plunge; but in fact Beckett seems to have had little fear as a diver either in the Forty-Foot or elsewhere. *Company* suggests that the quest for the exhilaration of the mid-air led him also to leap from his bedroom window into the branches of a larch tree (Beckett 1989: 17). At the age of fifty-two, Beckett still had the same relish for diving off high rocks (Knowlson 1996: 455).

However, for the most part, where Serres finds in sport an image for the many-angled star or corona of omnitude, Beckett seeks a different kind of equilibrium, in the ideal of an absolutely reversible game that would consume itself exhaustively. His ideal is absorption rather than exposure, and folded-over time rather than the expansion of the moment. The model for this is Mr Endon's game of chess in *Murphy*, in which he moves each piece one square forward and then moves them carefully all one square back. But the perfection of the retraction is not in fact available to Mr Endon, since pawns are not permitted to move backwards. The ideal of non-directionality, in which coming and going, backwards and forwards, will balance each other completely, is thwarted because the game must be played in time, which does not allow the complete return to initial conditions. The irreversibility of time is related to the necessary entanglement with others, or the other of the antagonist: having advanced into the other's territory, one can never retreat from it back into one's own space. In fact, one has no alternative but to play out the game, since every 'on' constitutes a move of a particular kind, with a particular aim, angle, spin and velocity, that can never simply be palindromically consumed by the 'no'. Serres celebrates the fact that, born a left-hander, he was trained to use his right, producing, not a stammering limper, but a 'lateral hermaphrodite' (Serres 1997: 13). Beckett's athletics is not the completion of the cack-handed looked for by Serres, but an expertise of the maladroit, the off-kilter, the ill-at-ease, the in-play. Beckett's work is full of these off-centred, unbalanced movements, most notably in Molloy's adjustment to stiffer and less stiff legs (Beckett 1973: 76–8) and the necessary asymmetry, or abandonment of the nautical principle Molloy calls 'trim' (Beckett 1973: 71) that enables him to find his solution to the sucking stones problem, even though it results in him 'being off my balance, dragged to the right hand and the left, backwards and forwards' (Beckett 1973: 74).

Of course, Mr Endon is not really playing chess at all. Rather, we may say, he is pretending to play chess, or playing at playing. The simple, hair's-breadth, but far-reaching difference between game and sport is that sport is real. There is no display in the play involved in sport, no il-lusion or al-lusion. It is in this sense that Beckett's work is sporting rather than ludic, athletic rather than aesthetic. If we needed another term to distinguish the intensity with which games must be played in Beckett, we might borrow one coined by Bernard Suits: Beckett's work is *lusive* rather than ludic (Suits 1973: 49).

Just a Game

Philosophy of sport has taken three forms: the ethnographic, which concerns itself with the social meanings of sport; the ethical, which investigates the social bonds and commitments enacted through it; and the phenomeno-logical, which attempts to derive an ontology of sporting behaviour. This last tradition, though the most promising for the understanding of the sporting life in Beckett, also throws up the greatest problems. The assumption which predominates in attempts to understand the ontology of sport is that sport involves a fulfilment or completion of the self. Often, sport is seen as a variety of play, which enables the athletic to be represented as cousin to the aesthetic. Clustering in the late 1960s and early 1970s as they do, phenomenological studies of sport often have a strongly existential cast, seeing sport as the arena of free and active human self-constitution *en situation*. As such, they follow Schiller:

> [H]ow can we speak of *mere* play, when we know that it is precisely play and play alone, which of all man's states and conditions is the one which makes him whole and unfolds both sides of his nature at once? . . . man only plays when he is in the fullest sense of the word a human being, and *he is only fully a human being when he plays*. (Schiller 1967: 107)

Surprisingly, Sartre has a similar formulation:

> What is play indeed, if not an activity of which man is the first origin, for which man himself sets the rules, and which has no consequences except according to the rules posited? As soon as a man apprehends himself as free and wishes to use his freedom, a freedom, by the way, which could just as well be his anguish, then his activity is play . . . His goal, which he aims at through sports or pantomime or games, is to attain himself as a certain being, precisely the being which is in question in his being. (Sartre 1984: 580–1)

This seems a long way away from Beckett's work, in which the attractiveness of play often seems to lie in the fact that it provides distraction, or, using the word that Beckett used in describing his turn to writing plays, relief. Play seems to offer the calm or consolation – factitious but locally effective – of pattern given to a disorderly and chaotic world, the booming, buzzing confusion of phenomena sorted into the syntax of move and countermove. Thus, it is possible to interpret M's words in *Play* as testifying to the longed-for insignificance of the unserious as a salve for the agony of responsibility: 'I know now, all that was just . . . play. And all this? . . . when will all this have been . . . just play?' (Beckett 1986: 313). But play is actually more serious than this in Beckett's work. Play is always absorbing, imperative, obligatory, never pastime, but the agonistic shaping of time's passage. The difference between game and sport is that, where games can be abstract, sports involve the putting into play of the body. It is the seriousness of this corporeal play in Beckett that seems to make it, in a perverse, but still recognisable sense, athletic.

The intensity of the lusive drive in Beckett comes from the fact that games are forms of world-making, which can sometimes violently displace the world of which they form a part. This is dramatised in the story of the birth of Larry, which is patched together between his mother (Tetty), his father (Goff) and Mr Hackett at the beginning of *Watt*. Having endured the pains of labour all the way through dinner, Tetty goes upstairs while the men retire to the snooker room, and delivers the child herself, snapping the cord with her teeth:

> We heard the cries, said Goff.
> Judge of their surprise, said Tetty.
> Cream's potting had been extraordinary, extraordinary, I remember, said Goff. I never saw anything like it. We were watching breathless, as he set himself for a long thin jenny, with the black of all balls.
> What temerity, said Mr. Hackett.
> A quite impossible stroke, in my opinion, said Goff. He drew back his queue to strike, when the wail was heard. He permitted himself an expression that I shall not repeat. (Beckett 1972: 13)

This is a replaying of the opening move of *Tristram Shandy*, but with the positions of biology and culture reversed. Here, it is not the mundane affair of winding the clock that interrupts the work of nature, but the untimely fact of human birth that botches Cream's masterstroke, jamming the paradigms of potting and parturition. The principle is enunciated some-what more pithily in Beckett's adaptation of Terence: 'Nothing human is foreign to us, once we have digested the racing news' (Beckett 1984: 80).

For Beckett, sport provides the impetus for the utter seriousness of a gaming in which everything, mind, body, world, is in play, which is not in the least to say up in the air, but rather to say risked, wagered, at stake. It is conventional for writers in the Schillerian tradition to associate play and art, but Beckett's play has little to do with art. In some sense art always stands apart from the world. But sport is lusive: it does not gesture to, or take up a relation to, the world it colonises or constitutes it. More than worldly, sport is, as we might say, *weltich*, 'worldive' because it forms a complete gestalt, with all the interrelated elements of the game necessarily present at once. It is this worldiveness which has often suggested the argument that play or sports create a kind of existential imperium, an arena in which humanity may make itself freely. But this 'arena' is also a space of subjection to necessity, the fascination of what's difficult and to the ever-present possibility of defeat.

Having Done with Losing

'There is always in sport an appropriative component', insists Sartre, in the course of the chapter in *Being and Nothingness* entitled 'Doing and Having' in which skiing features centrally as an instance (Sartre 1984: 581). However, the athleticism of Beckett's play is to be found principally in the intensity of this will to appropriation, or desire to win. This may seem counterintuitive, given the fierce determination with which Beckett's speakers claim to seek to lose or come unstuck. 'Old endgame, lost of old, play and lose and have done with losing', resolves Hamm (Beckett 1986: 132). Hamm wishes, like all of Beckett's carefully plotting, determined pseudo-failers, to follow to the end the rules of the game of the death-drive as set out by Sigmund Freud in *Beyond the Pleasure Principle*, whereby '[w]e have no longer to reckon with the organism's puzzling determination (so hard to fit into any context) to maintain its own existence in the face of every obstacle. What we are left with is the fact that the organism wishes to die only in its own fashion' (Freud 1968: 39). The will to appropriate one's failure, to live it and be it, is the effect of that absolute putting of oneself in play. The peculiar displaced athleticism of Beckett's writing is a way of mediating the contrary tractions of the appropriative aspiration of will on the one hand and the recoil from will's cruder dominion on the other. The losing that Beckett has in view is not defeat; rather it is an active striving and contriving to outwit, or win out against winning. In the end, the athletic qualities I have made out in Beckett – endurance, expertise, equipoise, exertion of will – are not simply exercised through his work, but are themselves put into play, or sported with, by it.

What kind of athleticism is this, so expertly unsure of its capacities, so supple in its mock-incompetences, so alertly self-defeating, so dextrously maladroit, returning with such indefatigable fatigue to the being that is in question in its being?

A kind of its own.

CHAPTER 3

The Nauseous Character of All Flesh

It should not be a matter of much amazement that Beckett studies should be playing so vigorous a part in the current revival of interest in phenomenology. The upsurge (to use a prime item of phenomenological lingo) of Beckett into literary and cultural awareness during the 1950s seemed to demand and handsomely to reward interpretation in terms of the then-dominant philosophies of Martin Heidegger, Sartre and Maurice Merleau-Ponty. It is hard to overstate the importance in particular of the Sartrean version of phenomenological philosophy. The extent to which Sartre's form of existential philosophy dominated the field can be measured by the negative imprint of his absence from the thoughts of not only philosophers but more particularly literary, cultural and social critics today. Sartre was not just lost to view – he was disappeared. Sartre was so ubiquitous that only a massive and sustained act of philosophical purging could scour him so completely from the field of intellectual reference.

The disappearance of Sartre from the field is all the more striking in the case of Beckett studies, given that 'Beckett and Sartre' was at one time as reliable a double act as Marks and Spencer or Abbot and Costello. For twenty years or so, it was almost impossible to make any sense of Beckett outside the paradigm of existentialist phenomenology, with its bifurcated emphasis on the themes of anguish, arbitrariness and absurdity on the one hand, and of choice, freedom and transcendence on the other. Above all, it was the figure of Sartre and the arguments he developed in *Being and Nothingness* that were the source of these principles. In 1970, Neal Oxenhandler could begin an essay on the nouveau roman, with Beckett as one of its most distinguished exponents, with the calmly assured statement that

> [w]hatever historical calipers one uses, it is hard to separate French literature of the sixties from that of the fifties and late forties. The major writers who follow existentialism – Beckett, Genet, Ionesco, Robbe-Grillet, Claude Simon – share a common ground of specific aesthetic tendencies which set them off from the pre-existentialist tradition. (Oxenhandler 1970: 169)

While objecting to the simple designation 'phenomenological' for the writers of the nouveau roman, Oxenhandler nevertheless assures us that '[w]hat we need is some kind of map, a map of what Samuel Beckett might call "the Sartre and Merleau-Ponty country"' (Oxenhandler 1970: 172).

The essay-flogging site 123helpme.com advertises its wares with a preview of an essay entitled 'Sartre's Existentialism in Samuel Beckett's *Waiting for Godot*' (which is rated 'Blue' for 'a powerful essay' and no doubt priced accordingly) (Anon n.d., 'Sartre's Existentialism'). But who sets essay titles like this any more? I suspect that this is a little-visited precinct of the site, a ghost town enlivened only by the eerie wail of a harmonica and occasional swirl of tumbleweed. Generations of students have been taught (some of them perhaps by some of the things I have written) both to condescend to and to be wary of 'existential-humanist' readings of Beckett. The superstitious dread of the empty space represented by Sartre is revealed by the fact that when phenomenology has again occurred to Beckett studies, it has been in a form relieved of its Sartrean thematics of choice, freedom and engagement. Where, in the 1950s, phenomenology had presented itself almost entirely in the compound form of 'existential phenomenology', in recent years, the specifically existential associations of phenomenology have been dropped.

Contemporary phenomenological readings (of Beckett and others) exhibit a strong preoccupation with the body, oddly, but conveniently enough a topic that attracts little sustained attention either from Sartre or from his explicators. Those contemporary critics who have turned to phenomenology have often done so in order to make out a more intimate and inward sense of embodied existence than poststructuralist criticism seemed to make possible, looking for a more fleshly 'phenomenological body' to supplement post-structuralism's body of signs. At this moment, Beckett studies appear to want from phenomenology what other new adopters of phenomenology want; not an invigorating account of man's absurd freedom, but a reassuringly holistic account of man's inherence in the 'flesh of the world', in Merleau-Ponty's conception (Merleau-Ponty 1968: 248). Discussions of Sartre and Beckett have tended to emphasise the anguish of subjectivity rather than the lived condition of the body. The existentialist themes made out by Edith Kern in the work of Beckett are limited to the absurdity of the outside world and the unavailability of the self to itself, as it represents 'the Sartrean pour-soi in futile quest of a Self that becomes a stranger, an en-soi, an object as soon as it is seen by an intelligence which classifies and judges it' (Kern 1970: 207). In this, she follows Richard Coe, who also saw the Beckettian self in terms of the Sartrean pour-soi (Coe 1964: 75). Even Lance St. John Butler, who provides a detailed explication of Beckett's work in the light of Sartre's

Being and Nothingness, nevertheless considers the question of the body only in a four-page afterthought (Butler 1984: 106–10). All this suggests that whatever utility there may be for Beckett studies from a reconsideration of his relations with Sartre may perhaps be derived from some close attention to the way in which Sartre treats the topic of the body that so animates the recent return to phenomenology.

Everywhere In the World

The problem with Sartre is that the body is such a problem for him, that the body is always a form of foreign body. This makes him less useful and congenial in this project of recovery than his associate and later critic Merleau-Ponty, whose work seems to articulate an altogether less hostile and agonistic view of embodied existence. To be sure, this may not at first appear from the way in which Sartre begins his chapter 'The Body' in *Being and Nothingness*. The first pages give what ought to be a soothing enough account of the priority of the lived body over the body as object of knowledge – this latter being simply 'the body for others', which Sartre will tell us is indistinguishable from a corpse (Sartre 1984: 303). My body is more than merely my own: as 'a living possibility of running, of dancing, etc'. (Sartre 1984: 305), it is me, it is my very individuation. Without my body, there would be no orientation, no perspective on or place in the world, there would *be no world*. That is to say, my body does not just happen to be in the world; it is my way of being enworlded, my being-in-the-midst-of-the-world. Sartre goes on to argue against the conventional view of the senses, which places them in some intermediary position between me and the world. This implies that, somewhere and somehow, I must have 'sensations' that correspond to my experience of the world. Sartre regards such a view as untenable, not least because none of us has ever had access to a 'sensation' as such. I may see that the cover of this book is green, but I can never get the greenness to appear to me on its own, as a subjective fact. In each case, what we take to be a subjective sensation is in fact an objective quality of the world that is revealed to me (Sartre 1984: 312).

This is another sense in which my body cannot be said to be 'in' the world, as the plant is in the pot or the pea is in the pod. Rather, as 'the point of view on which there can not be a point of view' (Sartre 1984: 329–30) my body is the entire way the world appears to me, and the world is therefore wholly impregnated with my body. I cannot subtract from my being-in-the-world from the embodied portion of it: 'Thus to say that I have entered into the world, "come to the world," or that there is a world, or that I have a body

is one and the same thing. In this sense my body is everywhere in the world'
(Sartre 1984: 318).

The list of examples Sartre provides of the way in which the world
ubiquitously indicates the body as my way of being in it (really, and more
briefly, my way of *being it*) not only has a Beckettian cast, it also employs
some distinctively Beckettian properties:

> My body is everywhere: the bomb which destroys my house also damages
> my body in so far as the house was already an indication of my body. That
> is why my body always extends across the tool which it utilizes: it is at the
> end of the cane on which I lean and against the earth; it is at the end of
> the telescope which shows me the stars; it is on the chair, in the whole
> house. (Sartre 1984: 325)

Viewed in this way, some of the experiences of the body detailed in Beckett's
writing may start into a different kind of sense. Two of Beckett's bedridden
characters in particular have an experience that is represented as a kind of
scattering or alienation of the body. In *Murphy*, Mr Kelly has some
difficulty in gathering together his scattered attention before he is able to
dispense advice to Celia: 'His attention was dispersed. Part was with his
caecum, which was wagging its tail again; part with his extremities, which
were dragging anchor; part with his boyhood; and so on. All this would
have to be called in' (Beckett 2003: 17). At the end of the novel, this will
be reversed, as Mr Kelly's body seems to soar out of sight at the end of his
kite-string. These experiences are recalled by Malone's probings with his
stick, themselves recalled by the speaker in *The Unnamable*, who imagines
investigating his circumstances with 'a stick or pole, and the means of plying
it, the former being of little avail without the latter, and vice versa' (Beckett
1973: 302):

> Then I would dart it, like a javelin, straight before me and know, by the
> sound made, whether that which hems me round, and blots out my world, is
> the old void, or a plenum. Or else, without letting it go, I would wield it like
> a sword and thrust it through empty air, or against the barrier. But the days
> of sticks are over. (Beckett 1973: 302–3)

Of course, the very possibility of projection is still available in whatever kind
of existence it is that here represents itself. The very experience of imagining
being able to project physically, even under circumstances where it is
impossible, is itself a kind of Sartrean project, a surpassing of the condition
of helplessness. This is temporal as well as spatial; reflecting on the simultaneous necessity of having a pole and 'a means of plying it', the speaker
remarks in passing, 'I could also do, incidentally, with future and conditional

participles' (Beckett 1973: 302). The voice in *The Unnamable* is never permitted, nor can it ever procure for itself, a fully out-of-body experience. Its projections beyond the body are always bodily projections and therefore as much bracing as scattering.

All this might suggest a conveniently post-Cartesian fusion of body, mind and world, with the body as 'that strange object which uses its own parts as a general system of symbols for the world, and through which we can consequently "be at home" in that world', as Merleau-Ponty puts it (1996: 237). For Sartre, however, I am never merely identical with my body, nor can the body and the world simply intersect. The most well-known, even notorious, aspect of Sartre's philosophy is his distinction between being 'in-itself', that is, forms of being that are simply and self-identically themselves, through and through, and the kind of existence he calls the 'for-itself'. The latter is distinguished by being a kind of active nothingness – a nihilation. Sartre intensifies Heidegger's claim that Dasein is outside of itself; this means, says Sartre, 'that *Dasein* "is not" in itself, that it "is not" in immediate proximity to itself, and that it "surpasses" the world inasmuch as it posits itself as *not being in itself* and as *not being in the world*' (Sartre 1984: 18). Man is therefore 'a being who causes Nothingness to arise in the world' (Sartre 1984: 24). My nihilation is the fact that I must always surpass or set at naught my contingent condition in the world. And it is my body, or my condition of being embodied, which represents this contingency – indeed, Sartre will define the body as 'the contingent form which is assumed by the necessity of my contingency' (Sartre 1984: 309). Thus, even though I am not anything but my body, the body 'is perpetually the surpassed' (Sartre 1984: 330). It was not, is not, will not have been necessary that I should be at all. There is no reason for the phenomenon that I know as me to have come into being. But, since I am in being, it is necessary that I should take some form or other, which will always prevent me from attaining to any kind of being-in-general. It is an easy but dangerous mistake to see the kind of negation of the body in which the for-itself must be involved as leading to a reinstatement of the Cartesian split between the inert body and the active but immaterial soul. For Sartre, existence is indeed split between the in-itself and the for-itself, between the form of being that is identical with itself and the '*being such that in its being, its being is in question*' (Sartre 1984: xxxviii). But inasmuch as this is a fissure within consciousness, which is never anything else than fully embodied, it is also a fissure within the body, not between it and something else.

I think that Stanton B. Garner is right to find a similar 'impossibility of transcendental self-possession' in the work of Merleau-Ponty and to recommend his philosophy as a way of understanding the 'problematic corporeality' to be found everywhere in Beckett's work (Garner 1993: 451, 453). Merleau-Ponty would therefore be the baby rescued from the gurgling outflow of phenomenology, the philosopher who shows 'the deconstructive possibilities inherent in the phenomenological stance itself' (Garner 1993: 453). But this maladjustment is much milder, more benign and much less dynamically anguished for Merleau-Ponty than it is for Sartre. Where, for Merleau-Ponty, embodiment can be spoken of as a condition, for Sartre, bodily existence is never anything but a project of striving.

Strides of Alimentation

There is one bodily action and associated affect that seems to be uniquely expressive of the split in embodied existence both for Sartre and for Beckett, namely, the experience of eating and, in its negative affect, that of nausea. In his 1946 essay 'Existentialism Is a Humanism', Sartre identifies a kind of nausea as the effect of existentialist fiction:

> [I]t appears that ugliness is being identified with existentialism. That is why some people say we are "naturalistic," and if we are, it is strange to see how much we scandalise and horrify them, for no one seems to be much frightened or humiliated nowadays by what is properly called naturalism. Those who can quite well keep down a novel by Zola such as *La Terre* are sickened as soon as they read an existentialist novel. (Sartre 1948: 24)

For both Beckett and Sartre, eating seems to be inseparable from the background or possibility of disgust, or nausea. The condition of the for-itself appears to be constitutionally dyspeptic.

In order to make out what may aptly be called a nauseous sensibility shared by Sartre and Beckett, it will help to distinguish more precisely what Sartre means by the term 'nausea', which certainly names something much more specific than what Rosette Lamont referred to casually as 'the sickness of the void' (Lamont 1959: 319). The term appears on a number of occasions in *Being and Nothingness* before finally being given a definition, at the end of the first section of the chapter on the body, that is devoted to 'The Body's Being For Itself'. It is the climax of a discussion of the ways in which the sufferer from pain or illness makes these conditions his or her own precisely by projecting him- or herself beyond them. It is not necessary for there to be a specific form of bodily experience in question in order for the body to be made one's own, for there will always be some kind of apprehension of the body within consciousness:

> Consciousness does not cease to 'have' a body. Coenesthetic affectivity is then a pure, non-positional apprehension of a contingency without color, a pure apprehension of the self as a factual existence. This perpetual apprehension on the part of my for-itself of an insipid taste which I cannot place, which accompanies me even in my efforts to get away from it, and is *my* taste – this is what we have described elsewhere under the name of *Nausea*. (Sartre 1984: 338)

The hint to readers of Sartre's 1937 novel seems clear: this, we are to understand, is the philosophical explication of the state of nausea experienced psychologically by Antoine Roquentin. The problem, however, as Richard Kamber (1983) lucidly indicates, is that the experience evoked in *Being and Nothingness* is not at all that repeatedly described in *Nausea*. In Sartre's novel, nausea is induced by the sudden awareness of the mute, irreducible, absurd facticity of things, which repels all efforts to ascribe to them sense or value. Nausea is provoked by the sense of being touched by objects:

> Objects ought not to touch, since they are not alive. You use them, you put them back in place, you live among them: they are useful, nothing more. But they touch me, it's unbearable. [. . .] I remember better what I felt the other day on the sea-shore when I was holding that pebble. It was a sort of sweet disgust. How unpleasant it was! And it came from the pebble, I'm sure of that, it passed from the pebble into my hands. Yes, that's it, that's exactly it: a sort of nausea in the hands. (Sartre 1976: 22)

There, nausea is something like the apprehension of the pure existingness of things, their resistance to being swallowed into human value and significance: 'Everything is gratuitous, that park, this town, and myself. When you realized that it turns your stomach over and everything starts floating about, as it did the other evening at the Rendez-vous des Cheminots; that is the Nausea' (Sartre 1976: 188). But, in *Being and Nothingness*, nausea names the apprehension, not of the simple existence of the in-itself, but of that specific form or phase of the in-itself that is an indissoluble component of the for-itself. Nausea is the persistent, vague but still unmistakable apprehension of the contingency, the *this*ness of my body. It might be regarded as the for-itself *of* the in-itself. If, for Sartre, it is no sooner there than it is necessarily surpassed, it is always nevertheless necessarily *there to be* surpassed, even as it clings and lingers through all my efforts to expel or outstrip it. Hence perhaps the name: for nausea is most commonly the designation not of the vigorously decisive, and divisive, act of vomiting, but rather of the unresolved desire for expulsion. We might say of nausea what Sartre says of illness, that it is transcendent but without distance. It is outside my consciousness as a synthetic totality and already close to being elsewhere. But on the other hand it is in my consciousness, it fastens on to consciousness with all its teeth, penetrates consciousness with all its notes; and these teeth, these notes, are my consciousness. (Sartre 1984: 336–7)

Sartre describes as 'the unique character of corporal existence' the fact that 'the inexpressible which one wishes to flee is rediscovered at the heart of this very wrenching away; it is this which is going to constitute the consciousnesses which surpass it; it is the very contingency and the being of the flight which wishes to flee it' (Sartre 1984: 333). The spectrality of Beckett's later works, the quality, manifest in such plays as *Footfalls* and . . . *but the clouds* . . . and such texts as *Ill Seen Ill Said*, of not being quite there, has been the subject of much attention in recent years, by critics who have related it to the 'ghosting' of the body in technology and media. Sartre's formulation helps us to grasp this spectrality in a different sense. These works are spectral, not because the body is erased or made less manifest, but because they are *body-haunted*. They are ghostly, not because, or not simply because they are no longer quite there; they are ghostly because they disclose the haunting of the body that is characteristic of the living.

Thus, nausea has two aspects: on the one hand a necessary subjection or submission to one's own bodily self-consciousness, or consciousness of oneself as body, and on the other hand the effort to project oneself beyond this identification with the bodily self. This twin relation of submission to and surpassing of the factical dimension of the for-itself is precisely the way in which the for-itself is, in that it is the way in which it becomes an issue for itself. What I am is my nausea at what I am. Lance St. John Butler is certainly right to see this 'permanent undercurrent of nausea', or 'contingency-sickness' as he calls it, as the status quo in Beckett's writing (Butler 1984: 109), but perhaps he underestimates the way in which, for Beckett as well as Sartre, nausea is also taken up positively into the nihilating project of the non-coinciding for-itself that is Beckett's writing. Sartre gives a curious name to this relation of simultaneous submission and surpassing, saying that this is the way in which, using the word in a transitive sense, 'consciousness *exists* its body' (Sartre 1984: 329). The body is brought into existence by the way in which consciousness exists as embodied, which is to say, in both necessarily recognising and refusing the body as itself. In a certain sense, Sartre seems to be saying that we give to ourselves the forms of our very subjection to the contingency of being embodied, the contingency that being embodied *is*. So the nauseous condition and effect of my self-sensing consists both in the fact that I can never be other than other to myself, and therefore must always apprehend my self-taste as a kind of nausea, a desire to expel the foreign body and also in the fact that this particular kind of revulsion is my very self, that the foreign body in question is by that very token my own.

So nausea is not just a passive condition, to which I am subjected, and against which I may or may not revolt. It is the revulsion itself; it is the self precipitated in revulsion from self. Sartre will not make this idea clear until the final chapter of *Being and Nothingness*. There we find the remarkable claim that tastes – whether applied to the object, as when one speaks of the taste of coffee or vinegar, or to the subject, as when one speaks of someone's 'taste for' a particular kind of food, or, metaphorically, for a particular kind of activity – are in fact part of the project of existing itself, and thus of world-making, in which each for-itself is engaged:

> [T]astes do not remain irreducible givens; if one knows how to question them, they reveal to us the fundamental projects of the person. Down to even our alimentary preferences they all have a meaning . . . the totality of the food proposes to me a certain mode of being of the being which I accept or refuse . . . We conclude that flavor . . . has a complex architecture and differentiated matter; it is this structured matter – which represents for us a particular type of being – that we can assimilate or reject with nausea, according to our original project. It is not a matter of indifference whether we like oysters or clams, snails or shrimp, if only we know how to unravel the existential significance of these foods. (Sartre 1984: 614–15)

For Beckett, as for Sartre, alimentation and appetite have a more than contingent relation to existence; for both of them, eating is the necessary form of my relation to my contingency, for it is one of the 'fundamental projects of the person', in which I may be said to exist my body (Sartre 1984: 614).

Relish of Disgust

However, we may have to draw a sharp distinction between Sartre and Beckett. Where, for Sartre, every taste or inclination will represent 'a certain appropriative choice of being' (Sartre 1984: 615), Beckett seems to enact through eating, or not eating, a fundamental refusal of the choice of being (even if this can never be a refusal of choice as such, since refusal in itself constitutes a choice). This refusal arises early in Beckett's work in the elaborate lunch prepared by Belacqua in 'Dante and the Lobster'. The meal can be seen as a parodic reprise of Leopold Bloom's moderate repast in 'Lestrygonians', in contrast to the carnivorous, even cannibalistic frenzies of eating that he sees around him in lunchtime Dublin – 'swilling, wolfing gobfuls of sloppy food [. . .] Every fellow for his own, tooth and nail. Gulp. Grub. Gulp. Gobstuff (Joyce 1986: 138, 139). Bloom takes a glass of Burgundy and a Gorgonzola sandwich, a meal that allows him a homeopathic dose of exposure to the nausea that he has encountered earlier, with the profit of a certain kind of 'relish' – reminding us of the very first thing we ever hear about Bloom, that he 'ate with relish the inner organs of beasts and fowls' (Joyce 1986: 45): 'Mr Bloom ate his strips of sandwich, fresh clean bread, with relish of disgust pungent mustard, the feety savour of green cheese. Sips of his wine soothed his palate' (Joyce 1986: 142).

Belacqua's lunch, by contrast, seems designed to effect, not a temperate interchange of contraries, but a violent self-cancellation. The bread he toasts must be completely incinerated, since '[i]f there was one thing he abominated more than another it was to feel his teeth meet in a pathos of pith and dough' (Beckett 1970b: 11). Pathos is precisely the point in this story, in which Belacqua seems to be doing everything he can to avoid the pang of pity. Belacqua cuts the bread on a spread-out newspaper that shows the face of Henry McCabe, who, at the time the story is set, had recently been convicted of murdering his employer and four other people in a house fire in Malahide. Much of the uncertainty of the case derived from the fact that the bodies had been partially consumed in the fire (Kroll 1977). The half-round of the bread becomes identified with the Dantean problem of the spots on the moon with which Belacqua has been tussling earlier that day. According to popular interpretation, the maculated moon was the face of Cain, 'fallen and branded, seared with the first stigma of God's pity, that an outcast might not die quickly' (Beckett 1970b: 12). Belacqua's toasting procedure is identified both with the putative arson that has led to the deaths of five people in 'La Mancha' (the Malahide house) and with the execution of McCabe that will take place the following morning: 'He laid his cheek against the soft of the bread, it was spongy and warm, alive. But he would soon take that plush feel off it, by God but he would very quickly take that fat white look off its face' (Beckett 1970b: 11). It is not at all a quick death for the slowly carbonadoed rounds of toast. Smeared with a fiery paste of mustard, salt and cayenne pepper, they are intended by Belacqua to enclose the round of high Gorgonzola that he will go out to procure. He is dissatisfied with the cheese reserved for him by the shopkeeper, this time however because it is insufficiently putrid:

> A faint fragrance of corruption. What good was that? He didn't want fragrance, he wasn't a bloody gourmet. He wanted a good stench. What he

wanted was a good green stenching rotten lump of Gorgonzola cheese, alive, and by God he would have it. (Beckett 1970b: 14)

If Belacqua wants the bread thoroughly carbonised, but the cheese leppingly alive, it is in order that there should be maximum resistance to the triumph of his assimilation. His meal, 'spiced' by the news that McCabe's appeal has been rejected, is an orgy of sadomasochistic oral rage: 'his teeth and jaws had been in heaven, splinters of vanquished toast spraying forth at each gnash. It was like eating glass. His mouth burned and ached with the exploit' (Beckett 1970b: 17).

This is an eating that seems designed at once to obliterate its object and to deny the very appropriation involved in alimentary consumption. It eagerly amplifies and embraces disgust, turning it into a principle of abjection. It is like not having one's cake and violently expelling it at the same time, as though one were assimilating the very refusal of incorporation. What will catch Belacqua off guard later in the day is the sudden pathos of the thought of the vulnerable internal body of the lobster's reassuringly crunchy carapace, a principle that introduces a real indigestibility.

Throughout his work, Beckett enacts the nihilation of the for-itself in the most literal way, as an anorexic rejection of the being which it has had imposed contingently upon it. In *Malone Dies*, Malone's version of the *gran rifiuto* is less grand than Belacqua's. In announcing 'I shall be neither hot nor cold any more, I shall be tepid, I shall die tepid, without enthusiasm' (Beckett 1973: 180), Malone is presumably looking forward with pleasure to the fate promised in Revelation 3.16 for the lukewarm soul: 'because thou art lukewarm, and neither hot nor cold, I will spew thee out of my mouth'. In the course of his valedictory statement, Arsene (in *Watt*) imagines a violent refinement of this procedure, in which the casting forth of the indifferent soul from felicity is replaced by a two-way spewing traffic, as meaning is alternately rammed into and violently rejected from the body of the subject:

> [I]t is useless not to seek, not to want, for when you cease to seek you start to find, and when you cease to want, then life begins to ram her fish and chips down your gullet until you puke, and then the puke down your gullet until you puke the puke, and then the puked puke until you begin to like it. (Beckett 1972: 43)

In *The Unnamable*, the refusing nihilation of being takes the form of a specifically verbal nausea, in which speaking becomes a voiding or vomiting of sense rather than the expression of it:

> It's a poor trick that consists in ramming a set of words down your gullet on the principle that you can't bring them up without being branded as

belonging to their breed. I never understood a word of it in any case, not a word of the stories it spews, like gobbets in a vomit. My inability to absorb, my genius for forgetting, are more than they reckoned with. Dear incomprehension, it's thanks to you I'll be myself, in the end. Nothing will remain of all the lies they have glutted me with. And I'll be myself at last, as a starveling belches his odourless wind, before the bliss of coma. (Beckett 1973: 327)

Ann Banfield reads this as a rejection specifically of the surrogate mother tongue (English rather than Irish): 'Since English, like the forced feeding of the hunger striker, is thrust upon the Irish speaker [...] that attack reduces the language-milk taken in against the will to an excrement' (Banfield 2003: 9). *Au contraire*: it is hard to believe that Beckett's lactose intolerance could have been lulled at the breast by the lilt of Erse, Bantu, or any other candidate mother tongue.

The emetic aesthetic is maintained through *Texts for Nothing*, with its determination to turn aside from every 'guzzle of lies piping hot' (Beckett 1984: 105), and, indeed, alimentary forms of lessening and worsening survive to the end of Beckett's writing, for example, in the bulimic rhythm of filling and evacuation used by *Worstward Ho* to express its sense of serial negations and returns:

First the body. No. First the place. No. First both. Now either. Now the other. Sick of the either try the other. Sick of it back sick of the either. So on. Somehow on. Till sick of both. Throw up and go. Where neither. Till sick of there. Throw up and back. The body again. Where none. The place again. Where none. Try again. Fail again. Better again. Or better worse. Fail worse again. Still worse again. Till sick for good. Throw up for good. (Beckett 1989: 101–2)

Edith Fournier's French version of this passage opts to make the sickness and the throwing up, which may be read metaphorically in the English, entirely literal: 'Dégoûté de l'un essayer l'autre. Dégoûté de l'autre retour au dégoûte de l'un ... Vomir et partir ... Jusqu'à être dégoûté pour de bon. Vomir pour de bon. Partir pour de bon' (Beckett 1991: 8–9). But this loses what we might think of as the specifically nauseous nature of the project of worsening or sickening meaning, for nausea in fact never permits the full and definitive separation of throwing up 'for good'.

The Slimy

Sartre articulates in the final pages of *Being and Nothingness* a horror at the prospect of absorption by the indeterminate condition he names the *visqueux*, translated by Hazel Barnes as the *slimy*. The slimy is a quality of the in-itself that threatens the freedom and nihilating self-determination of the for-itself. There is a 'tactile fascination' in the indeterminate substance that seems to be docile to my touch, but wants to appropriate me as I attempt to appropriate it (Sartre 1984: 609). To absorb this kind of substance is to encounter what Sartre calls 'a poisonous possession', in which

> there is a possibility that the In-itself might absorb the For-itself; that is, that a being might be constituted in a manner just the reverse of the 'In-itself-For-itself,' and that in this new being the In-itself would draw the For-itself into its contingency, into its indifferent exteriority, into its foundationless existence. (Sartre 1984: 609)

So captivating, so overwhelmingly gluey is Sartre's evocation of his own disgust at the threat to the projective powers of the for-itself posed by the slimy, that it is easy to see why he has frequently been accused of a neurotic desire to shore up the integrity of the self in the face of formlessness, an accusation sharpened by his unabashed characterisation of the slimy as female. What this misses is the fact that all this is represented as a *taste* for Sartre, a way of choosing, that is, *existing*, his body, not the way in which bodies exist as such (as in so much else, for Sartre, there is no *as such* about it). The point of this final discussion in *Being and Nothingness* is not to assert the universality of this mode of the for-itself, though one can be forgiven for thinking so; rather it is to show that, even in this most proximal, reflex or even 'instinctual' affect, there is always a kind of choosing of being, a choice that is never free, in the sense of being entirely unconstrained, but which must always be made precisely because it is subject to the general constraint that I cannot choose not to make a choice as to how to exist my body, how to live in and live out my nausea.

Indeed, Sartre even allows the possibility of a choice of the slimy. The kind of existential psychoanalysis that he sketches in the final chapter of *Being and Nothingness* must orientate itself, not to the fundamental 'symbols of being', like holes, slime, snow and shine, but rather 'the free project of the unique person' in relation to them (Sartre 1984: 614):

> If the slimy is indeed the symbol of a being in which the for-itself is swallowed up by the in-itself, what kind of person am I if in encountering others, I love the slimy? To what fundamental project of myself am I referred if I want to explain this love of an ambiguous, sucking in-itself? (Sartre 1984: 614)

Sartre's question may help us describe a form of nauseous sensibility different from that we have so far made out in Beckett's work. Where Sartre insists on the primal horror at being sucked or swallowed up in mess or mire – the mire of 'Bouville', for example, that compound of La Rochelle and Le Havre, which forms the setting of his *Nausea* – Beckett's writing at times seems to find some accommodation with, and even a kind of appetite for, the mess. Sartre seems to want above all to distance himself from this indistinctness. In the final pages of *Being and Nothingness*, this distance is given a temporal form, as projection rather than Beckettian disjection:

> It is horrible in itself for a consciousness to become slimy . . . A consciousness which became slimy would be transformed by the thick stickiness of its ideas. From the time of our upsurge into the world, we are haunted by the image of a consciousness which would like to launch forth into the future, toward a projection of self, and which at the very moment when it was conscious of arriving there would be slyly held back by the invisible suction of the past and which would have to assist in its own slow dissolution in this past which it was fleeing . . . The horror of the slimy is the horrible fear that time might become slimy, that facticity might progress continually and insensibly and absorb the For-itself which *exists it*. (Sartre 1984: 610–11)

The occupants of *How It Is* seem, by contrast, like the inhabitants of Chandrapore at the beginning of E. M. Forster's *A Passage to India*, to be 'of mud moving' (Forster 2005: 5), and the very text to be a metabolic amalgam of mud, body, mouth and murmured words, past, present and future, churning and percolating into each other. The words that we read declare themselves to be simply the regurgitations of the voices the speaker hears, both within him and abroad. It is a 'continuous purgatorial process', as Beckett puts it at the conclusion of his essay on Joyce's *Finnegans Wake*, in which neither 'prize nor penalty' is to be expected and in which 'the partially purgatorial agent' is the 'partially purged' (Beckett 1983: 33). Here, it seems, time itself has indeed become slimy.

There are two opposite conditions in *How It Is*, which alternate in what seem like peristaltic spasms. On the one hand there is the slow oozing together of things – the body sinking into the mud, alimentation and excretion becoming simply phases of each other, everything slowly subsiding into everything else. On the other hand, there are the sudden 'existings', accesses of image and miracle, which stand clear of the indeterminate subsiding into equivalence. The first condition, in which nothing is to be distinguished from anything else, is figured by the image of a population crawling across the miry terrain, each dragging a sack with a burst bottom: 'those dragging on in front those dragging on behind whose lot has been whose lot will be what your lot is endless cortège of sacks burst in the interests of all' (Beckett 1977b: 53). But the sack with its bottom intact, which still contains cans of sardines and tuna, along with the vital 'opener', figures the principle of local separation from the general metabolism, the possibility of an opening in, or nihilation of, the general condition of metamorphic decay. An unruptured sack is a kind of negentropic pocket in things, which scoops out a state of exception from all the otherwise undifferentiated slurping and oozing. If there are sacks with the bottoms unburst, there is the possibility still of local variation, or an upsurge of existence out of the mud, which will allow in turn the possibility of time, an existence that takes the form of a kind of miraculous nausea: 'or a celestial tin miraculous sardines sent down by God at the news of my mishap wherewith to spew him out another week' (Beckett 1977b: 53).

Beckett is, if possible, even closer than Sartre to that proximal relation to self that Sartre designated as nausea. The problem under such circumstances is how to achieve or safeguard any kind of exteriority. Since I endlessly consume myself, there is no object outside me for me to assimilate; in just the same way, there is no possibility of my emptying myself of myself. There is no interchange of self and other, but only a kind of autophagy, of the kind that Beckett described in the course of a letter to Georges Duthuit of 9–10 March 1949, explaining why it is impossible for him, not just to write about Bram van Velde, but to 'write *about*' ('écrire *sur*' Beckett 2011: 137) at all, in that action of assisted exteriorisation which in his brief 'Homage to Jack B. Yeats', he will call 'the lenitive of comment' (Beckett 1983: 149):

> I shall tend irresistibly to pull Bram's case over towards my own, since that is the condition of being in it and talking about it, and then for other reasons less easy to admit. Let us say that what is at issue is the enjoyable possibility of existing in diverse forms, all of them, as it were, confirming the existence of the others, or each in turn confirmed by the one designated for that purpose and which, bursting with the visions thus obtained, indulges from time to time in a little session of autology, amid greedy sounds of suction. (Beckett 2011: 139) [gorgée des visions ainsi obtenues, se livre de temps en temps à une petite séance d'autologie, avec un bruit goulu de succion (Beckett 2011: 135)]

Beckett's self-reproach here introduces a new dimension to the question of the body: namely, the dyspepsia induced by the body of the Other.

Incorporation

Sartre does not regard the question of the body as exhausted by his explication of the body for itself. There are two further sections of 'The Body', one devoted to my apprehension of the body of the Other, and the other devoted to the being-there for the Other of my body. Beckett's writing may be said to follow something like the same trajectory, in its shift from the intensely interiorised account of the body-for-itself to an account of the body of and for the Other. In one sense, the body of the Other is just like my body for the Other – it is a pure object of knowledge. But there is a complexity, for it seems to be possible for me to share in some sense in the Other's nauseous self-relation:

> This facticity is precisely what the Other *exists* – in and through his for-itself; it is what the Other perpetually lives in nausea as a non-positional appre-hension of a contingency which he is, a pure apprehension of self as a factual existence. In a word, it is his *coenesthesia*. (Sartre 1984: 342)

Of course, my relation to the Other's body is different from his own, since for me it is a matter of something known. But, sooner or later, says Sartre, a new kind of nausea comes about, in which I take on or into myself some of the Other's nauseous relation to his own contingency:

> What for the Other is his *taste of himself* becomes for me the *Other's flesh*. The flesh is the pure contingency of presence. It is ordinarily hidden by clothes, make-up, the cut of the hair or beard, the expression, *etc*. But in the course of long acquaintance with a person there always comes an instant when all these disguises are thrown off and when I feel myself in the presence of the pure contingency of his presence. In this case I achieve in the face or the other parts of a body the pure intuition of the flesh. This intuition is not only knowledge; it is the affective apprehension of an absolute contingency, and this apprehension is a particular type of *nausea*. (Sartre 1984: 343–4)

Sartre here seems to hold out the prospect not just of knowing the fact of the other's contingency to himself, his taste of himself as an object, but also of feeling it in a kind of shared coenesthesia, in which I affectively (nauseously) participate in the Other's nauseated self-tasting. I get a taste of the Other's taste of himself.

In the final section of 'The Body', which is devoted to the ways in which 'I exist for myself as a body known by the Other' (Sartre 1984: 351), Sartre gives another version of this shared nausea. Discussing the ways in which 'a being-for-others haunts my facticity' (1984: 357), Sartre evokes the kind of disgust that I may be prompted to feel for my own body in light of my knowledge of other people's viewpoint on it, though he then immediately modifies the nature of this disgust, claiming that it is not strictly my own:

> I am not disgusted by all this. Nausea is all this as non-thetically existed. My knowledge extends my nausea toward that which it is for others. For it is the Other who grasps my nausea, precisely as *flesh* and with the nauseous character of all flesh. (Sartre 1984: 357)

Even worse for the voice in *The Unnamable* than 'the inestimable gift of life [that] had been rammed down my gullet' is the prospect of ingesting the body, or the idea of the body of others: 'What they were most determined for me to swallow was my fellow-creatures' (Beckett 1973: 300). In Beckett's writing after *The Unnamable*, the nauseous relation with the body comes more and more to implicate the body for, and the bodies of, others: the nausea of coenesthesia becomes the more complex nausea of heteraesthesia.

Sartre's final considerations of alimentation, assimilation and expulsion in general, as they are expressed in the final chapter of *Being and Nothingness*, bring to a climax his argument about the nature of possession, through which the for-itself attempts to make good the deficiency which decrees that '[t]he for-itself is the being which is to itself its own lack of being' (Sartre 1984: 565). Doing, Sartre declares, is always in fact a kind of having. Sartre assimilates knowledge to possession, since the urge to know is the urge 'to devour with the eyes' (Sartre 1984: 578). The most complete form of possession is that which takes the appropriated object into the body, through consumption. But an even more complete form of assimilation offers the magical prospect of eating one's cake without depleting it. Sartre finds in certain kinds of object and condition – snow or shininess, for example – the promise of the 'digested indigestible ... the dream of the non-destructive assimilation' (Sartre 1984: 579):

> The known is transformed into me; it becomes my thought and thereby consents to receive its existence from me alone. But this movement of dissolution is fixed by the fact that the known remains in the same place, indefinitely absorbed, devoured, and yet indefinitely intact, wholly digested and yet wholly outside, as indigestible as a stone. (Sartre 1984: 579)

This ideal, says Sartre, amounts to the desire to become God, or to have the same relation to the world as God has – both possessing it, and yet allowing it to be in full independence. This relation is indeed an ideal and scarcely to be achieved in the world – indeed, Sartre doubts if even God could manage it: 'The tragedy of the absolute Creator, if he existed, would be the impossibility of getting out of himself, for what he created could be only himself' (Sartre 1984: 590).

There is a particular Beckett text in which this relation seems to be aimed at, if not acted out. In *Ill Seen Ill Said*, something like a revival or limited rehabilitation of appetite seems to be permitted. The siege of the figure of the woman by the wooing eye is represented as a kind of hunger: 'Finally the face caught full in the last rays. Quick enlarge and devour before night falls' (Beckett 1989: 69). The alternating rhythm of opened and closed eyes becomes a rhythm of ingestion and digestion, with visual and alimentary assimilation being assimilated to each other:

> Having no need of light to see the eye makes haste. Before night falls. So it is. So itself belies. Then glutted – then torpid under its lid makes way for unreason ... While the eye digests its pittance. In the private dark. The general dark. (Beckett 1989: 69)

The most extended imaging of the woman shows her eating:

> The eye closes in the dark and sees her in the end. With her right hand as large as life she holds the edge of the bowl resting on her knees. With her left the spoon dipped in the slop. She waits. For it to cool perhaps. But no. Merely frozen again just as about to begin. At last in a twin movement full of grace she slowly raises the bowl toward her lips while at the same time with equal slowness bowing her head to join it. Having set out at the same instant they meet halfway and there come to rest. Fresh rigor before the first spoonful slobbered largely back into the slop. Others no happier till time to part lips and bowl and slowly back with never a slip to their starting points. As smooth and even fro as to. Now again the rigid Memnon pose. With her right hand she holds the edge of the bowl. With her left the spoon dipped in the slop. (Beckett 1989: 78–9)

The narrative here evinces disdain for the content of the eating (slop), while expending great labour on capturing and enacting its mobile form, which reads like a slowed-down, statuesque redemption of the furiously autonomous mechanism, with its 'flying arms, and champing mouth, and swallowing throat', of Mary the parlourmaid's ceaseless eating in *Watt* (Beckett 1972: 54). The coming together of mouth, hands and bowl, and then their parting, mimic the slow, respiratory rhythm of the opening and closing eye. The two extremes of the movement are 'grace' and 'slobber', separation and commingling. The alimentary churning of self and other found in *How It Is* has become slow, sepulchral and separated out. In place of the allergic expulsion or annihilation of the other to be found in Belacqua's lunch or the omnivorous assimilations of *How It Is*, the text here makes a space for the body of another, which hovers between assimilation and abandonment. At the heart of the movement is a kind of miniature nausea, in the 'spoonful slobbered largely back into the slop', which will be recalled in the 'suspicion of pulp' at the corner of the woman's mouth when seen later (Beckett 1989: 89). This nausea is a way to register within the field of the visible the woman's way of existing her body, neither abandoning nor accepting it. It is a momentary taste of her own self-taste, an internal sapience.

As the text approaches its end, the analogies between eating, seeing, seeking, seeming and speaking become closer and closer. The narration imagines closing itself off from external stimulus to protect itself from 'the vicissitude of hardly there and wholly gone' (Beckett 1989: 80), though then immediately acknowledges the possibility that it might have to find some relief in external vision: 'No more unless to rest. In the outward and so-called visible. That daub. Quick again to the brim the old nausea and shut again. On her. Till she be whole. Or abort. Question answered' (Beckett 1989: 80). Perhaps the 'old nausea' of the visible world is what will fill the eye 'to the brim'. Perhaps, on the contrary, it is open to us to see this as the eye, perhaps like the woman's own eyes, later described as 'fit ventholes of the soul that jakes' (Beckett 1989: 96), itself filling the outward scene with its own effluence. In a similar way, it is possible to read 'Shut on her' as meaning both shutting her off and enclosing her (Beckett: 1989: 80), in the way in which a mouth closes on what it means to consume – not to mention the possibility of a conjugation of *shut* into *shit* and *shat*.

Finally, the extraordinary finish of the text seems to allow an acknowledgement of the famishing that has driven it throughout:

> First last moment. Grant only enough remain to devour all. Moment by glutton moment. Sky earth the whole kit and boodle. Not another crumb of carrion left. Lick chops and basta. No. One moment more. One last. Grace to breathe that void. Know happiness. (Beckett 1989: 97)

The unpredictable lurches of register make the pitch of the writing extremely hard to catch. There is savage relish at the prospect of finally consuming the woman ('moment by glutton moment') combined with a kind of disgust (if she is carrion, then he is less predator than scavenger). But this suddenly gives way to a suspension, a graceful, grateful holding back of the swallow, as the saying of grace defers the beginning of the meal, an exquisite interval between appetite and assimilation, in a simultaneous solicitation and seeing off of the woman who we know well enough by now has anyway been all along no longer of this world. We may be reminded here of Sartre's suggestion that destruction can in fact be an ideal form of assimilation. The destroyed object 'has the impenetrability and sufficiency of being of the in-itself which it *has been*, but at the same time it has the invisibility and translucency of the nothingness which I am, since it *no longer exists*' (Sartre 1984: 593). Here, the tarrying, the epoch, the suspension, the catch in the throat, is perhaps itself a kind of reversed nausea, for what is nausea but the indefinite abeyance of the violent desire for definitive expulsion? This is not a passing beyond nausea, but an existing of it, a resiling against revulsion. Here, Beckett finds a way to hold to the nausea that is embodiment, of the body for-itself, the body for the other and the body of the Other for itself.

For both Beckett and Sartre, embodiment takes the form of a nausea, a proximity-to-self that can neither be purged nor absorbed. For both writers, alimentation is the way in which notions of embodiment and worldedness are 'existed'. Existence is indigestion. For Sartre, remarkably, this is a matter of much more – or perhaps one should say less – than a metaphor. The nausea of self-tasting is no symbol drawn from bodily experience, but rather the origin of that experience:

> We must not take the term *nausea* as a metaphor derived from our physiological disgust. On the contrary, we must realize that it is on the foundation of this nausea that all concrete and empirical nauseas (nausea caused by spoiled meat, fresh blood, excrement, *etc.*) are produced and make us vomit. (Sartre 1984: 338–9)

Nausea is itself because it has no mediating form, or because it is the form of immediacy itself, for it allows us no distance from ourselves. You cannot escape that desire for escape from yourself which is nausea, precisely because you are that desire. It is the very being of the subject that must be what it is not and not be what it is. Alimentation and disgust are the privileged expression of that relation of primal, proximal revulsion, that internal 'coefficient of adversity' (Sartre 1984: 328) which is at the heart of the not-quite-issueless predicament articulated in Sartre's phenomenology, in 'the fact that I am nothing without having to be what I am and yet in so far as I have to be what I am, I am without having to be' (Sartre 1984: 309).

Sartre's and Beckett's writings converge, not on a neutral set of beliefs or philosophical principles, but rather in a kind of cognitive tonality, in which nausea is nevertheless given some form, in something of the way in which Sartre describes the parsing of a sickness as my own. For both Sartre and Beckett, nausea becomes a kind of melody of malady (Sartre 1984: 336, 338). Phenomenology in general helps to explicate Beckett's attempt to find a way to write of and from the proximal heart of being. But perhaps only Sartre's version of phenomenology allows us to understand the impossibility of self-coincidence, the proximal revulsion from what is most proximate, in that part of me from which I can never pull apart, which Beckett finds at that heart. And it does not do so by giving us a set of transferable terms by which to explicate Beckett's representation of embodiment. Rather, Sartre provides an opening into an understanding of the conditions under which Beckett's writing is prompted always ('on') to its own project of being, its existing of its body. And Beckett will find, at the almost-last, that if existence is always haunted by the body, then embodiment demands to be existed as incorporation.

CHAPTER 4

Making Flies Mean Something

In 1982, Samuel Beckett replied to an academic who had sent him an essay he had written on animals in his work that flies – of which there had been not a whisper in the essay, but of which Beckett gave a couple of examples – 'might have been made to mean something' (Beckett 1982). This chapter is an effort to make flies mean something, or, failing that, at least to make out something of their bearing on meaning. Flies have traditionally been thought of as the opposite of thought, as unmeaning. The meaning of flies is their meaninglessness, their meanness, their insignificance, their negligible not-mattering. Flies are a maddening but trivial distraction – maddening, of course, just because they are trivial. To undertake the enterprise of making flies mean something may, of course, be to blunder flylike into a sticky little trap, since it could easily be that what Beckett meant was that making even flies mean something, in the sense of forcing them into meaning, was just the kind of miniaturist *i*-dotting explicitation that might be expected of academics with nothing better to do, or plenty better to do but the indolent indisposition to do it.

Implicit in this little sally may be a reminder that flies have often been thought of as a kind of threshold creature, a test-case for the idea of animality itself. Flies mark and make, not so much a boundary between humans and animals, as a boundary between animals and non-animals. Flies are, in this sense, not the animal other but the other of the animal. Flies, like ticks, maggots and fleas, were believed for many centuries to be spontaneously generated from purulent matter, to arise, for example, from drops of sweat dripping into dust. The belief in spontaneous generation was often linked to the idea that it produced imperfect creatures, creatures that do not belong to the domain of created nature. Aristotle was oddly uncertain about flies: although he observed and reported accurately on the life cycle of certain of the insects, he also thought that there were spontaneously generated flies, which, though they could copulate and reproduce, could never reproduce themselves identically:

[W]hensoever creatures are spontaneously generated, either in other animals, in the soil, or on plants, or in the parts of these, and when such are generated male and female, then from the copulation of such spontaneously generated males and females there is generated a something – a something never identical in shape with the parents, but a something imperfect. For instance, the issue of copulation in lice is nits; in flies, grubs; in fleas, grubs egg-like in shape; and from these issues the parent-species is never reproduced, nor is any animal produced at all, but the like nondescripts only. (Aristotle 1910: 539a–539b)

Flies may have been of interest to Beckett not just because of the possibility they held out for anthropomorphic identification, but more particularly because humans and flies were analogously anomalous. Both humans and flies are nonce- or nonesuch creatures, creatures of exception and accident. There is, in fact, a long tradition of identification between humans and flies. If flies are in one sense the opposite or negative of human beings, literally living in and off our deaths, they are also for that very reason our familiars and fellow-travellers, their wide dispersal across the world shadowing that of their human hosts and partners. Flies have for centuries been taken as emblematic of human weakness, vulnerability and susceptibility to frivolous pleasures. Some of Beckett's early representations of flies seem to come out of this emblematic tradition. For this tradition, flies were dedicated to light, life and libido and, thus, usually, neglectful of more spiritual truths. As dawn breaks at the end of *Watt*, flies, whose presence in such large numbers perhaps has something to do with the strange unlocatable smell of decomposition that assails Watt on first entering the waiting room (Beckett 1972: 234), gather and cluster longingly at the window:

> The flies, of skeleton thinness, excited to new efforts by yet another dawn, left the walls, and the ceiling, and even the floor, and hastened in great numbers to the window. Here, pressed against the impenetrable panes, they would enjoy the light, and warmth, of the long summer's day. (Beckett 1972: 236)

Flies have a prominent position in two poems Beckett wrote in the 1930s, 'Serena I' and 'La Mouche'. Both of these poems flirt with the kind of sentimentality that is always in the offing when an individual fly – 'my brother the fly' in 'Serena I' – is singled out for poetic attention and identification. The poem begins in the Regent's Park Zoo, with views of lugubrious weaver-birds, condors, elephants and adders, and proceeds in a mock-Dantean pilgrimage across various London locations. Its menagerie-itinerary comes to rest (as it may be in the garden of Kenwood), with an ominous, valedictory view of a less exotic creature:

> my brother the fly
> the common housefly
> sidling out of darkness into light
> fastens on his place in the sun
> whets his six legs
> revels in his planes his poisers
> it is the autumn of his life   (Beckett 2012: 17)

The possibility of fly-human identification is rather oddly suggested by Beckett's 1935 remark to Tom MacGreevy, following a lecture Beckett had heard by Carl Jung: 'I can't imagine his curing a fly of neurosis' (Beckett 2009b: 282). If one of the ways in which flies have been made to mean is by means of their meanness, then another is in the way in which they can be made to measure, or used to focus ideas of relative scale, and to make perspectives collide. During the nineteenth century, the fly, which had been thought to mark the limit of viability for life, began to be seen as the creature that inhabits the precise middle point of the scale of creation, holding the line between and macrocosm with just as many creatures above it, all the way up to the blue whale, as there are microscopic creatures below it. The real drama of 'La Mouche' is not that of an identification, but that of a sudden convulsion of scales, with the fly on its transparent screen, caught between death and life, as the connector and converter of the two immensities on either side of it, the crushing thumb and the vast void of sea and sky. Crushed against the pane, the fly seems magnified, precisely through being the only item in view. By the end of the poem, it has suddenly expanded to cosmic proportion, capsizing the relations between near and far, small and large, local and universal.

> entre la scène et moi
> la vitre
> vide sauf elle
> ventre à terre
> sanglée dans ses boyaux noirs
> antennes affolées ailes liées
> pattes crochues bouche suçant à vide
> sabrant l'azur s'écrasant contre l'invisible
> sous mon pouce impuissant elle fait chavirer
> la mer et le ciel serein   (Beckett 2012: 95)

> [between the vista and me
> the pane
> void save it
> belly down
> strapped in its black guts

crazed antennae, bound wings
legs crooked mouthparts sucking on void
slashing the blue crushing itself against the invisible
under my helpless thumb it convulses
sea and quiet sky] (my translation)

The fly also marks out a convergence or mingling of timescales. The speaker in *Texts for Nothing* remarks, '[T]hat's the way with those wild creatures and so short-lived, compared with me' (Beckett 1984: 72); but in *Molloy* Moran feels himself 'ageing as swiftly as a day-fly' (Beckett 1973: 149). In Beckett's later work, the fly becomes a much more ambiguous presence, a much less definitive and more dubious kind of possibility. Beckett often imagines a fly as the last possible accompaniment to his solitary creatures. In 'Imagination Dead Imagine', a fly represents the minimal, meremost flicker of life and the flickering of vision and imagination that may bring it into being:

> And always there among them somewhere the glaring eyes now clearer still in that flashes of vision few and far now rive their unseeingness. So for example as chance may have it on the ceiling a flyspeck or the insect itself or a strand of Emma's motte. Then lost and all the remaining field for hours of time on earth. Imagination dead imagine to lodge a second in that glare a dying common house or dying window fly, then fall the five feet to the dust and die or die and fall. No, no image, no fly here, no life or dying here but his, a speck of dirt. (Beckett 1984: 120)

A similar flickering of existence, between assumption and extinction, attaches to the putative or hypothecated fly in *Company*. The narrator imagines his story enlivened by the creation of a fly:

> Some movement of the hands? A hand. A clenching and unclenching. Difficult to justify. Or raised to brush away a fly. But there are no flies. Then why not let there be? The temptation is great. Let there be a fly. For him to brush away. A live fly mistaking him for dead. Made aware of its error and renewing it incontinent. What an addition to company that would be! A live fly mistaking him for dead. But no. He would not brush away a fly. (Beckett 1989: 22–3)

A sentimental reading might be that the fly indeed provides company in the darkness and silence, another living creature. But that 'let there be a fly' flickers between the permissive and the directive, since in Beckett's cosmos there may be as much cruelty in the *fiat musca* as charity. The word 'company' hints at a more sombre reading too, for it literally means eating or taking bread together. If the life of the fly seems in many ways incommensurable with that of humanity, not measurable on the same scale (and we have seen that questions of measure and scale will always be provoked by the thought of the fly), then it is certainly intimately commensal, taking its meals at the same table (we are a table spread for it).

The passage in *Company* also recalls the climax of Nathaniel Hawthorne's *The House of the Seven Gables*, though almost certainly unintentionally, so strong are the parallels. The penultimate chapter of Hawthorne's novel is all addressed to the solitary figure of Judge Jaffrey Pyncheon as he sits dead in his chair, clutching his ticking watch. Just as the figure in *Company* entertains a series of ghostly companions, so Hawthorne imagines a host of Pyncheon's ancestors processing through the death-chamber. In the end, the appearance of a fly and the judge's failure to brush it away mark the abandonment of the narrative's pretence that its addressee will ever respond to its jeerings and remonstrations:

> What! Thou art not stirred by this last appeal? No, not a jot! And there we see a fly – one of your common house-flies, such as are always buzzing on the window-pane – which has smelt out Governor Pyncheon, and alights, now on his forehead, now on his chin, and now, Heaven help us, is creeping over the bridge of his nose, towards the would-be chief-magistrate's wide-open eyes! Canst thou not brush the fly away? Art thou too sluggish? Thou man, that hadst so many busy projects yesterday! Art thou too weak, that wast so powerful? Not brush away a fly? Nay, then, we give thee up! (Hawthorne 1991: 283)

My editing of *The Unnamable* for Faber & Faber produced plenty of difficulties as well as delights. Among the less absorbing parts of the process was checking the Calder editions against the Olympia and Grove editions, particularly the punctuation. The problem was to distinguish commas from full stops, especially with the Calder edition, in which the otherwise admirably yeoman-like font does not always easily allow one to distinguish the tadpole tails of the commas from the emmet's eggs of the full stops. After an hour of close reading, some of the later pages of *The Unnamable* started to wriggle and shimmer under the pulsing eye like the lake-water under Antonie van Leeuwenhoek's microscope. I thought it might help to automate the process by scanning the texts and using the excellent JUXTA open source software to collate them. The problem here is the usual one – that scanning from less than immaculate copies of the text gives the OCR operation much to contend with, since the accidental maculae are so apt to be construed as punctuation marks.

There is a long tradition that associates the bodies of flies with just this kind of scriptive mark-making. Ambrose Bierce's *Devil's Dictionary* proposes that punctuation derives from fly-specks, the small traces of dipterous excrement:

FLY-:SPECK:, n. The prototype of punctuation. It is observed by Garvinus that the systems of punctuation in use by the various literary nations depended originally upon the social habits and general diet of the flies infesting the several countries. These creatures, which have always been distinguished for a neighborly and companionable familiarity with authors, liberally or niggardly embellish the manuscripts in process of growth under the pen, according to their bodily habit, bringing out the sense of the work by a species of interpretation superior to, and independent of, the writer's powers. The 'old masters' of literature – that is to say, the early writers whose work is so esteemed by later scribes and critics in the same language – never punctuated at all, but worked right along free-handed, without that abruption of the thought which comes from the use of points. [. . .] In the work of these primitive scribes all the punctuation is found, by the modern investigator with his optical instruments and chemical tests, to have been inserted by the writers' ingenious and serviceable collaborator, the common house-fly – *Musca maledicta*. (Bierce 2000: 83)

For Beckett too, we might surmise, flies are what bibliographers call accidentals, as opposed to substantives, a kind of noise, or automatic writing, neither figure nor ground, part of the fabric of the work, without quite partaking of its substance.

The visual noise of the fly is matched by its aural noise – that humming which indeed gives it its name in Romance languages, Greek *muia* modulating into Latin *musca*, Italian *mosca*, French *mouche* and English *midge*. Hebrew and Arabic hear a different kind of noise in the fly, more buzz than whine – the *zvuv* which gives *Beelzebub*. Beckett borrowed William James's phrase to refer to Murphy's vision of Mr Endon as a 'big blooming buzzing confusion or ground, mercifully free of figure' (Beckett 2003: 138; James 1981: 462). In *Not I*, buzzing is used to conjure something like the ground bass of existence, that which prevents the relapse into full and perfect insentience. But the buzzing can never be discerned as ground, for it keeps breaking in on the speaker – crossing the line between ground and figure, insisting on being recognised and acknowledged – though presumably it is not the buzzing itself, but some voice making reference to, raising the matter of the buzzing, that keeps breaking in:

> till another thought … oh long after … sudden flash … very foolish really but– … what? … the buzzing? … yes … all the time the buzzing … so-called … in the ears … though of course actually … not in the ears at all … in the skull … dull roar in the skull [. . .] no part– … what? … the buzzing? … yes … all silent but for the buzzing … so-called … (Beckett 1986: 377–8)

And yet the buzzing becomes a correlative of the voice itself, which indeed begins and ends as indeterminable noise at the opening and close of the play.

In aural as well as visual terms, the fly is a phenomenon of the in-between, a fact to which Beckett draws our attention in alluding in *Proust* to that author's treatment of flies:

> his faculties are more violently activated by intermediate than by terminal – capital – stimuli. We find countless examples of these secondary reflexes. Withdrawn in his dark cool room at Combray he extracts the total essence of a scorching midday from the scarlet stellar blows of a hammer in the street and the chamber-music of flies in the gloom. (Beckett 1970c: 83)

Another respect in which the fly can be regarded as a hinge or liminal creature is in relation to its uncertain singularity. Like all insects, flies appear to us as species-creatures, in that they do not have distinguishable individual appearances. *The* fly is always just *a* fly. And yet flies do not quite subsume their individual existences into that of the mass. It is common for human beings to refer to swarms of flies, but in reality flies do not form swarms, if by swarms we mean a collective form, or a form of behaviour that is more than a mere aggregation of individuals. Flies cluster, when they do, near a food source, or a source of warmth or coolness, not because their massing gives them any concerted mutual benefit. Fly swarms are contingent rather than constitutive, aggregative rather than associative. Yet flies seem to partake of plurality, most notably in their proverbial deaths (we die like flies, not like a fly) in a way that, for example, spiders and beetles do not.

In this respect, the fly is consubstantial with the many insects that scurry through Beckett's work. It is in *The Unnamable* that we find the insect, in the form of the ant, embodying the threshold or interstitial condition of the narrator, who is neither in nor out of language or being:

> In at one ear and incontinent out through the mouth, or the other ear, that's possible too. No sense in multiplying the occasions of error. Two holes and me in the middle, slightly choked. Or a single one, entrance and exit, where the words swarm and jostle like ants, hasty, indifferent, bringing nothing, taking nothing away, too light to leave a mark. (Beckett 1973: 357–8)

There seems to me to be a strong affinity between the swarming and jostling of words – often thought of in *The Unnamable* as a kind of semi-animated dust, ash or other particulate matter – and the swarming insects that the text evokes at moments like this. 'I'm like dust, they want to make a man out of dust', the voice says (Beckett 1973: 351). For the voice to be nothing but his voice, *vox et praeterea nihil*, is for it to be a swarm-entity, since a voice is the postulated synthesis of all the swirling bits and divisions of language, words, vocables, punctuation marks:

> I'm in words, made of words, others' words, what others, the place too, the
> air, the walls, the floor, the ceiling, all words, the whole world is here with
> me, I'm the air, the walls, the walled-in one, everything yields, opens, ebbs,
> flows, like flakes, I'm all these flakes, meeting, mingling, falling asunder,
> wherever I go I find me, leave me, go towards me, come from me, nothing
> ever but me, a particle of me, retrieved, lost, gone astray, I'm all these words,
> all these strangers, this dust of words, with no ground for their settling, no
> sky for their dispersing, coming together to say, fleeing one another to say,
> that I am they, all of them, those that merge, those that part, those that never
> meet. (Beckett 1973: 390)

There is in fact a link between atoms and insects, which in earlier times had
often been thought of as marking a kind of limit in terms of possible size, as
though animalcules represented the irreducible motes or corpuscles of life.
Fleas and flies were thought to be able to generate spontaneously, from dust
or dirt. This link is etymological as well as atomic: for an atom is that which
is *a-tomos*, without a break, while an insect, from *in* + *sectare*, to cut, is a
precise translation of the Greek *en-tomos*, that which has a cut or division
within it. Beckett's work often seems to be driven by the urge to atomise, to
slice, split and divide, in pursuit of the ideal of maximal disarticulation, or
what Wilfred Bion (1993) calls an 'attack on linking'; as Beckett told Lawrence
Harvey: '[Y]ou break up words to diminish shame' (Harvey 1970: 249).
The shame that Beckett seems to have in mind is the shame attaching to the
pride or presumption that he sought to guard against precisely with disarticulation, telling Harvey in 1961 or 1962 'I can't let my left hand know
what my right hand is doing. There is a danger of rising up into rhetoric.
Peak it even and pride comes. Words are a form of complacency' (Harvey
1970: 249–50).

Insects seem to be closely associated with all the many heaps or piles of
loosely sifting stuff, dust, millet, sand, lentils that appear so frequently
throughout Beckett's work as an image of the loose and provisional aggregation of selfhood, neither wholly dispersed, nor fully holding together.
Two of the most beautiful associations between flies and dust are to be
found in Moran's narrative in *Molloy*. The first is Moran's memory of seeing
the minimal breath of a fly's passage: 'And I note here the little beat my
heart once missed, in my home, when a fly, flying low above my ash-tray,
raised a little ash, with the breath of its wings' (Beckett 1973: 163). The
second is the little cluster of decomposed bees that Moran finds in his hive at
the end of his disastrous journey – though bees evolved from wasps and
were thought of for centuries as a kind of fly, bees are in fact, as the French
miel-mouche confirms, hymenoptera and not diptera – an experience

analogous, perhaps, to the discovery of the neglected hedgehog in *Company* (Beckett 1989: 24):

> I put my hand in the hive, moved it among the empty trays, felt along the bottom. It encountered, in a corner, a dry light ball. It crumbled under my fingers. They had clustered together for a little warmth, to try and sleep. I took out a handful. It was too dark to see, I put it in my pocket. It weighed nothing ... The next day I looked at my handful of bees. A little dust of annulets and wings. (Beckett 1973: 175)

This recalls an earlier passage in which the thought of dying like a fly has prompted in Moran himself the thought of crumbling into dust:

> And on myself too I pored, on me so changed from what I was. And I seemed to see myself ageing as swiftly as a day-fly. But the idea of ageing was not exactly the one which offered itself to me. And what I saw was more like a crumbling, a frenzied collapsing of all that had always protected me from all I was condemned to be. (Beckett 1973: 149)

The speaker in *Texts for Nothing* makes a similar copula between dust and the life and death of flies: 'Well look at me, a little dust in a little nook, stirred faintly this way and that by breath straying from the lost without. Yes, I'm here for ever, with the spinners and the dead flies, dancing to the tremor of their meshed wings, and it's well pleased I am, well pleased, that it's over and done with' (Beckett 1984: 90). Insects are of a piece with Beckett's highly developed feeling for the pulverous or particulate, which is drawn to and organises itself around the diffuse movements and massings of comminated matter, its siftings, shiftings, slippages, stirrings, swellings, erosions, undulations, dissolutions, agglomerations and agitations. A particulate mass is a mixed body, a median form between a body and the space it occupies – it is a body suffused by space, and a space saturated by bodies, which has its outside on its inside and whose inside is all outerness. The fizzy, sizzling sensation appropriate to these shifting masses is Willie's 'formication' in *Happy Days* (Beckett 1978b: 423).

There may be another, more particular reason for the association of flies with dust. At the end of their lives, usually after about three months or so, house flies will become infested by a fungus, which will slowly consume them from the inside out. They can often be seen, motionless on window panes or ledges, the desiccated effigies of themselves; sometimes the spores of the fungus will surround them in a faint white smudge of dust; touching the fly can be enough to crumble it into dust. The action of the fungus, known as *Empusa muscae*, was first described by Goethe in 1828. Those short-lived autumn flies, which Moran thinks of as having hatched out, may in fact be at the end of their lives. They certainly end in the dust-pan:

> You see them crawling and fluttering in the warm corners, puny, sluggish, torpid, mute. That is you see an odd one now and then. They must die very young, without having been able to lay. You sweep them away, you push them into the dust-pan with the brush, without knowing. That is a strange race of flies. (Beckett 1973: 166)

Appropriately, given its dipterous contour, the agent of verbal granulation in the trilogy and especially in *The Unnamable* is the comma – the word is derived from the Greek *kopma*, from *koptein*, to strike or cut – the mark of elementary division, dividing off the smallest unit of grammatical sense, that is nevertheless itself not quite entire; like the insect, the comma has duality or division within it, between body and tail, and therefore lacks the punctual absoluteness of the full stop or period.

The comma fulfils a dizzying multiplicity of functions in *The Unnamable*: interrupting, retarding, accelerating, clarifying, confirming, questioning, iterating, intensifying, interpolating, taking and making exception. Perhaps its principal function, though, like that of the fly, is to *distract*, to draw apart or internally divide an utterance that both does and does not wish to round on, to come round to itself. The comma performs in Beckett the labour of what Roland Barthes proposed in his *Elements of Semiology* to call 'arthrology', which he glossed as 'the science of apportionment', though the word really signifies the knowledge of joints and articulations – arthrology was used in the seventeenth century by John Wilkins and John Bulwer to mean a manual sign language. We may perhaps recall the speaker in *Texts for Nothing* looking at his own writing hand: '[I]t comes creeping out of shadow, the shadow of my head, then scurries back, no connexion with me. Like a little creepy crawly it ventures out an instant, then goes back in again' (Beckett 1984: 86). The comma articulates, in both senses, opening and occupying the intervals between units of sense. The comma has no sound in itself, but it exerts its influence on the sound and the sense of everything around it.

Unlike the period, however, the comma exerts only a short-range influence. The full stop draws together an entire span of words into a single, elastically sprung, intentional arc, turning it precisely into a *period*, literally, *peri + odos*, a turning way, a time that turns back on itself. The comma, by contrast, effects something like what Beckett, referring to Winnie's loose hold on time in *Happy Days*, calls the 'incomprehensible transport' from one moment to another (Beckett 1978b: 150). The sentences in *The Unnamable* have nothing like an organic closedness; rather they are like Hamm's 'moment upon

moment, pattering down, like the millet grains of … that old Greek'
(Beckett 1986: 126). Commas effect that weak syntax or 'syntax of weakness'
that Beckett told Lawrence Harvey he sought (Harvey 1970: 249). Beckett's
commas are appositional rather than compositional, they bring about
coordinated rather than subordinated syntax, in which items are added to
each other with the exhilarated, improvised forgetfulness of the fly in flight,
rather than layered or levelled. There is no subordination in this syntax, there
are no real enclosures; it is made up of what might be called leaking parenthesis, closed on one side and open on the other, as though the comma were
an abbreviated form of an opening bracket that never finds its corresponding
closing form, just as Beckett, following Joyce, uses commas rather than
inverted commas to introduce speech, the mark therefore inhabiting the
same plane as what it introduces, rather than being lifted above it.

At one point, Beckett seems to suggest an affinity between the non-finite
unfolding of his sentences and the similarly unfinished business of biological
evolution: 'my good-will at certain moments is such, and my longing to have
floundered however briefly, however feebly, in the great life torrent streaming
from the earliest protozoa to the very latest humans, that I, no, parenthesis
unfinished' (Beckett 1973: 324). When the voice congratulates himself on
keeping hold of an intention through the turbid spate of his discourse, it is in
terms that suggest to us the entomological nature of its form – 'what a
memory, real fly-paper' (Beckett 1973: 385). But, for much of the time, the
paper itself seems to lack this adhesiveness, as well as to be characterised by the
scribbling, riddling flight of what, in a poem that weaves together flies and
words, Ciaran Carson calls 'His dizzy Nibs' (Carson 1996: 42) The fly means
this prolonged meanwhile, incessantly coming unstuck, in a movement that
turns on itself without ever quite intersecting with its own flight.

The fly is a figure of distraction, of a dehiscent or internally divided
interiority, as in the cries of the patients in the Magdalen Mental Mercyseat
heard (and ignored) by Murphy: 'The frequent expressions apparently of
pain, rage, despair and in fact all the usual, to which some patients gave
vent, suggesting a fly somewhere in the ointment of Microcosmos' (Beckett
2003: 102). As a result of Mr Endon's erratic switching on and off of the light
to his room, '[t]he hypomanic bounced off the walls like a bluebottle in a
jar' (Beckett 2003: 139). Thoughts, so apt to be torn from their moorings by
the interference of the fly, are often themselves figured as flylike. Moran, for
all his tender curiosity about insects, does not tolerate them for long: 'That
there may have been two different persons involved, one my own Mollose,
the other the Molloy of the enquiry, was a thought which did not so much
as cross my mind, and if it had I should have driven it away, as one drives

away a fly, or a hornet' (Beckett 1973: 113). When hornets reappear in *The Unnamable*, they are not so easily to be evicted from thought, since they are now thought's own spasmodic, impassioned substance: 'For others the time-abolishing joys of impersonal and disinterested speculation. I only think, if that is the name for this vertiginous panic as of hornets smoked out of their nest, once a certain degree of terror has been exceeded' (Beckett 1973: 353).

The fly performs its work as a figure of distraction, of unintact, disfigured or discomposed thought, mostly through the idea of its infant form, the maggot, in which every fly begins its days. For centuries human beings have lived with a dread of their skulls and brains being invaded by worms or maggots. In the sixteenth and seventeenth centuries, the word 'maggot' was commonly used to mean a whim or fantastical obsession, that, once having taken up nibbling residence in the mind, could not easily be expelled. In this sense, the most developed dipterous doppelgänger in all of Beckett's works is the crepuscular non-figure of Worm in *The Unnamable*, whose role seems to be to bore out a pure space of hypothetical existence, which is meant never to be real enough to be falsified: 'Worm, I nearly said Watt, Worm, what can I say of Worm, who hasn't the wit to make himself plain, what to still this gnawing of termites in my Punch and Judy box' (Beckett 1973: 342).

I would like finally to revert to the postcard, or fly-leaf, of 1982 with which I began. Beckett recommended two examples of flies in his work that 'might have been made to mean something' (Beckett 1982) – 'the unswottable fly in La Mouche and the flies in the waiting room in *Watt*' (Beckett 1982). Of course, it is possible for 'swotting' to be spelled with an 'o', but it is surely much more usual to spell it 'swat'. In tipping this wink to the earnest young swot who had written to him, Beckett may have wanted simultaneously to offer up his flies to the loutishness of learning and protectively to hold them back. The first sentence of the postcard, alluding to the title of the article Beckett had been sent, 'Beckett's Animals', read 'Thank you for "my" animals, read with interest'. The fly at the end of 'Serena I' may allude to this question of ownership, for we hear that the fly 'fastens on his place in the sun' (Beckett 2012: 17). As Lawrence Harvey reminds us, the phrase 'place in the sun' is an allusion to one of Pascal's *Pensées* (no. 64) that deals with the theme of human ownership and appropriation (Harvey 1970: 90n.29):

> Mien. Tien. – Ce chien est à moi, disaient ces pauvres enfants, c'est là ma place au soleil. Voilà le commencement et l'image de l'usurpation de toute la terre. (Pascal 1962: 65)

[Mine, yours. – 'This dog is mine', said those poor children; 'that is my place in the sun.' Here is the beginning and the image of the usurpation of all the earth.] (my translation)

It seems as though the role of the fly, especially as bodied forth by the maggot – that incipient, almost-creature, in which the fly has its beginning, and we are like to find our end – is to be an image of the unconstruable, of that which cannot be made to mean, or might hold out against the eclipse of its being by meaning. Beckett prefers the inscrutable Worm to the creature occupying its place in the sun, in the burning light of scrutiny. Why, I wonder, does Beckett call the fly of 'La Mouche' unswottable'? Harvey, coached perhaps by Beckett, tells us that:

> He has been unable to act the part of fate. At the critical moment his thumb becomes paralyzed, incapable of visiting destruction on the helpless fly. While the poet wisely leaves it at that, we can easily imagine the experience preceding the poem, the sudden intuition of the unity of all living creatures in a common earthly destiny. (Harvey 1970: 198)

Hugh Kenner, by contrast, sees a very different ending to the poem: 'Having delineated the beast with precise repulsion, he squashes it, and the heavens, for no clear reason, are reversed in their courses. He is playing God, perhaps, and the fly (sucking the void, sabring the azure) is being made to play man' (Kenner 1961: 54). Both of these readings are perhaps right. For why is the fly, first so frenzied and yet so trapped, also immobile enough to be crushed by a thumb? I think it is plausible that the fly has already been swatted once and is here in its death throes, the only circumstances in which a fly may be crushed by a thumb, which makes the prolonging of its life scarcely as merciful as it seems to Harvey. Knowing, owning and owning up are perhaps not easily to be distinguished here.

Let me recall some of the claims I have been trying to get to stand up. First, that, as a kind of anomaly-animal, flies are fitted to embody the anomaly of the animal itself. Second, that flies are a kind of mean, a mediator and converter of scales and gradations. Third, that Beckett moves from an identificatory focus on the fly as singular entity to the indistinctness of the multiplicity – from the form to the swarm. Finally, the fly focuses a reproach to the usurpation of animality into the sphere of meaning.

The figuring of flies in Beckett's work allows us to imagine a different configuration of the relation between human and animal, that is neither the simple usurpation of the animal for human purposes – through what Derrida calls the 'animot', the singular-general name-word that names that which cannot name itself (Derrida 2008: 37) – nor the sentimental fantasy of ceding to the animal its existence *an sich*, its place in the sun, which is itself another mode of custody, making over to the animal as it does a being that it can never own. During Beckett's life, as the lives of humans and flies became indissolubly compounded, through the knowledge of our own composition furnished by *Drosophila melanogaster* (the fruit fly), the fly comes to allow an understanding of humans and animals, not as others or brothers, but as chimerical assemblages, constituted in their mutual interferences with each other, living out each other's lives and deaths.

PART II

Timepieces

CHAPTER 5

'I Switch Off': The Ordeals of Radio

Listening In

The question that a radio aesthetics can never for long set aside is that of location. Where is radio? Where does radio take place and what place does it occupy when it does?

There are two standard answers to this question, both in their way amounting to the answer 'noplace' and thus utopian. The first is given by F. T. Marinetti and Pino Masnata in the futurist manifesto 'La Radia' of 1933. According to this manifesto, the proper habitation of radio is everywhere. Its power is that of delocalisation, such that radio itself names a greater power of radiation, diffusion, dispersal – 'La Radia' – which it instantiates, and to which it is itself subject. La Radia, Marinetti says, abolishes 'the space and stage necessary to theater' such that '[n]o longer visible and framable the stage becomes universal and cosmic.' It promises '[a] pure organism of radio sensation ... An art without time or space without yesterday or tomorrow' (Marinetti and Masnata 1992: 267). Radio means the dispersal of all punctualities and particularities, of space and of time.

The second answer is that radio space is mind space: that radio is always enacted in the mind of the listener, and that the signified or assumed locations of radio are in fact surrogates for this mind space. The cosmic space of Marinetti's radiations shrinks to the booming round O of the skull.

The strangeness of radio comes from the fact that contingency is of its essence. Where the telephone establishes a connection between two determinate interlocutors – travelling through space but moored securely at both ends of the line – and the phonograph fossilises the act of listening and communication in a specific material form (the record as well as the apparatus needed to play it), radio occurs at the coincidence of two asymmetric actions – a broadcast that sends a signal out, with no clear idea of where it will be received, and a reception that always has the sense of an overhearing of an address that is not specifically directed at oneself. Hence, perhaps, the long survival of the phrase – well beyond the 1940s – of the expression 'listening in to the radio'. Listening in, as opposed simply to listening to, implies that the programme has been come upon by chance, or even surreptitiously. One eavesdrops on a programme that can never entirely be meant for one. One might even see the tendency to think of radio space as mind space as another kind of listening in, in a more appropriative sense – as a kind of deliberate incorporation or making one's own of what has been come upon.

This may also account for the fact that the radio has been thought of both as the most intimate of communications and as the most impersonal. Perhaps we can say that radio is characterised both by the intimacy of its impersonality and the impersonality of its intimacy.

In processing radio space as mind space, we make it possible to believe in the priority of the latter – to believe, in other words, that radio has the power it does because it happens to resemble the interior auditory dramas we all already experience. This is perhaps an auditory version of what Daniel Dennett has called the fallacy of the 'Cartesian theater' – the idea that somewhere inside the mind, behind its mechanical processes of perception, there exists a kind of primal scene or final instance in which everything is played out, for the solitary benefit of a mind's eye, or mind's ear, itself the organ of some homunculus, who is a miniaturised version of the mind itself (Dennett 1993: 101–38). This, of course, simply reinstates the problem of what perception actually is at a deeper level, and would require an infinite series of Cartesian theatres-within-theatres and homunculi-within-homunculi.

Beckett's radio worlds are indeed highly interior, and many critics have been tempted to see the principal use of the sensory deprivation or sensory concentration of radio as affording Beckett an opportunity to focus undistractedly on the interior workings of the mind. For Martin Esslin, this makes possible a kind of immediacy or tuning-together of the experience represented in the radio play and the experience of the listener: 'radio can create a subjective reality halfway between the objective events experienced and their subjective reflection within the mind of the character who experiences them' (Esslin 1982: 130–1). Nearly everybody who has written about Beckett's radio plays seems to agree that their ultimate location is the mind, or at any event, somebody's mind: 'the mental landscape that radio, unencumbered by visuals, is so good at' (Frost 1999: 322).

Beckett's most extended statement on the nature of radio expresses a slightly different perspective. Refusing permission for his first radio play, *All That Fall*, to be adapted for the stage, Beckett wrote to his American publisher Barney Rosset that

> *All That Fall* is a specifically radio play, or rather radio text, for voices, not bodies ... Even the reduced visual dimension it will receive from the simplest and most static of readings ... will be destructive of whatever quality it may have and which depends on the whole thing's *coming out of the dark*. (Quoted in Zilliacus 1976, n.p.)

Here, the emphasis is not upon the space which radio occupies or constitutes, but rather on its emergence from nothing and nowhere. It is in radio that Beckett seems to have found the possibility of writing without ground – that is to say, writing in which the spoken words are at once figure and ground. Under such conditions, to retire from utterance is to lapse from existence, a point made all the more intensely by Mrs Rooney's insistence in *All That Fall* that she is indeed still there even when she is not speaking: 'Do not imagine, because I am silent, that I am not present, and alive to all that is going on' (Beckett 1986: 185). Characters in *All That Fall* surge up out of nowhere or rather, perhaps, arise in their words, entering the sound space of the play with no announcement and vacating it just as abruptly. Existence in sound is the only existence possible. And yet, the comic overstatement of certain sounds, like the '*exaggerated station sounds. Falling signals. Bells. Whistles. Crescendo of train whistle approaching*' which mark the passage of the up mail in *All That Fall* (Beckett 1986: 187) also suggests a desperate need to convince, as though sound itself, even in this medium in which sound is everything, could never be enough. (The ostentatiously synthesised sounds of '*Sheep, bird, cow, cock*' that open and punctuate the play (Beckett 1986: 172,) also suggest the dubiousness of the sound-background.)

Radio Work

If radio does appear to come from nowhere, it can never in fact do so, setting apart the radiophonic fantasies of mystics and psychotics, without any material intermediary or apparatus – even if, like the legendary tooth filling, its radiophonic action is accidental or unwilled. Radio can come out of nowhere only because it passes between. Radio, just like cinema, always requires an apparatus, an array or arrangement of elements that is prepared in advance. To be sure, the material forms and arrangements of the radio are much more variable than the cinematic apparatus, as classically described by theorists like Jean-Louis Baudry (1985). Although, as a basic condition of cinema, one must, however minimally, subtract or absent oneself from involvement in the world (one must at the very least be facing forwards), one can nowadays listen to radio as one runs, irons, eats and makes love. Nevertheless, just as in the cinema, the apparatus is more than the support

or technical framework of radio. Surprisingly few writers – one of them being
Alan Beck in his *The Death of Radio?* (2002) – have attempted to adapt the
idea of cinematic apparatus to radio. The array or syntactic disposition of
elements of which radio is compounded, including the writer, the speaker,
the transmitter, the medium, the receiver, the context of reception and the
listener, spreads through the whole of radio, dividing and in the process
constituting that homogenous dark or nothingness out of which it seems
to come.

The apparatus of radio has slipped out of the picture, as radio has got the
reputation of being an immaterial art. This really began in the rise of public
broadcasting during the 1930s and with the impetus of war in the 1940s, as
listening became an ever more diffuse and involuntary activity. Radio provided more and more of an environment in which to live, and sank more and
more into the background, while listening became correspondingly less
focussed, more peripheral, more compounded with other things. Radios
themselves became smaller, lighter and more portable with the development
of midget radios during the Second World War, including one that was
designed to be operated from within a gas mask (Hill 1978: 85).

Beckett's work for and with the idea of radio reactivates an earlier tradition
in which listening to radio was an active, absorbing and laborious undertaking. By the 1950s, all the work of radio had passed across to the production
and transmission side, with listening requiring little in the way of preparation or active attention. But, in the early days of radio, before the advent of
broadcasting, radio was mostly the preserve of hobbyists and adventurers,
for whom listening was an intricate and expensive undertaking. During the
1910s and the early 1920s, radio listeners, like early motorists and computer
users, had often built their own apparatus, which needed to be carefully
maintained. Once the designs of radio had stabilised and been commer-
cialised, the radio set, often disguised as a piece of furniture, was merely a
way-station through which sounds and voices could pass on their way to the
listener. But before this, the apparatus was no mere accessory to the act of
listening. Apparatus and act were closely imbricated and reciprocally trans-
forming. Listeners to crystal sets had to cope with the susceptibility of the
apparatus to de-tuning. G.E. Mortley described the fragility of crystal reception in an article in the short-lived *Weather and Wireless Magazine* in 1924:

> [A] crystal is somewhat 'uncertain, coy and hard to please' with regard to
> location and pressure of contact, and it not infrequently happens that just as
> one reaches an important point during a communication, some slight
> vibration caused by traffic or what not can cause the crystal to become
> displaced, and the signal will be lost. (Mortley 1924: 13)

The arrival of valves freed operators from the problems of adjusting crystals, but brought problems of their own:

> [T]he valve has brought many knotty little points with it. The most difficult part of the whole set are the accumulators. They require constant watching. Their importance need not be described in full, since we all know that if they fail 'out goes the light!' (Allison 1924: 42)

One listened not only with the ear, but also with the vigilant eye and with patient, painstaking fingers and even with the tongue – the author of this article recommended developing the trick of tasting the strength of the charge remaining in the battery by applying the wires to the tongue (Allison 1924: 43).

Radio listening of this kind was described often and explicitly as 'work' requiring active, vigilant and inventive attention: 'The purity of music and speech where crystal rectification is employed is usually considerably greater than with valve rectification, unless the latter is in skilled hands . . . positive reliability is essential when working on weak signals or distant stations' (Mortley 1924: 13). Add to this the fact that the radio frequency bands were so sparsely populated with signals to listen to, causing radio enthusiasts to tune eagerly into transmissions from ships and military sources in their search for communications, and one has the sense that the ratio of activity is concentrated firmly on the reception rather than the transmission side. Beckett's work for radio activates this archaic sense, very literally, of the work of radio, the strenuous, solitary ardours of audition.

Beckett's work for radio is concentrated into a short period of his writing career. His first play for radio was *All That Fall*, written on invitation for the BBC in late 1956 and broadcast in January 1957. This seemed to trigger an intense period of reflection on and writing for radio, which occupied him from early 1959, when he wrote the play *Embers*, through to 1962. During this period he completed a sequence of closely related radio works: *Rough for Radio I* (written in French in late 1961 and first published as *Esquisse radiophonique*), *Rough for Radio II* (written in French in the early 1960s and published as *Pochade radiophonique*), *Words and Music* (written at the end of 1961, first broadcast by the BBC November 1962) and *Cascando* (written in early 1962 and first broadcast by the French ORTF in October 1963). The last of Beckett's engagements with radio occurred in 1963, when he produced an English version of a play by Robert Pinget, *La Manivelle*, as *The Old Tune*.

I think Stanley Richardson and Jane Alison Hale are right to say that 'Beckett's radio plays are not only for radio, they are about radio' (Richardson and Hale 1999: 285). Perhaps the most important feature of Beckett's work for the radio is the fact that it can also be thought of as a kind of work *on* radio, a working through of the grounds of possibility for radio, and what radio itself makes possible. Although Beckett's work for radio is concentrated into the space of about five years, the forms of radio radiate or diffuse throughout his work for other media. The work on radio works, we may say, on Beckett's work as a whole.

Alternating Currents

Gilles Deleuze and Félix Guattari have habituated us to the idea that machines are not merely analogous to the actions of desiring, but may also be generative of it – that desiring is no more or no other than a machinery, by which they usually seem to mean a conjuncture of relations (Deleuze and Guattari 1983: 1–2). But desiring-machines, like machines in general, are rarely apprehended as such and as a whole, just as the new experiences of 'communication', 'broadcasting' or 'transmission' never present themselves directly. Rather, they appear through certain approximations or synecdoches which stand for the entire ensemble of arrangements that makes up the machinery in question, just as Kleinian part-objects are both detached from and stand in for the body in its ungraspable wholeness. Among these mechanical part-objects are the screen, the wire, the lever, the wheel, the joystick, the pedal and the mouse. Perhaps no object of this kind is more pregnant of power and portent than the switch. Whether in the form of button, rocker, slider, tap, knob or cord, the switch is the executive means by which the apparatus is moved abruptly from one state to another – from 'off' to 'on'. In one sense, the switch is part of the apparatus; in another sense, because it has the power to bring the entire apparatus into working configuration, it is a kind of meta-apparatus, a machinery for communicating with the machine and making it work. When the machinery is itself concerned with communication, the means by which one communicates with it takes on an added significance.

We have become so familiar with the states of being off and on and the patterns of alternation between them that we no longer grasp their strangeness or newness. I am not suggesting that, before there were switches, people had no conception of absolute or strongly counterposed either/or alternative states. In this sense, off is to on as black is to white, death is to life, absence is to presence and nonbeing is to being. But switches made such absolute transitions easy and familiar. Devices for turning things on and off more or less instantly began to multiply through the mechanical age, and, by the beginning of the twentieth century, switches and valves and taps for gas, water and electricity were common.

The first use of the word 'switch' to mean a crossing over or redirection was in 1797, to refer to railway points (Curr 1797: 27). The OED also records a reference in the 1845 *Annual Register* to 'a "switch" which, when turned in one direction allows the train to pass direct on'; the word was still appearing with inverted commas as though to indicate that the usage was still not widespread. During the second half the nineteenth century, the word itself started to be switched across to other mechanisms and then, increasingly, to various forms of electrical appliance.

Perhaps the most culturally powerful of these devices was the electric chair, invented as a more humane – because more instant – way to execute felons. This method of execution seems first to have suggested itself in 1881 to a dentist and former steamboat engineer called Albert Southwick, who was surprised by how quickly and apparently painlessly a drunken man died when he touched the terminals of an electrical generator. In that year, discussions began about the use of electrocution to replace hanging. These discussions became caught up in the rivalry that developed between Thomas Edison, who had established a direct current (DC) service, and the system of alternating current (AC), which had been developed by Nikola Tesla and provided by Westinghouse. As part of his efforts to show how dangerous AC was compared with DC, and therefore appropriate for capital punishment but not domestic use, Edison conducted dozens of public electrocutions of dogs and other animals (including an elephant). When execution by electricity passed into law in 1889, George Westinghouse, whose company supplied AC electricity, campaigned against the law and refused to supply generators for the execution process. The fact that electrocution briefly became known as 'Westinghousing' shows that his fears were well founded.

Of course the rapid alternations of AC – at around fifty cycles a second in Europe and 60 in the United States – were and are not directly apprehensible. But devices like the electric bell seemed to offer an enactment of its power and fluctuating form. Perhaps alternating current proved acceptable in the long run because it seemed to be in accord with the many forms of undulation or oscillation with which people were increasingly made familiar from the late 1890s onwards, as explored by Shelley Trower in her *Senses of Vibration* (2012). The pain and danger of oscillation rapidly gave way to forms of pleasure, with the first development of vibrators for medical and then domestic use in the late 1880s (Maines 1999). By the 1940s, the word 'buzz' was also being used to describe the pleasurable sense of arousal

derived from the use of drugs, as though the organic-chemical world were
being electrolised. Increasingly, turning 'on' and 'off' came to be applied to
affective states. 'Turning on', meaning experiencing the high of intoxication,
dates from about the mid 1950s. Turning on sexually followed in short order.

There are different kinds of alternating current in Beckett's work. First of
all, there is the ideal of an alternation between absolute states of on and off.
But this itself alternates in Beckett's work with much more unpredictable
and capricious comings and goings, which seem to be emblematised in the
slapstick reading lamp in *Rough for Theatre II*. Here, two Pinteresque
investigators, placed at either end of the stage, each at a table with a reading
lamp, are investigating the life and probable suicide of an unnamed subject.
Their attempts to make out the documentary evidence of morbid sensitivity
in their subject are comically accompanied by a similar sensitivity in one of
the reading lamps:

B: I'll read the whole passage: '. . . morbidly sensitive to the opinion of others –'
   [*His lamp goes out.*] Well! The bulb has blown! [*The lamp goes on again.*] No
   it hasn't! Must be a faulty connection. [*Examines lamp, straightens flex.*]
   The flex was twisted, now all is well. [*Reading.*] '. . . morbidly sensitive –'
   [*The lamp goes out.*] Bugger and shit!
A: Try giving her a shake. [*B shakes the lamp. It goes on again.*] See! I picked up that
   wrinkle in the Band of Hope. [*Pause.*]
B: }   '. . . morbidly sensitive –'
   }[*Together.*]
A: }   Keep your hands off the table.
B: What?
A: Keep your hands off the table. If it's a connection the least jog can do it.
B: [*Having pulled back his chair a little way.*] '. . . morbidly sensitive –'
   [*The lamp goes out. B bangs on the table with his fist. The lamp goes on again.
   Pause.*]
A: Mysterious affair, electricity.

                                            (Beckett 1986: 242–3)

In Beckett's work, the states of being on and off are at once starkly counterposed, and capriciously unpredictable. If much of his work is dedicated to the
effort to get on, or at least keep going on, much is also concerned with the
effort to turn things off – the 'buzzing' doubts in the mind of the speaker in
Not I, for example, or the strange electronic susurration of the sea in *Embers*.

There is a particular salience to the on/off switch of the radio that makes
for a new understanding, a new experience of 'offness'. For something to be
switched off is for it to be in a state of suspension or abeyance. Offness
signifies a certain kind of readiness, an imminently actualisable possibility,

rather than a simple negative. 'Off' does not mean idle or at rest: it means standing by, being able, even about, at any moment, to be turned on.

When words fail on the stage, the stage, characters and scenery are still visibly, if mutely, still there. In this, the stage is like Freud's unconscious, in which, he wrote, 'we never discover a "no" ' (Freud 1961a: 239). When words and sounds die away on the radio, there is broadcast silence – what has come to be called 'dead air'. What one hears during broadcast silence is not exactly the sound of the radio when it is off; rather it is a kind of radiophonic offness, an offness that is nonetheless on. Interestingly, broadcasting regulations distinguish sharply between being 'off-air' and the broadcasting of nothing, of dead air or what is known as 'unmodulated carrier'. The broadcasting of dead air is nowadays an offence; under British broadcasting laws, any radio station that transmits more than ten minutes of dead air without any warning announcement or explanation is liable to legal penalty, or a fine of up to £25,000 per minute.

Unspeaking characters are not simply equivalent to characters who are offstage; rather, they resemble *Hamlet*'s Polonius behind the arras, in that they are on stage without being evident in the only way in which one can be evident in radio, namely by signifying their presence through sound. Where the stage provided a kind of relief, in its palpability, its three-dimensionality, its necessities of space and action, for a Beckett tormented by the uncertainties of his trilogy, the radio let in something like the opposite, in which absence and presence enter each other's condition. Indeed, we can say that this is part of the demand of radio – that its off condition enter into the broadcast. Later on, Beckett played a variation on this notion in the screenplay for his film *Film*, which specifies that '[t]he film is entirely silent except for the 'sssh!' in part one' (Beckett 1986: 323). The soundtrack is not off, or absent, as it might be said to be in a silent film, but rather is replete with silence, or offness. For radio differs from other devices for transmitting or reproducing sound. Whereas lifting the telephone or switching on the phonograph itself initiates the sound that is to be heard, in radio, the signal to which one tunes must already be there, unheard, but ready-to-be-heard, and by others in addition to oneself.

This uncertain condition of the radio switch is dramatised in Freud's famous description of playful alternation, the fort/da game of his grandson, described in his *Beyond the Pleasure Principle* (1955: 14–16). It is not often remembered that Freud describes two versions of this game. First Freud says that, in his game of alternately releasing and retrieving a cotton-reel flung out from his cot, the child gains pleasure from mastering the pain caused to him by the periodic disappearances of his mother. He then adds a footnote relating an episode that, he says, 'confirmed this interpretation fully' (Freud 1955: 15n1):

> One day the child's mother had been away for several hours and on her return was met with the words 'Baby o-o-o-o!' which was at first incomprehensible. It soon turned out, however, that during this long period of solitude the child had found a method of making *himself* disappear. He had discovered his reflection in a full-length mirror which did not quite reach to the ground, so that by crouching down he could make his mirror-image 'gone' (Freud 1955: 15n1).

Far from confirming the interpretation of the first game – in which the cotton-reel represents the mother, whom the child is able in play to treat like a puppet on a string – this footnote seems to describe a very different set-up, Whatever motive the child might have for toying with and joying in his own disappearance, it seems unrelated to his cotton-reel game. What is more, where the cotton-reel game seems to depend upon a simple alternation between the visibility and invisibility of the object/toy, with the child continuously present throughout and able to appreciate and enjoy the coming and going of his mother surrogate, it is the enjoying subject in the mirror game who makes himself appear and disappear and who derives pleasure from that. All that holds the child together in the intervals of invisibility is the fact that, crouching down, he is able to say that he is 'o-o-o-o!' – *fort*, away, gone or 'off'. In other words, in the second game, the child accedes to something like the condition of the radio body, that is there only if and when it utters, even as that utterance may testify to the fact that, in spite of all, it is not really or fully 'there'.

Switchboards

A number of actual switching devices feature in Beckett's work for radio. In *Rough for Radio I*, a woman is given a demonstration of the two 'needs' of a man she has come to visit, in the form of two knobs which, when turned to the right, produce the faint sound of music and a faint voice, whether singing or speaking is not made clear (Beckett 1986: 268). Daniel Albright suggests that, in contrast to the Beckettian stage settings that seem like magnified interiors of a skull, here 'he conceives an imaginary theatre space as a magnified version of a radio receiver' (Albright 2003: 112). This produces strange convolutions. The woman who has come to hear the sounds is astonished by what she finds in this scenario. First of all she discovers the asymmetry of transmission and reception, and the fact that, even though listening may be discontinuous, radio itself is unremitting:

SHE: Is it true the music goes on all the time?
HE: Yes.
SHE: Without cease?
HE: Without cease.
SHE: It's unthinkable! [*Pause.*] And the words too? All the time too?
HE: All the time.
SHE: Without cease?
HE: Yes.
SHE: It's unimaginable. So you are here all the time?
HE: Without cease.

(Beckett 1986: 267)

And then, seemingly forgetting the fact that she is on, or perhaps rather in radio, she asks if it would be possible to see the sources of the sound:

SHE: May one see them?
HE: No, madam.
SHE: I may not go and see them?
HE: No, madam.

(Beckett 1986: 267)

Here, Beckett's English translation adds a little extra detail that is not in his original French version: the woman asks, 'May we have a little light?' and is refused with the same 'No, madam', seeming to indicate that, despite the odd specificity of detail relating to the setting (the woman asks if she may squat 'on this hassock', and enquires as she leaves whether the carpet is a Turkoman), there is actually nothing to be seen, or to see with, in this eyeless place. When she asks if the sounds she is to hear are live, her French interlocutor wearily replies 'Mais bien entendu, madame', but she receives no answer to her query in the English version (Beckett 1978a: 90; Beckett 1986: 268).

The visitor's attention then turns to the apparatus to be used for hearing the sounds. She is told that she must twist the knob to the right rather than pushing it. We hear a click as she activates the sounds of the faint music with one knob, and another click as she turns on the sound of a single voice with the other. These knobs seem peculiar in their functioning. First of all, they do not seem to allow for alteration of volume, so that the voice and music remain distressingly faint, despite the woman's cries of 'Louder!' Secondly, they do not seem to stay on of their own accord, but rather, they lapse into silence after a few seconds, as though metered, or perhaps like the automatically returning dial of a telephone. So we hear the click as the knobs are turned repeatedly to the right, but never an answering click as they are turned off. The knobs are the only audible and executive parts of whatever apparatus is being used to convey and listen to the sounds. In a sense, they control the whole play, which then becomes an apparatus for tuning into the agon of listening to radio.

These switches are unusual in their literalness. But metaphorical switches and switchings also abound in Beckett's work, which is governed by alternation and oscillation. One might say that this is one of the most insistent forms in which the spectral apparatus of the radio radiates through his work, a work that might then be designated, not just as literally radio-phonic, in that Beckett wrote some of his most significant works for the radio, but also radiophoric, in that there is a kind of warping, or carrying away of the forms of the work by the phantasmal apparatus of radio. The inhabitants of the cylinder in *The Lost Ones* are subject to an artificial climate in which light and temperature rise and fall in regular coordinated cycles. Every now and then, at unpredictable intervals, the fluctuations of both light and temperature cease for a short period, as though both were 'connected somewhere to a single commutator' (Beckett 1984: 171). Beckett's odd term is a literal translation of the French 'commutateur', which, given the judicial associations of switch-throwing, allows the faint flicker of a suggestion that a penal sentence is being commuted. After the densely unparagraphed spate of *The Unnamable*, Beckett began to favour writing in short segments, separated by blank spaces. *How It Is* gives the impression of spasmodic bursts of murmuring, broken up by silences; later prose works like *Company*, *Ill Seen Ill Said* and *Worstward Ho* suggest a more measured pacing, with the gaps in the text seeming to be filled more with rumination than desperate, panicked lockjaw. But in all these cases, there is a rhythm of remission and resumption, in which the idea and experience of switching between alternate states of silence and utterance are to the fore. The very last words that Beckett wrote, or published, to be spoken in the theatre seem to designate a closing down of transmission not just of the particular work in which they feature, but of Beckett's work as a whole: 'Make sense who may. I switch off' says V at the end of *What Where* (Beckett 1986: 476).

Often, there is the suggestion that to be switched off and, more espe-cially, on in this way is very painful. Being suddenly switched into speech is like the awakening suffered by King Lear – 'you do me wrong to take me out o' the grave' (*King Lear* IV.7, 51). In *Happy Days*, the harsh bell that wakes Winnie and summons her to another 'happy day' of maundering yap is an instance of this kind of on-switch. In *Ohio Impromptu*, a Listener sits opposite a Reader and employs knocks on the table both to activate the reading when it has lapsed and to 'rewind' the reading to an earlier point. The most literal form of switching on is perhaps in the radio play *Rough for*

Radio II, in which the interrogation of the unfortunate Fox is initiated by the thudding of a ruler and pencil on a desk and then, when he proves too taciturn, the '[s]*wish and thud of pizzle on flesh*' (Beckett 1986: 278). This may remind us that the principal reference for the word 'switch', up until the nineteenth century, was to a whip or lash, usually made of a flexible twig or branch. The early form of the word was *swits* or *switz*, apparently variant of Low German *zwuksen*, which means to bend up and down, but is also imitative of the swishing noise of the lash.

The experience of switching, or being switched, is not just a matter of being activated or deactivated. In many of Beckett's works, the drama is developed and sustained through a switching between voices, characters or states. In *Play*, an inquisitory light switches restlessly between the three different witness-narrators, either in order to stitch together the sordid tale of adulterous deception they severally recount, or in quest of some truth unspoken by any of them. The second movement of the text has the three enurned characters addressing the light that comes on and off, prodding them into speech. We are to assume that none of the three knows of the presence of the other two, despite the fact that their urns are touching and that they are all contributing to the unfolding of their shared story. Theirs is a condition of non-coincident participation. For both characters and spotlight, existence is a matter of patterned intermittency. For the characters, there is the arbitrary and unintelligible switching on and off of the light. For the light, there is the restless switching between channels, anxious not to let a crucial word be uttered unheard.

Keep That Sound Down

The on/off switch in radios and other such appliances was often combined with a volume control. In Beckett's work, there is an equivalent linkage. Voices can suddenly be amplified, as in the moments in *Embers* in which Henry appears to be able to summon and amplify sounds in his mind:

HENRY: A drip! A drip! [*Sound of drip, rapidly amplified, suddenly cut off.*] Again! [*Drip again. Amplification begins.*] No! [*Drip cut off.*]

                                                       (Beckett 1986: 255)

HENRY: Hooves! [*Pause. Louder.*] Hooves! [*Sound of hooves walking on hard road. They die rapidly away.*] Again! [*Hooves as before.*]

                                                       (Beckett 1986: 257)

More usually, voices are subject to slow, agonising diminishment, as at the end of *Eh Joe*. In this play for television, we hear a voice telling Joe of his own efforts to switch off the voices in his head. When the stage directions call for 'the mounting tension of *listening*' (Beckett 1986: 362), all we are given to see is Joe screwing up his attention to make out the final words of the speaker describing what we presume is the suicide of one of Joe's lovers (or perhaps even her own suicide) as the volume diminishes. As the camera moves in more and more tightly on Joe's face, and the volume diminishes, it is as though a volume control were being turned up to its maximum to counteract the effect of the fading out, which is both dreaded and desired:

> [*Voice drops to whisper, almost inaudible except words in italics.*] . . .
>   *Breasts* in the stones . . . . and the *hands* . . . . Before they go . . . . *Imagine* the hands . . . . What are they at? . . . . In the *stones* . . . .
> [*Image fades, voice as before.*]
>   What are they fondling? . . . . Till they go . . . . There's love for you . . . . Isn't it Joe? . . . . Wasn't it Joe? . . . . *Eh Joe?* . . . . Wouldn't you say? . . . . Compared to us . . . . Compared to Him . . . . *Eh Joe?* . . .
> [*Voice and image out. End.*] (Beckett 1986: 366–7)

An anxiety about the diminishment or augmentation of volume is to be found in other Beckett plays, for various media. In *Happy Days*, the earth-bound Winnie tests the reception of her words on her partner Willie through a careful modulation of volume:

> WINNIE: Can you hear me? [*Pause.*] There! [*All these directions loud. Now in her normal voice, still turned towards him.*] Can you hear me? [*Pause.*] I beseech you, Willie, just yes or no, can you hear me, just yes or nothing.
>   [*Pause.*]
> WILLIE: Yes.
> WINNIE: [*Turning front, same voice.*] And now?
> WILLIE: [*Irritated.*] Yes.
> WINNIE: [*Less loud.*] And now?
> WILLIE: [*More irritated.*] Yes.
> WINNIE: [*Still less loud.*] And now? [*A little louder.*] And now?
> WILLIE: [*Violently.*] Yes!
>   (Beckett 1986: 147–8)

Winnie's concern is that her words should not be wasted – should not, one might say, be broadcast in vain, without a listener or receiving apparatus. For many, the volume control instantiated a world in which the normal physical limitations of distance and audibility can be overridden – in which the sound of the world could in principle be infinitely augmented. For Beckett, volume control is more likely to create inaudibility, or near-inaudibility. This makes it very hard to accept Everett Frost's suggestion that '[o]ntologically speaking, in radio sound not only makes sense, but *essence. Esse est audiri* . . . To be is to be heard (or, better, to be heard it to be; and not to be heard is not to be). It is significant that Beckett's characters often go blind, but seldom deaf' (Frost 1999: 316). By contrast, much of Beckett's world, and many of his characters and dramatic set-ups, are decidedly hard of hearing, with variability of volume making for a kind of structural deafness in the radio apparatus.

The television play *Ghost Trio* also evidences a concern with the conditions of audibility:

v: Good evening. Mine is a faint voice. Kindly tune accordingly. [*Pause.*] Good evening. Mine is a faint voice. Kindly tune accordingly. [*Pause.*] It will not be raised or lowered, whatever happens.

(Beckett 1986: 408)

Asking the listener to 'tune' suggests that establishing the right volume – a kind of ideal equipoise, perhaps between transmission and reception, neither one predominating – is equivalent to finding the right auditory focus, locking on to the station rather than in between stations. A little later on, the voice menacingly reminds the listener of the slightly uncomfortable optimum that it demands: 'Forgive my stating the obvious. [*Pause.*] Keep that sound down' (Beckett 1986: 408).

Tuning

The switch is an executive device, one that puts one in a position of control over the machinery that is thereby put into motion or discontinued. But the radio incorporates a more specific and sensitive form of executive control than either the on/off or volume switches. Listening to the radio also requires *tuning*. This makes the machinery of radio – especially early radios in which tuning could be a delicate and troublesome affair, subject to the vicissitudes of atmospherics and the physical condition of the apparatus itself – both more forensic and more volatile than that of other devices such as the gramophone or the telephone. In tuning, the listener to the radio actively and repeatedly constitutes his or her relation to the device and the transmissions to which it gives access. Tuning is perhaps a mechanical version of the phatic function, in which the contact between listener and signal is established, checked and confirmed. The uncertainty and fragility of Beckett's radiophoric apparatus means that the functions of switching and adjustment of volume often in fact approximate to that of tuning, or attempting to bring together in the same zone of reception, or frequency band, the listener and the transmitter. Beckett returns this musical

metaphor to its source at the beginning of *Words and Music*, in which the
controlling or summoning voice attempts to synchronise the two agencies
or faculties (Joe and Bob) who represent words and music.

The apparatus of radio also includes the interference or atmospherics
that, according to a well-known story, made it difficult for Beckett, listening
in Paris, to hear the first BBC broadcast of his play *All That Fall*. Interference,
scrambling, fading of signal, detuning, all the vicissitudes that beset the
listener to radio, are made part of Beckett's writing for the medium, which
features a large number of inchoate or unintelligible sounds. Perhaps the
most striking of these is the sound of the sea in *Embers*. As long as it is 'the
sound of the sea', it is an interpretable signal, emerging from the noise of
contingency. But for Henry, the sound of the sea does not quite correlate
with 'the sound of the sea':

> That sound you hear is the sea. [*Pause. Louder.*] I say that sound you hear is
> the sea, we are sitting on the strand. [*Pause.*] I mention it because the sound
> is strange, so unlike the sound of the sea, that if you didn't see what it was
> you wouldn't know what it was. (Beckett 1986: 253)

The sound is an anguished kind of interference, which is both less and more
than an identifiable sound or signal. His spectral interlocutor Ada is not at
all disturbed by the sound, which she finds peaceful and describes as 'like
another time, in the same place' (Beckett 1986: 258). But for Henry the sea
seems to be the sound of indeterminacy itself, corroding and decaying the
clarity of signals, hence his desire for definite sounds that stand clear of their
background, rather than including their background in themselves, or being
assimilated to it – the thumps of the music master's ruler, the stabbing of the
F-key on the piano, his father's slamming of the door and the clashing of
stones:

> Thuds, I want thuds! Like this! [*He fumbles in the shingle, catches up two big
> stones and starts dashing them together.*] Stone! [*Clash.*] Stone! [*Clash. 'Stone!'
> and clash amplified, shut off. Pause. He throws one stone away. Sound of its fall.*]
> That's life. [*He throws the other stone away. Sound of its fall.*] Not this . . .
> [*Pause.*] . . . sucking! (Beckett 1986: 260–1)

Writing for radio seems to have attuned Beckett to the effects of interference
or sonorous murk in his writing for other media. *How It Is* imagines a
speaker murmuring his words in the mud, the words strained and slobbered
as though they were themselves a kind of primal soup. *Not I* arises out of an
inaudible gabble and subsides at the end of the play back into it, as though
we had come to rest in a temporary slot of clear reception. *Play* begins with a
'chorus' in which all three characters speak unintelligibly all at once, before

the spotlight is able to separate the three stations or channels. Part of the point of the repetition of the play is to give the listener a chance to piece together a story that is unlikely to make much sense on first listening, as though signal were emerging from noise.

It is odd how bulkily bodily Beckett's work for this allegedly abstract medium can be. This is especially true of *All That Fall*, with its panting, shoving, straining, sniffling and shuffling. But, as Daniel Albright has noted, there is another dimension of physicality that is repeatedly evoked in the play – the physicality not of clear and distinct forms, but of soft edges, of the drift into indistinctness: it is, he says 'a soft sort of piece, a play about erosion' (Albright 2003: 110). But the play also correlates softness with declension, with the falling that is alluded to in its title and remorselessly played with throughout the text. Raising bulk upwards costs huge and extravagantly audible effort, whether it is Mrs Rooney being shoved into the seat of Ms Slocum's van, or her purgatorial toilings up the Matterhorn of the station steps. The principle of inertia ensures that these risings are only ever temporary and achieved at great cost, compared with the universal tendency of the material world to sink and settle:

MRS ROONEY: Suppose I do get up, will I ever get down?
MR SLOCUM: [*Breathing hard.*] You'll get down, Mrs Rooney, you'll get down.
We may not get you up, but I warrant you we'll get you down.
(Beckett 1986: 178)

Distinctness is correlated with uprightness, while the irresistible lapse and drift of things downwards suggests merging, decomposition, the loss of distinguishable form, just as Mrs Rooney imagines herself flopping down on the road 'like a big fat jelly out of a bowl' (Beckett 1986: 174). And this parabolic motion of alternation between up and down has sonorous correlatives. Articulate speech belongs to uprightness, just as descent is accompanied by cacophony and confusion, as in the directions for the sound of the descent of the Rooneys down the station steps – '*Confused noise of their descent. Panting, stumbling, ejaculations, curses. Silence*' (Beckett 1986: 190). These confused or inarticulate sounds are the aural correlative to the 'lingering dissolution' evoked by Mrs Rooney, which is followed directly by her observation that '[n]ow we are white with dust from head to foot' (Beckett 1986: 175). Sound is also an irritant, which has the power to raise the dust that Mrs Rooney despairs 'will not settle in our time. And when it does some great roaring machine will come and whirl it all skyhigh again' (Beckett 1986: 176). The logic here is perhaps that the effect of the roaring sound is as much to pulverise as to lift into distinctness. The subsiding tendency even extends to Mr Tyler's bicycle: 'My back tyre has gone down again. I pumped it hard as iron before I set out. And now I am on the rim' (Beckett 1986: 175). We do not hear the sound of the air escaping from Mr Tyler's tyre, but it is doubled by the general inarticulate windiness of the play, with all its panting, tittering, cackling and groaning, including Mrs Rooney blowing her nose *violently and long* (185) and the sudden enforced deflation of) Tommy: '*Loud titter from TOMMY cut short by MR BARRELL with backhanded blow in the stomach. Appropriate noise from TOMMY*' (Beckett 1986: 184). Of course, Beckett's attraction to the fart and its minor form, the fizzle, is well known, but there is evidence that on at least one occasion he associated it with the capacities or liabilities of radio in particular. In September 1938, during the anxious period leading up to war, Beckett described in a letter to George Reavey the effect on him of listening to Adolf Hitler: 'I heard Adolf the Peacemaker on the wireless last night. And thought I heard the air escaping – a slow puncture' (Beckett 2009: 642).

We do not think of sound as having weight, but Beckett's sound world exhibits a kind of declensive ballistics. If radio is normally a sublimating device, which turns material forms and objects into the events and energies of sound, radio sound here does not radiate outwards, but lapses downwards, as though energy were being converted into dead luggage, and clarity, like brightness, were falling from the air. In the end, the polyphony of voices and animal cries so comically picked out from their background, like a conductor, by Mrs Rooney – 'the birds – [*Brief chirp.*] – are tired singing. The cows – [*Brief moo.*] – and sheep – [*Brief baa.*] – ruminate in silence' (Beckett 1986: 192) – are swallowed up in the '*Tempest of wind and rain*' that ends the play (Beckett 1986: 199).

The pneumatic entropy of *All That Fall* is matched by *The Old Tune*, Beckett's English, or rather Irish, rendering of Robert Pinget's play *La Manivelle*. This is not usually included in accounts of Beckett's work of radio, though it has some striking continuities with it. The two wheezing old geezers – Cream and Gorman – whose rambling, spasmodic gassings by the side of a road are followed out through the play, struggle to make out what each other is saying against the deafening roars of traffic. Gorman's complaints about the traffic ('They'd tear you to flitters with their flaming machines' – Beckett 1986: 338) are reminiscent of the 'great roaring machine' that Mrs Rooney anticipates (Beckett 1986: 176) The other voice scored in the play is an unreliable, asthmatic barrel-organ, which Gorman's voice is clearly meant to mirror: 'Old man's cracked voice, frequent pauses for breath even in the middle of a word, speech indistinct for want of front teeth, whistling sibilants' (Beckett 1986: 337). The end of the play replaces the men's speech with a contest staged between the barrel organ and the traffic noise that threatens to engulf it. Though the victory goes to the tune, it is a tune that is itself made up of noise rather than being wholly distinct from it.

For Marinetti and other early radio enthusiasts, the radio represented the promise of an intoxicating dissolution of boundaries and limits. Where Marinetti projects an 'immensification of space' and a 'pure organism of sensations', others celebrated the capacity of radio to synthesise sound worlds, which would no longer, as in the theatre, need to be assembled from disparate elements like sound, light, music, movement and speech (Marinetti and Masnata 1992: 267). Radio means joyous moreness and exceeding of limit for many of its early practitioners and theorists. It is as though radio were, like radiation, a source of limitless, expansive energy. According to Daniel Tiffany, Ezra Pound was suspicious of radio's powers to enchant and fascinate, and to interrupt and disfigure the voice; therefore, he sought to take control of and channel the new form. Nevertheless, Pound recognised the odd affinity between the fluidity and shiftingness of *The Cantos* and the machinery he called 'a God damn destructive and dispersive devil of an invention' (Pound 1971: 342; Tiffany 1995: 280–8).

Some have seen Beckett taking advantage of the same freedom in his work for radio. Kim Conner, for example, argues that Beckett develops a 'radioactive voice', which, freed from the anchors of the body, 'is procreative precisely because of its disembodiment' and concludes that

> [t]hrough the technology of sound recording and broadcasting, the matter of the voice can be separated from the matter of the body, transmuted into energy, stored, and reconverted at will back into the matter of sound. Therefore, so can the multivalent associations and significance of that voice (indeed of all sound) be separated from its context, withdrawn from the passage of time and transported across space. (Conner 1997: 311)

But there is little sense of anything being done 'at will' in the radio work of Beckett. The sound world evoked by Beckett, not just in his works specifically for radio, but also in the ways in which the radio condition is propagated throughout his work, is tenuous, infirm, impeded, difficult, discontinuous. For Beckett, radio is projected as lessness, as liability and estrangement. Focussing on the distributed and distributing body of the radio apparatus, by means of which voices are abruptly terminated and painfully revived, Beckett finds in radio an anguished intermittence of being, in which neither transmitter nor receiver can ever be at peace or in one piece.

CHAPTER 6

Looping the Loop: Tape-Time in Burroughs and Beckett

The tape recorder is untimely. Though magnetic tape might seem like the orderly and inevitable successor to the phonograph, ushering in the new world of ubiquitous recording and playback following the Second World War, the principles of magnetic recording had been established since the beginning of the twentieth century, and forms of tape recording had been in use in the United States and Britain during the 1930s. Far from lying unsuspected in the womb of technological time, tape seemed to have been discovered, but then left undeveloped for some four decades. When Beckett conceived the idea of a play built around a character looking back on a lifetime of tape-recorded diaries, he realised that he would have to give it the only historical temporal specification to be found for any of his plays: '*a late evening in the future*' (Beckett 1986: 215). This now seems even odder than it did in its own time, for it is becoming every year less and less likely that such a future could now ever come about, that is to say, a future with a long and continuous history of tape recording behind it, so abrupt has the eclipse of tape been, and so imminent does its absolute extinction appear to be. It may have looked as though tapes were inevitably going to overtake records in 1958, and for a couple of decades after that, with the development of the cassette in the early 1960s, sales of which almost reached parity with those of gramophone disks by the beginning of 1982 (Millard 2005: 320). But this was the year in which the CD appeared, which quickly caused the demise of cassettes. The history and prospects of the phonograph seem, by contrast, and surprisingly, unbroken and assured.

This rapid occultation of the tape recorder may account in part for its remarkable neglect in the recent explosion of studies in the culture of sound reproduction. Despite the fact that modern electronic media would have been unthinkable without the possibilities of storage and editing that were opened up by magnetic tape technology, Steve Wurtzler's *Electric Sounds* (2007) contains only one reference to magnetic tape. In placing Beckett's *Krapp's Last Tape* at the end of an account of the anxiety and mistrust shown by modernist writers towards the phonograph and the gramophone, Sebastian Knowles seems simply to assimilate the tape recorder to the phonograph, seeing the tape recorder as just a technical variant in the history of phonography (Knowles 2003).

There are of course obvious analogies between the phonograph and the tape recorder, not the least of them the fact that both are analogue rather than digital media. Like tinfoil, shellac or vinyl, tape is what Michel Serres refers to as hard rather than soft (Connor 2009), since it relies on a material inscription of an acoustic signal rather than a digital encoding of it. However, from the beginning, the materiality of tape has seemed enigmatic or anomalous, relying as it does not on any visible tracing of the sound but on magnetic fluctuations that are analogous to or isomorphic with a variable electrical signal, which in itself is as much an encoded transformation as a physical trace or effect of the vibrations of sound. The difference between analogue and digital recording resolves in the end into the difference between a continuously varying waveform, in its various physical analogies, and a discontinuously encoded form. The fluctuations of the electrical field seem in some ways closer to a digital than an analogue encoding, since they are so easy to render as quantitative variations in a single continuous quality than qualitative variations. And the most important development in tape recording – which accounts for much of the difficulty in putting magnetic recording to wide use in Britain and America before the war, before the Allies were able to benefit from, or plunder, the technical developments made by German industries – was the technique of coating cellulose-acetate tape with ferric oxides in the form of a powder. This means that, at the microscopic level, tape recording involves not a continuously variable waveform, as analogue forms are supposed to, but the tracing of magnetic patterns in discontinuous bits, which are tiny (about 0.5 of a micrometre wide) but still distinct. The shape and size of these particles proved to be crucial to the quality of the sound reproduction: the ferric powders developed in Germany produced particles that were mostly regular cubes; the versions developed in the United States had a longer, sticklike shape, which allowed for better sound reproduction at lower speeds (Morton 2004: 114, 121).

The idea that one might be able to read off sound from the scorings in a phonograph record might always have been a fantasy, but gramophone records do allow for a certain kind of quasi-legibility, sounds of greater amplitude resulting for example in visibly deeper and wider indentations; DJs are able to drop the stylus very accurately on to a particular point in a piece of music using this kind of legibility. Tape offers much less opportunity for this, since the dispositions of the magnetic particles on the tape are not visible, meaning that one length of tape looks and feels pretty much identical to another. One of the reasons that magnetic recording was not adopted as quickly by editors of film sound after World War II was precisely that it did not offer a visible set of undulations on the film print as the optical soundtrack did (Morton 2004: 126). So although tape recording is like the gramophone in requiring some material analogue in which the trace or memory of the fluctuations in a magnetic field can be deposited, what is memorised seems only quasi-material. This may be why the concept of digital audio tape seems so much more plausible and comprehensible than that of digital vinyl.

Gramophone records have a reputation for being more corporeal than tape. This may be an accidental after-effect of the development of the cassette tape, which made the process by which the tape is read by the tape heads much less visible than the reading of the grooves of the gramophone record by the stylus, and also of the exploitation of the manipulability of the record in 'scratching' and DJing tactics and techniques from the 1980s onwards. This reputation may have been gained, not because gramophone disks are more susceptible to manipulation than tapes, but because disks are more vulnerable to damage. Indeed, tape requires and permits a much greater and more varied range of affordances, of bodily tactics and conducts than the phonograph. Gramophone disks are fascinating, but tape is intriguing – remembering the relation of that word to knitting (*tricoter*), trickery and intricacy, which connects to the whole tangled thematics of thread in the human imagination. Once the disk had been selected and removed from its wrapper, most record players will do most of the work thereafter. The problem with, but also the performative opportunity and provocation of, the tape recorder lay in the fact that one was required to do so much in relation to it – most particularly in the ticklish ritual of threading the tape into the machine, and then the even more exquisitely satisfying task of securing it on the empty or receiving spool. There were those who were prepared to create an extravagantly long trailer of tape to secure it in the notch provided for the purpose, but I always felt that efficiency, economy and grace all demanded that one attempt to secure the tape by the clasp of its own friction alone, which is perfectly possible to achieve. Use of the notch always struck me as both indolent and inelegant, and I quietly scorned the bunglers who needed to create a flapping kiss-curl in order to get the tape started, in much the same way as I looked down on those who needed a machine to help them roll cigarettes, the manual version of which, come to think of it, requires a very similar tucking-in technique.

Records are two-sided, but in a rather literal and visually intelligible way; one has only to flip the record to play the other side. The imaginary space of the tape seems more complex. There is really no 'other side' of the tape, since the reverse track is usually recorded in a strip that runs parallel, but in the reverse direction, to the first 'side'. Thus one does not so much play the other side, as the other direction of the tape, turning it back on itself. In a malconfigured tape recorder, these two tracks could bleed across into each other. It is not surprising that, when cassette tapes automated the process of tape listening, they replicated the experience of the gramophone record, allowing one simply to flip and play again. To play the reverse side of a tape means sometimes to wind through to the end, take the tape from the right hand side spool, swap it with the now empty tape on the left hand spool, rethread and play again. The tape instantiates and occupies a space that does not so easily surrender or reduce to visuality. It is a soft, semi-imaginary space. The obvious disadvantage of tape, which it shares with the scroll, partially overcome by the book and the gramophone record and now (almost) fully overcome by the searchable electronic text, is that it locks one into the continuum of recorded sounds, making it hard to get from one part to another except by going through the sequence once again, like someone trying to remember a line from the middle of a song. But this disadvantage is in fact a hidden opportunity; for the plasticity and mutability of tape means that it allows one to rework, to work against or work across its given conditions, to overcome or outwit its resistances. The advantage of tape is precisely that it is pedagogical; it is a technic that teaches technique.

It is perhaps this tactile involvement with the intrigues of the tape that accounts for the fact that almost all sound editing software retains the virtual image of the unrolling tape in its graphical form. In part, this has to do with the influence of film editing, which accustomed sound editors to the idea that editing was fundamentally a matter of coordinating two dimensions: the vertical one of cutting and splicing, and the horizontal one of the sound-stream. Behind both, surely, lies the visual grammar of the musical stave. In the early days of digital editing, sound editors found it very hard to let go of the physical process of editing, and in a BBC editing studio as recently as 2009, I saw an emulator in use that allowed editors working on digital files to continue to experience the feel of working on the larger scale of quarter-inch tape.

The materiality of the gramophone record allows one to cut, to skip, to retard, accelerate and reverse, but only as variations in an already predetermined form, in a record that has always already been cut. Tape allows many more opportunities to interrupt, to intervene in and to transform the signal as it is being formed. Record 'scratching' allows one to interfere with the reproduction of a recorded signal; tape editing allows one to start again and produce a new signal entirely. As N. Katherine Hayles observes, 'whereas the phonograph produced objects that could be consumed only in their manufactured form, magnetic tape allowed the consumer to be a producer as well' (Hayles 1999: 210). Whereas gramophone disks remained technologies of sound reproduction, tape became an instrument of production, changing the technologies and practices of recording in fundamental ways, which emphasised, not the faithful capture of sound, but its manipulation (Morton 2004: 142). One of the most important features of the tape recorder for post-war writers was surely the analogies it suggested with the typewriter. Here, too, the operator needed to wind the material to be inscribed around a drum (a complex operation when making carbon copies). The inked tape unrolled similarly underneath the keys from a spool on the left to one on the right, and then back again. Once again, this suggested a medium that provided ongoing opportunities for intervention and transformation. One can compare gramophonic modification to medical treatment that works at the level of the body, through grafting, amputation and other forms of local therapy, and tape recording to treatment at the level of the chromosome. The gramophone is revisionist; the tape recorder is regenerative.

The other determining feature of the tape recorder is that it is reversible, and in a number of different senses. I do not mean by this simply that it allows one to hear things backwards, significant though this capacity is, for the phonograph also allows this. It is reversible in the sense that the tape recorder allows both recording and playback. Of course, this too was true of the phonograph as opposed to the gramophone, and the recording capacities of the phonograph and various other recording devices were not completely forgotten or swept away by the gramophone. But the tape recorder does more than double the function of the phonograph. It also allows one to connect recording to playback and playback to recording in various ways, as well as simply alternating between them. If one imagines playback as the verso of the act of recording, which is its recto, then the tape recorder allowed the formation of something like a Moebius strip, in which recording and playback could feed into and bear upon each other. This metaphor is deployed by N. Katherine Hayles too, who sees tape as inviting us to see passive inscription and active incorporation 'not as static concepts but as mutating surfaces that transform into one another' (Hayles 1999: 220). The canonical demonstration of this is Alvin Lucier's *I Am Sitting In a Room*, in which a voice was recorded in a room, then the output tape of that recording was broadcast back into the room and rerecorded, this input then providing the output for a further recording, and so on, through dozens of iterations, in which playback and recording are simultaneous and indistinguishable. This arrangement is theoretically possible with a series of phonographs, of course, but is much easier to do with a tape recorder. It was not long before tape recorders were available that allowed one to do this kind of rerecording on to the same tape, using the playback and recording heads of a single machine. The result was that a kind of reflexive self-relation becomes tightly wound up in the experience and meaning of the tape recorder. The tape remains soft, and 'live' in a sense that the groove of the record does not, the proof of this being that tape is vulnerable not just to damage (damage-ability is central to the understanding and experience of many forms of recording media), but also to deletion. The disk is a fossil record; the tape is much more like Freud's Wunderblock (1961b), susceptible at any point to modification and erasure. The disk lays sound out for manipulation and modification. Tape allows sound to turn back on, and in on itself. This could sometimes happen without human intervention. One of the most mysterious effects of old tapes was the phenomenon of 'print-through', caused by the fact that, when wound on top of one another, the magnetic patterns deposited in one part of the tape could print themselves by induction on a neighbouring part of the tape. Normally this faint ghost-ing of the sound is buried by the principal signal, but it can become audible in blank passages of tape, causing a curious anticipation of the first second or so of a track before it actually begins. Tape embodies not just the stopping of time, but the spreading and thickening of the present moment.

Most importantly, tape seems to allow for real-time manipulations and transformations, folding together the real and the reel. There are many different variants of this. In the early 1950s, Jacques Poullin invented a device known as a 'morphophone'. The morphophone played a loop of tape in a circle, in which were set an erasing head, a recording tape and ten playback heads, the positions of which could be adjusted to allow different kinds of delays. Another technique devised by Brian Eno and Robert Fripp was called 'Frippertronics'. This involves hooking up two tape recorders alongside each other; an input is recorded on the left-hand machine, and the tape is fed to the right-hand machine, which plays back the sound that has just been recorded, though with a few seconds' delay. This signal can then be fed back to the first tape recorder and replaced by or mixed with whatever new sound may be being played. Similar looping systems were used by artists such as Roy Harper and, most notably, John Martyn, though by now the tape had been replaced by the Echoplex echo delay unit. An entire language of reverberation and echo effects is owed to tape, in the history of reverberation which remains deliciously to be written. What happens under these circumstances is not the simple, two-stage recording and retrieval of the phonograph, but the rapid alternation of past, present and future, in a kind of eddy. Tape then becomes an image of time susceptible of being looped as well as lopped, knotted as well as pooled. If the gramophone disk is an impassioned surface, tape is an ideal, phantasmal fabric.

But the tape recorder is reversible in a more radical sense still, namely that it allows things to be erased and re-recorded. Gramophones can play sounds backwards, but cannot unsound them. They can allow you to go upstream in the continuum of sound, but not backwards from the stream of sound itself into the state of the tabula rasa. If you play a gramophone disk backwards, you will have to do so in real, elapsing time. If you erase a tape, it will be as though time itself were being rewound. It is this capacity of tape to be reused that explains why so much post-war broadcasting was lost. If one had been able to reuse film in the same way, many more early works of cinema might similarly have vanished. 'Dubbing', a term that derives from post-production synchronisation of dialogue, is almost certainly derived from 'doubling', but the customary spelling suggests an association with rubbing, and rubbing out.

Indeed, we might say that the awareness and possibility of loss is built into tape in a way that it is not in gramophone recording. This is precisely because of the capacity that tape offers of layering and alternating recording and playback, building up multitrack recordings. Of course, the problem of decay certainly exists in gramophone recordings, and the best reproduction will still always be from a cutting that is as few generations as possible removed from the master disk. But the fact that rerecording in the case of the gramophone tends to be a matter of reproduction rather than of primary production means that loss and decay are less of a constant issue than they are in magnetic recordings in which the mixing together of live and recorded elements is commonplace. The fact that magnetic tape allows one to do more editing at every stage means that the question of loss and degradation is also much more pressing. It also makes it possible for such effects to be exploited, as in Alvin Lucier's *I Am Sitting In a Room*. In such media, loss is more. In a melancholy play like Beckett's *Krapp's Last Tape*, the function of tape indeed seems to be to 'link us to our losses', in Philip Larkin's phrase (Larkin 1988: 106). Beckett discovers for himself this layering structure in *Krapp's Last Tape*, the early drafts of which indicate that his plan was to have Krapp simply listening to a series of separate instalments from different moments of his life. The play developed its distinctively nested or sprung structure when Beckett collapsed two tapes into one, with his thirty-nine-year-old self acting as an intermediary for the mid-twenties Krapp, whom we never hear directly (Gontarski 1977: 64).

The most distinctive feature of the tape recorder arises from the combination of its extreme plasticity and its corporeality. For William Burroughs, who used tape recordings extensively in his early writings, the tape recorder was not an image or facsimile of sound reality, it was continuous with it. Burroughs borrows from his friend Brion Gyson the view that writing is fifty years behind painting because 'the painter can touch and handle his medium and the writer cannot. The writer does not know what words are' (Burroughs 1969: 12). The various 'cut-up' techniques that Burroughs devised, both with the use of tape recorders and with the manipulation of printed text, were intended in part to give the writer a kind of plastic, elastic contact with his medium: 'These techniques can show the writer what words are and put him in tactile communication with his medium', said Burroughs (12).

Burroughs believed that the link between tape-recorded sounds and ideas and real sound and ideas was so tight that cut-ups could have a kind of prophetic power, through revealing splices and fault-lines in the fabric of reality that would ordinarily be concealed or forgotten. Burroughs gives as an example of this a cut-up he made from a text by John Paul Getty which produced the sentence 'It's a bad thing to sue your own father'. Three years later, Getty indeed found himself being sued by his son. 'Perhaps events are pre-written and pre-recorded and when you cut word lines the future leaks out', commented Burroughs (Burroughs 1969: 13). The magical thinking here involves a familiar reversibility of the relation between reality and representation. When the recording seems so tightly bound to and even consubstantial with the reality that seems spontaneously to give rise to it, it can appear that the recording can reciprocally give rise to or revise a reality. This reversibility seems to be a mirror of, and to be mirrored in, the reversibility of tape.

Burroughs's use of tape exploits the two sides of the editing process, which are the same as the two alchemical principles of *solve et coagula*, disjoining and joining, cutting and pasting. Burroughs developed a weird and frankly rather wearisome political psychophysics, according to which all human beings were programmed by external messages. Burroughs sees language as a kind of tape system, so that thinking itself is a kind of playback, or rather perhaps a simultaneous recording and playback. Burroughs is not the only person to have borrowed from the tape recorder to understand mental functioning. Recent work suggests that these kinds of hallucinations may have their origin in some kind of distortion in the perception of time, for which the tape recorder has sometimes provided an apt analogy. A recent review of work on déjà vu suggests (while warning that this is just an analogy, which seems to have no anatomical basis), that '[i]f the brain's memory system is like a tape recorder, it is as if the recording head has got muddled with the playback head' (Phillips 2009: 28). Other work suggests that ordinary temporal apprehension may involve the coordination of several time tracks; schizophrenics tend to display poor coordination of time events, leading to the suggestion that sensations of being controlled by external forces may actually derive from a failure of neurological synchronisation that leads to somebody experiencing the evidence or 'playback' of one's own actions before the sensation of having initiated or 'recorded' them, rather than vice versa (Fox 2009: 36).

For Burroughs, there is no simple way to eject or escape from this apparatus, but it is possible to reprogramme it. The cuts and displacements that Burroughs introduces are aimed at jamming the system, freeing subjects from their sense of having been preprogrammed. Rather than attempting to remove the tape, the tape is cut, ravelled and sabotaged. This is one side of what tape manipulation can bring about. The other side is the creation of new kinds of continuities, especially through sexual couplings. Burroughs's work plays with the idea of splitting people down the middle and resuturing them, either with themselves or with each other. With its interchange between left and right reels, the tape recorder provides a suggestive image of this process:

> Small microphones were attached to the two sides of his body the sounds recorded on two tape recorders – He heard the beating of his heart, the gurgle of shifting secretions and food, the rattle of breath and scratches of throat gristle – crystal bubbles in the sinus chambers magnified from the recorders. – The attendant ran the tape from one recorder onto the other to produce the sound of feedback between the two body halves – a rhythmic twang – soft hammer of heartbeats pounding along the divide line of his body. (Burroughs 1968: 72)

An even more suggestive rhyme may be that between the two hemispheres of the brain and the two spools of the tape recorder. In fact, the relation between the right and left brain has sometimes been understood in terms, not only of the circulation of recording and playback functions, but also of the difference between two different kinds of recording, namely the analogue and the digital:

> The right hemisphere encodes data according to its total configurational similarity to other available gestalts, whereas the left hemisphere encodes

stimulus configurations according to verbal codes and categories. Human hemispheric specialization is not unlike the difference between magnetic analogue tape recording and digital tape recording. The left hemisphere works like a digital audio recorder, using words as the medium for an encoding-decoding process, with words functioning as the "digital" units of meaning, much as the digital audio recorder breaks the complex acoustic waveform down into pieces that can then be encoded into numbers. The right hemisphere works more like an analogue recorder, which records a magnetic analogue of the whole acoustic waveform. (Watt 1990: 493)

Another metaphor that Burroughs frequently employs to express the invasive capacity of tapes is the tapeworm, which literally takes up residence in the human body, coiling itself through the intestines and sharing its nutrition. In the end, the tapeworm comes to double the shape of the human body itself, the auditory channel isotropic with the alimentary canal.

There are striking differences between the different uses of tape made by Burroughs and Beckett. Though Burroughs met and admired Beckett, he seems not to have alluded to Beckett's use of tape in *Krapp's Last Tape*. But the two writers have in common a sensitivity to the powers of tape to induce bodily hallucinations. Krapp's tape-erotics are of a rather less magical kind than those of Burroughs, though the movement of the tape back and forth is a kind of mechanical masturbation for him (Beckett noted in his production notebook 'Tape-recorder companion of his solitude. Masturbatory agent' [Beckett 1992: 181]). As Krapp winds back and forth, coming up short, overshooting, circling back, the tape is violently shuttled back and forth, in a sort of chronic, clonic frottage. This onanistic association is highlighted by a change that Beckett made in 1969 when directing the play in German in the Schiller-Theater in Berlin. Where the published text has Krapp say of his recent concourse with Fanny, the obliging 'bony old ghost of a whore' that it was 'better than a kick in the crutch' (Beckett 1986: 222), Beckett substituted 'etwas besser als zwischen Daumen und Zeigefinger' ('a bit better than between thumb and forefinger') (Beckett 1970a: 98). A similar change was introduced in the French production Beckett directed in the following year, 'mais sans doute mieux qu'un coup de pied dans l'entre-jambes' becoming 'mais quand même un peu mieux qu'entre pouce et index' (Beckett 1992: 36), while Beckett substituted 'better than the thumb and forefinger' in the English production he directed in Berlin in 1977 (Beckett 1992: 36). Beckett enjoins a particular attention to the work of hands and fingers in manipulating the tape and tape recorder, making it clear, for example, when winding forwards and backwards is to be done mechanically, and when it is to be done manually, with a single, dialling finger in the spool. The shimmying back and forth of revelation and concealment, of *fort* and *da*, is intensified by the bipolar structure of the tape recorder, which may make manifest the association that Lynda Nead notices in the word 'strip', which 'refers both to the first ribbons of perforated film and to the ritual performance of staged nudity' (Nead 2007: 186). Beckett specifies in his directing of the play that Krapp is to keep hold of the play and wind buttons as he listens to the lake episode, this making the tape recorder correspond to the imagined body of the woman. The erotic relation between the tape and the body is also brought to the fore in the pun in the title of the French version of the play, *La dernière bande*; since *bander* is to get an erection, the last tape is also the last stiffy. (I remember once remarking to the critic Christopher Ricks that this was a rare example of Beckett enriching rather than inhibiting comic possibilities in translating from English to French; Ricks thought for a moment and then said, 'Oh I don't know – *Krapp's Last Tape* – Custer's Last Stand?'). However, the tape recorder in *Krapp's Last Tape* (and which one, by the way, *is* his last tape?) also has something of the metamorphic quality of Burroughs's soft machine, for Beckett indicated that it should also at times be identified with the earlier selves whose voices speak through it.

But Krapp's movements also seem to relay those of the tape recorder. These involve repeated turns and returns, like the pacing and wheeling up and down of the woman in *Footfalls*, 'revolving it all' (Beckett 1986: 403). Krapp listens to his younger self describe how he likes to get up and move about in the dark, in order to return to the sanctuary of his lighted desk (Beckett 1986: 217), the rotary motion being emphasised in the French text: 'J'aime à me lever pour y aller faire un tour, puis revenir ici à . . . (*il hésite*) . . . moi' (Beckett 1977a: 15). Beckett introduced a number of turning movements to look backwards over his left shoulder into the dark (where, he said, rather stagily, death was lurking for Krapp), and, in the Schiller-Theater production attempted to formalise the alternation between these anticlockwise movements and the rest of Krapp's movements about the stage, which he wanted always elsewhere to be clockwise. On a page headed 'CIRCULATION', Beckett's production notebook contains rotary diagrams of Krapp's movements' and the note 'Principe: K. ne tourne pas à gauche' ('Principle: K does not turn to the left') (Beckett 1992: 171). Some of the sentimentality of the episode in the punt is diffused if one attends to the rhymes between the movements of the lovers and the oscillations of the tape:

> We drifted in among the flags and stuck. The way they went down, sighing, before the stem! [*Pause.*] I lay down across her with my face in her breasts and

my hand on her. We lay there without moving. But under us all moved, and moved us, gently, up and down, and from side to side. (Beckett 1986: 221)

Just as Krapp lingers on the word 'spool', the word being a veritable ideogram of the tape recorder itself, so the lovers here seem to be becalmed in a kind of pool (the palindrome of loop). Krapp loops a phrase from this into his own recorded discourse, 'Lie down across her', just before breaking off his recording and returning to listening. The French is a little more suggestive: 'Coule-toi sur elle' (Beckett 1977a, 31). *Couler* is to flow, slide, slip or glide, while *couloir* is to strain or separate, as the younger Krapp imagines himself 'separating the grain from the husks' (Beckett 1986: 217), and the younger Krapp looks back 'vers l'année écoulée' (Beckett 1977a, 19) – the word 'crap' originally meant chaff, husks or offscourings. This contrasts with the Sturm und Drang of the 'wind-gauge spinning like a propeller' (Beckett 1986: 220) in the younger Krapp's recounting of his spiritual vision. In successive productions of *Krapp's Last Tape* with which he was involved, Beckett saw more and more opportunities to deepen the relationship between Krapp and his apparatus. He is reported to have been particularly pleased by the effect of the turning spool reflecting light on to the face of the listening Krapp during the final moments of the play, an image which may ironically recall the whirling wind-gauge of Krapp's vision, which, by the end of the play, seems to matter so much less than the love he has set aside for his art.

In a sense, the tape recorder is simply the inversion of the gramophone, in that here, rather than the tracking device moving through the track of the sound, the track moves across the tracking device (the tape head). But much more seems to be in play in this process. The sliding of the tape is a kind of decantation, with each passing inch a diminishment of the supply tape and an equivalent accumulation on the receiving spool. At the end of the play, as Krapp listens to his younger self arrogantly celebrating his freedom from his past, the tape runs on, and then, inevitably, exhausts the supply spool, suggesting the pouring out of some emblematic vessel. The mixture of panic and pathos induced by the sight of a spinning tape reel disconnected from its partner is evoked by Christian Marclay's *Tape Fall* (1989), in which tape spills out from a single-reel tape recorder mounted on top of a step-ladder, playing the sound of falling water, as the tape gathers in a beautiful tangled heap below it. Readers of *Krapp's Last Tape* have often sought to connect it to Beckett's discussions of time in *Proust*, the first book he published, in 1931, and it is as though Beckett had anticipated in that book an apparatus like the tape recorder, when he speaks of the self subjected to time as 'the seat of a constant process of decantation, decantation from the vessel containing the fluid of future time, sluggish, pale and monochrome, to the vessel containing the fluid of past time, agitated and multicoloured by the phenomena of its hours' (Beckett 1970c: 15).

I proposed earlier that if the gramophone disk suggests the plate, placard or surface of inscription, the tape connects sound recording much more to the many processes of weaving. The word 'spool', which Krapp so relishes (the French *bobine* is a bit harder to draw out with such lasciviousness) originally referred, like 'bobbin', to spinning and weaving, processes that have been bound symbolically to the unfolding of time. The other word on which Krapp dwells, the puzzling 'viduity', which he hears his self of thirty years earlier use, but has now forgotten the meaning of, is threaded through with some of these issues. 'Viduity', Krapp discovers on consulting his dictionary, is the '[s]tate – or condition – of being – or remaining – a widow – or widower' (Beckett 1986: 219). Beckett is at pains to remind us of the association between widows and weaving, having Krapp refer to a non-existent quotation 'deep weeds of viduity', which improves the 'deep weeds of widowhood' he would have found as an illustrative quotation from Bulwer-Lytton's *Lucretia* (1846) in the OED, and also having him come upon a reference to the 'vidua-bird', also known as the 'widow-bird' or 'weaver-bird'. The arachnid associations of widowhood and weaving are unspoken but operative. Viduity, from *viduare*, meaning to deprive, means the opposite of undividedness or individuality. Itself bereft of its familiar prefix, 'viduity' seems to mime the condition of bereavement it signifies. So the play seems simultaneously to activate weaving and cutting, splicing and slicing.

The patterning of the action of the play also doubles the operations of the tape, with its alternations of continuity and discontinuity. Krapp not only violently chops into the body of the tape that he listens to, he also constantly interrupts his own thoughts, words and actions, to fetch bananas, to brood or to shamble to his cubbyhole for restorative snifters. The sequencing of his actions also exhibits some of the temporal loopings and alternation of before and after that the tape recorder effects. Krapp prepares for his annual retrospect by listening to an earlier retrospect, and what he hears in that retrospect is that his earlier self has adopted precisely the same tactic of *reculer pour mieux sauter*. As in his frantic and furious efforts to find the right place on the tape, Krapp rewinds in order to be able to make his play.

In fact, winding features at intervals in Beckett's writing. There is, for example, 'St-Lô', the lovely but cryptic little poem Beckett wrote about the hospital amid the devastation of Northern France where he worked after the war. 'Vire' is the name of the river that runs through St-Lô:

> Vire will wind in other shadows
> unborn through the bright ways tremble
> and the old mind ghost-forsaken
> sink into its havoc   (Beckett 2012: 105)

There is also the winding that features in the cover blurb (Beckett's) to *Lessness*, the only text in which Beckett ever approached anything like the aleatory methods of the Burroughs cut-up. 'Ruin, exposure, wilderness, mindlessness, past and future denied and affirmed, are the categories, formally distinguishable, through which the writing winds, first in one disorder, then in another' (quoted in Knowlson 1996: 564).

Perhaps the most important kind of reversibility attaching to tape in the play is that of sense and the senseless. I have already noted the relation between the remarks about grain and chaff and Krapp's own name. Beckett seems here to play on the possibility, noted by many, that sound-recording processes can preserve very much more than what appears to have been said. Beckett plays between silence – passages in which nothing is said, or no sound is made – and recorded silence, the one being an absence of sound, the other the presence of silence, in a little gag at the beginning of Krapp's chronicle:

> Thank God that's all done with anyway. [*Pause.*] The eyes she had! [*Broods, realizes he is recording silence, switches off, broods. Finally.*] Everything there, everything, all the – [*Realizes this is not being recorded, switches on.*] Everything there, everything on this old muckball, all the light and dark and famine and feasting of . . . [*hesitates*] . . . the ages! [*In a shout.*] Yes! [*Pause.*] Let that go! Jesus! Take his mind off his homework! (Beckett 1986: 222)

Krapp seems to mean here, how could his earlier self have let go everything for the sake of his art ('ses chères études' in the French [Beckett 1977: 28]). The French text seems once again to have seen an opportunity to link retrieval and letting go to the process of the tape, for 'Let that go!' is rendered as 'Laisser filer ça!' (Beckett 177: 28). *Filer* means to slide or drift away, *le temps file* being a perfectly familiar way of saying 'time flies, or slips away', but its primary reference is to processes of spinning, drawing or paying out of some thread, rope or cable. Younger Krapp has let everything go in favour of his vision of the friendly powers of darkness, which he records 'against the day when my work will be done and perhaps no place left in my memory, warm or cold, for the miracle that . . . [*hesitates*] . . . for the fire that set it alight' (Beckett 1986: 220). There is indeed no place in Krapp's memory for this; instead, what he wants are the tiny remaining traces of what younger Krapp has discarded. The tape records both the grain and the detritus, and by preserving both, allows for the bitter inversion of one into the other. Iron (magnetised particles of ferric oxide) enables irony. Beckett dramatises this first by having Krapp record his own brooding silence, and then by having him enunciate unrecorded.

The play between sound and silence, intelligibility and unintelligibility, meaning and meaninglessness – all variants in signal-to-noise ratio – is also embodied in a particular feature of the tape recorder that Beckett capitalised upon in his Schiller-Theater production. Beckett noticed that, when fast-forwarded or fast-reversed, a high-pitched gabble could be heard (this was a common feature of early tape recorders, which tended to be removed from later models, though it was actually very useful as a navigational device). The published versions of *Krapp's Last Tape* make no mention of this feature, but Beckett specifies very clearly in the revised stage directions he produced for the Schiller-Theatre production when he does and does not wish the winding to be '*mechanical with gabble*' (Beckett 1992: 32). What is more, he even provides equivalents for this in Krapp's own actions. Krapp's isle, like Caliban's in *The Tempest*, is full of noises – grunts, growls, sighs, gasps, howls. In his notebook Beckett wrote,

> Toutes manipulations magnétophone, recherches d'endroits registre et dictionnaire, peuvent raccompagner de petits bruits de bouche (soupirs, colère, impatience). (Beckett 1992: 99)
>
> [All manipulations, of tape recorder, searches for the place in the ledger or dictionary, may be accompanied by little noises of the mouth (sighs, anger, impatience)] (my translation)

Indeed, for Krapp's searching through the dictionary for a definition of the word 'viduity', which the lapse of years has orphaned of intelligibility, Beckett actually provided a few words of subvocal scanning for the French and German productions with which he was involved: 'vice-président, vicieux, vidange' (vice-president, vicious, draining-away) for the French (Beckett 1992: 29) and, for the German, 'Wickel, Wiesel, Wischwasch' (roll, weasel, drivel) (Beckett 1992: 225). Tape not only includes words and gabble, silence and speech, it also makes it possible to wind them into each other. Beckett noted that his entire play formed a balance between speech and silence: 'With the silence of the listening phase these form a balance in terms of sound with the duo immobility-agitation' (Beckett 1992: 101). He even went to the trouble of timing the periods of immobile listening, and mobile non-listening on the part of Krapp, noting with satisfaction that the play broke down into '2 fairly equal parts – listening and non-listening' (Beckett

1992: 201). This economy involves a physical interchange between Krapp and the tape recorder, as between the two spools of the tape recorder itself; when it is moving, he is motionless; when it is still, he is in motion and audible.

Michel Serres has offered a reading of narrative and history in terms of the irreducible relation between code and information. Any instance of information requires the existence of some channel or medium, which Serres identifies with the principle of repeatability itself. Serres notes that this relation involves the mixing together of the principles of the continuous and the discontinuous. On the one hand, there is the repeatable, of the flow that remains itself through every change; on the other hand, there is the sudden and entirely unprecedented event of a change that comes from nowhere. The word 'tension', and the family of words with which it is associated, has this ambivalence at its heart: 'the Greek roots of this word *teinô*, which means to be stretched, to be drawn out continuously, as in the long flow of a paste or a fluid, contradicts the other possible root, *temnô*, which means to cut into tiny, quasi-atomic pieces' (Serres 2006: 135; my translation).

The development of the tape recorder required a material that could maintain a balance between these two principles: some materials were too stretchy, others, like metal, resisted stretching but had a tendency to snap (the first tape recorder used by the BBC in 1932, which used metal tape with razor-sharp edges, had to be operated in a locked room, since the risk of snapping, along with the fact that the tape had to travel at 90 metres a minute to ensure adequate sound quality, made playback too dangerous for bystanders). The tape recorder only became a feasible proposition with the development of a material that balanced brittleness and elasticity. But Serres's structure applies at another level, too, for it seems to encode the cooperation between code and information: 'continuous extension can act as the channel and the granular sections . . . give information' (Serres 2006: 135; my translation).

We have seen that, in both Burroughs and Beckett, tape and its apparatus involve fantasies of male and female coupling. This code-information coupling is also regularly sexualised. For Serres, the principle of redundancy is that of the creative Logos, while information arrives with the first, bifurcating disobedience of Eve. Burroughs, too, makes the identification between woman and error or aberration. Asked how he felt about women, Burroughs replied, 'In the words of one of the great misogynists, plain Mr Jones, in Conrad's *Victory*: "Women are a perfect curse." I think they were a basic mistake, and the whole dualistic universe evolved from this error. Women are no longer essential to reproduction' (Burroughs and Odier 1969: 113). But I think that woman actually functions in a more systematic way for

Burroughs as the redundancy of repetition. In a sense, woman is the matrix, the channel, the tape apparatus, insofar as this is devised to make dissent and discontinuity impossible, by ensuring that everything is programmed, pre-recorded. Or rather, perhaps, woman means the irreducibility of the dualism, whereby every discontinuity requires there to be a continuity, every signal requires a channel, every message emerges from a background. Woman means the necessity of this coupling; she is the looped tape that is required for every reproduction. Against this, Burroughs will assert and in his work attempt to enact the life of a thousand cuts, of a kind of pure discontinuity, atomising, granulating, never falling back into repetition.

We might link this impulse to what W.R. Bion called the attack on linking (Bion 1993), which might be said in informational terms to resolve into an attack on the idea of a background against which any two things might seem relatable or become commensurable – Bion describes in the essay the sleep of a schizophrenic, in which 'his mind, minutely fragmented, flowed out in an attacking stream of particles', and his dreams were 'a continuum of minute, invisible fragments' (Bion 1993: 98). Burroughs' struggle is against indifference, numbness, regularity – hence the importance in his writing of spasmodic movements, like vomiting or ejaculation or explosion. The apparatus of control and anticipation that the tape repre-sents is atomised and exploded, but so relentlessly that the paroxysms start to be patterned, to form a new kind of redundancy, against which more, and more violently spasmodic, struggles will always be needed. Burroughs thus strives, not only to assert discontinuity against continuity, but also to vaporise the link between continuity and discontinuity. *Solve et coagula*: the tape becomes the carrier wave for its own dissolution, which feeds back into itself to form a structure that is made of dissolutions. The discontinuous becomes continuous, such that the writing approaches the condition of a tape recorded on to itself over and over again: pure, unrelieved information coagulating into a stiff sludge of noise.

Beckett, too, reads the encounter between Krapp and his tapes in sexual-ised terms. But, where Burroughs struggles against the duality of continuity/discontinuity, Krapp, for all his misogyny, encounters what Beckett in his production notebook calls 'das Weibliche' (Beckett 1992: 97), an allusion to the 'Ewigweibliche' referred to in Goethe's *Faust*, as Beckett confirmed to Martha Fehsenfeld. This is part of an alternation through the play of continuity and interruption, moments when Krapp surrenders himself to listening and moments when he breaks off from that listening (sometimes combining the two, as when he switches off in order to lose himself in reverie). In the end, Beckett's Krapp has no choice but to inhabit the predicament that Burroughs struggles to cancel or evade. Krapp sits in silence and darkness, drowned in dreams of the lake episode he has just played through again, not listening to the confident affirmation of his younger self of discontinuity: 'Perhaps my best years are gone. But I wouldn't want them back. Not with the fire in me now. No, I wouldn't want them back' (Beckett 1986: 223). Discontinuity interrupts continuity; continuity interrupts discontinuity; the young man who declares himself in his opening words to be 'sound as a –' is interrupted by Krapp scattering his pile of tapes to the floor before his phrase – 'sound as a bell' – is completed (Beckett 1986: 217). The joke seems even better to me in the French, in which the younger Krapp is interrupted in saying that he is 'solide comme un pont' ('solid as a bridge') (Beckett 1977a: 13–14), a phrase that looks forward to his vision 'at the end of the jetty' (Beckett 1986: 220). The tape provides Krapp with a bridge to his lost past, which he can nevertheless never cross. The play ends with Krapp sitting in silence, and the audience listening to the empty tape running on – until, presumably, it runs off its reel, cutting through the thread of continuity, and the liberated spool starts its blind, fluttering freewheel. As he himself revolves it all, wound up in internal playback, Krapp's last tape, and *Krapp's Last Tape*, is played out.

Tape brings together the continuous and the discontinuous; more, it disallows the discontinuity between the continuous and the discontinuous. For that reason, it is the medium that most seems to embody the predicament of temporal embodiment – by linking us to our losses, making it possible for us to recall what we can no longer remember, keeping us in touch with what nevertheless remains out of reach, making us remain what we no longer are. Tape extends and attenuates us, distributing us through the time, or times, that we are, without ever being able to have. In this sense, tape might also seem to provide an allegory for its own broken, looped temporality, being, as it must be henceforth, at once all over and still somehow going on. And, as Beckett's Molloy wonders, is there any tense for that? (Beckett 1973: 36)

CHAPTER 7

'In My Soul I Suppose, Where the Acoustics Are So Bad': Writing the White Voice

As we tune our ears to the patterns of chatter and clatter in literature and the hesitations and lapses that mark their abeyance, we may easily forget the most important defining condition of most literary writing, namely that it is itself stonily mute, and that it exists in a world in which it is assumed that it will be read by a similarly silent reader. The exceptions to this – like the public readings of his work undertaken by Dickens, and the new popularity of audiobooks – seem to reaffirm this powerful background condition in the very way in which they break from it. Literature elaborately and attentively concerns itself with sound, but does not itself make a sound. Georges Bataille once remarked that '*the word silence is still a sound*' (Bataille 1988: 13); it is the opposite point that I am proposing; that the noise of literature is itself mute. It is this strangely resounding silence, this garrulous dumb show, that the sentences that follow will try to turn up.

It seems to be widely agreed and regularly affirmed that literature has not always been silent. The story of the move from voiced to silent reading usually draws on the account in St Augustine's *Confessions* of the very distinctive manner in which Bishop Ambrose of Milan read:

> But when he was reading, he drew his eyes along over the leaves, and his heart searched into the sense, but his voice and tongue were silent (*sed cum legebat, oculi ducebantur per paginas et cor intellectum rimabatur, vox autem et lingua quiescebant*). Ofttimes when we were present (for no man was debarred of coming to him, nor was it his fashion to be told of anybody that came to speak with him) we still saw him reading to himself, and never otherwise: so that having long sat in silence (for who durst be so bold as to interrupt him, so intentive to his study?) we were fain to depart. We conjectured, that the small time which he gat for the repairing of his mind, he retired himself from the clamour of other men's businesses, being unwilling to be taken off for any other employment and he was wary perchance too, lest some hearer being struck into suspense, and eager upon it, if the author he read should deliver anything obscurely, he should be put to it to expound it, or to discuss some of the harder questions; so that spending away his time about this

work, he could not turn over so many volumes as he desired : although peradventure the preserving of his voice (which a little speaking used to weaken) might be a just reason for his reading to himself. But with what intent soever he did it, that man certainly had a good meaning in it. (Augustine 1912: 1.273–5)

This passage is the lynchpin of a consensus that the move to silent reading was an innovation of the fourth century, meaning that, before that date, at least in the classical world, books were read out loud. The move from sounded to silent reading has been explicated in terms of a move from the ear to the eye, particularly in the development of punctuation. It is usually maintained that the development of punctuation and the development of silent reading are simultaneous and closely connected. The argument seems to be this: that there was no need for texts and inscriptions written in the era of sounded reading to be punctuated, since the very work of bringing them to utterance would itself supply the pauses and breaks required. Hence the extraordinary practice, to modern eyes, of rendering written texts in *scriptio continua*, without breaks between words or sentences. It was only when this structuring support of orality was removed that the need for spacing and pacing started to be felt and supplied. It is possible to run this argument the other way round, too. The absence of spacing made it necessary to adopt what Paul Saenger, who has done most to substantiate this case, calls the 'tunnel vision of orality' (Saenger 1997), groping one's way blindly along the line with the probings of the tongue.

I have never really seen the force of this explanation. For surely silent reading is precisely what is required to sieve and riddle the sense of *scriptio continua* (and here it will be appropriate perhaps to remember that the word *sens* in French means direction as well as meaning), while unrehearsed reading out loud exposes one to multiple possibilities of error as one sets out on one tonal path, only to find the syntax taking another. This point is well made by A. K. Gavrilov, who observes that 'when a reader of any experience reads aloud – especially when it is someone whose job it is to make public announcements or give artistic performances from written texts – the habit of reading to oneself is presupposed. Indeed, it is itself an essential element of reading aloud' (Gavrilov 1997: 59). Only a small amount of reflection is needed to show that it is only the habitually silent reader who is capable of scouting out and construing the passage of text to be read in advance and, of course, necessarily in silence, since the tongue will be preoccupied with its work of word-by-word enunciation – and only this kind of reader who is capable of performing the extraordinary trick of parsing a complex text in this apparently *en passant* fashion. This is made all the more remarkable since almost all reading of this kind would have been of texts in a Latin and Greek characterised by inflection and complex subordination of syntax. This fact is acknowledged by Saenger in the course of his detailed account of the link between visual punctuation and the development of silent reading. Even though Saenger argues that the unpunctuated blocks of prose of early writing required slow and laborious oral unpicking, he also recognises that much of the labour consists of 'the onerous task of keeping the eyes ahead of the voice while accurately reading unseparated script, so familiar to the ancient Greeks and Romans' (Saenger 1997: 6). This, he says, 'can be described as a kind of elaborate search pattern. The eye moves across the page, not at an even rate, but in [a] series of fixations and jumps called "saccades"' (Saenger 1997: 6–7). But what is going on in these anticipatory leaps if not a kind of silent reading? There is no need to doubt that silent reading is materially assisted by spacing and punctuation. There is equally no need to infer from this that silent reading required its development, or that its absence necessarily enjoined reading out loud. The idea that before the development of this visual architecture readers had to rely on their voices alone to sound out the sense of what they were reading is neither necessary nor actually easy to justify. The fact is, punctuation assists every kind of reading, oral as well as silent.

One might wonder, too, why Latin became syntactically simpler, and therefore more adapted to oral delivery, during the period in which silent reading was becoming widespread. Perhaps the kind of reading involved in sounded reading was not in fact of the kind that we would recognise today; that is, perhaps there was much less attempt to inhabit and dramatise the sense in the orderings and inflections of the voice. Perhaps the kind of sounded reading that allegedly came before silent reading was a word-by-word sounding (though some kind of on-the-fly analysis would have been necessary even to separate out words in the absence of spaces), rather than a reading which constructed synthetic or intensive arcs of sense across sentences.

Despite all these difficulties, the story of the silencing *d'un seul coup* of the act of reading is constantly told and retold, even if there is strikingly little agreement about precisely when this process is supposed to have occurred. For Alberto Manguel, it occurs during the life of St Augustine, in AD 386, for book 8 of his *Confessions* records an act of silent reading on Augustine's own part that seems to mimic that of Ambrose described in book 6 (Manguel 1996: 44–5). Stephen Roger Fischer is similarly convinced that '[f]or most of written history, reading was speaking', until this condition was suddenly revoked at the beginning of the ninth century when, he says, 'Western Europe's scriptoria fell silent' (Fischer 2003: 159). For Elspeth

Jajdelska (2007), it is the increasing ownership of books during the eighteenth century that makes possible the definitive moved to silent, private reading on a wide scale. Just as the silent reader is said to need punctuation to orientate themselves to a soundless text, so historians of reading seem to need the semi-colon provided by the idea of the switch from sounded to silent reading to orientate their histories, even though that historical hinge may be placed at different points.

The idea that silent reading is a distinctly modern experience is tied to some strong presuppositions about the nature of that modernity. The first is that silent reading brings about a withdrawal from the oral world of sonorous collectivity. Walter Ong argues that this scoops out a space of interiority, the fine and private place of the solitary subject, that had simply not previously existed (Ong 1967: 126). This is a space of suspension, reservation, exception, delay, a space of spacing itself, in which the subject becomes able for the first time to put a distance between itself and the world and to project alternatives to the authority of the world as it is collectively construed and reproduced through mimicry, iteration and policing. Silent reading is identified with the Protestant spirit of sceptical thinking for oneself. This is at once an alienation and an emancipation – for the subject will have henceforth to make out the grounds of his being for himself, and give himself the law. The subject will be free, but in a state of wounded loss, having gained his soul at the cost of a richly sonorous being-in-the-world.

Though the myth of the epochal shift from sounded to soundless reading is regularly restated, a great deal of work has been done in the last decade or so to cast doubt on it. The first to enter reservations was B. M. W. Knox in 1968, who drew attention to a number of references to or depictions of reading in classical texts that make no sense unless one assumes that silent reading is occurring. This work has been extended by Gavrilov and M. F. Burnyeat (1997), the latter of whom continues to prosecute with missionary zeal the cause of rescuing the Greeks from the myth of reading out loud (Fenton 2006).

It seems sensible to assume that sounded and silent reading have always coexisted, and that what happens historically is not a simple shift from one to the other – in which an increase of sound necessarily means a deficit of visualisation and vice versa – but rather a readjustment of the ecology of eye, tongue and ear involved in the process of reading (not to mention all the other members of the mixed body of reading, heart, fingers, toes and stomach among them). We may also need, as William A. Johnson (2000) has suggested, a more nuanced and particularised sense of the many different kinds of practice, going far beyond the cognitive procedure of extracting the sense from strings of words on a page, that 'reading' may involve.

This might allow us to grasp the move from sounded to silent reading as not simply a move from noise to quiet. Rather, perhaps, it is a move from one kind of sound to another. The one who reads aloud is silent inside, for the outer voice will tend to drown out or shout down the inner. The one who reads silently, by contrast, is suffused by his or her inner sonority, if inside is exactly where it is, if sonorous is exactly what it is. Those who read aloud make themselves deaf, abolishing their ear into the sound that actuates their tongue. Those who read silently still their tongues the better to sound out what they read.

The usual way in which this is thought to be done is through what is called subvocalisation. This may be regarded as the vestigial traces of speech that accompany any act of reading or writing. According to this view, what readers may feel as a sounding in the mind may be due at least in part to the effect of very small impulses sent by the brain to the larynx and the tongue. The 'tip-of-the-tongue' experience, when one is searching for the word that seems to be just out of reach, seems to provide experiential confirmation of this. More physiological proof is supplied by subvocal speech recognition systems, which would allow us to capture and overhear subvocalised speech (Armstrong 2006). Subvocalisation seems to provide some kind of indication of, or at least correlation with, what has been called 'inner speech'. Most readers will report or at least recognise the experience of some kind of 'hearing' of some kind of 'voice', or 'speaking' when they read.

It may be nevertheless that this phenomenon of the internally sounded voice, that inner speech itself, is in the process of fading out, and that our difficulty in describing its qualities is due to the fact that we are hearing its last dim spasms and whispers. Perhaps, following the stilling of our external lips, we are undergoing a slow quelling of the internal voice. And yet, for us still 'the voice without a mouth still stirs in the head', as Denise Riley has put it (Riley 2004: 95). Riley has gone further than most towards capturing the strange condition of the inner voice, caught between the auditory and the non-auditory. Of course, the inner voice is experienced whenever consciousness cocks an ear to itself, but her comments are useful since it seems to be activated or at least attended to with particular intensity in the act of reading, during which the inner voice is not quite mine, nor yet entirely not mine either. In a similar way, the peculiarity of the inner voice is that it is never quite a matter of hearing, while never quite not hearing either:

> Among its convoluted qualities, the inner voice, however ostensibly silent, is still able to be heard by its possessor. Where it resonates, no air is agitated.

No larynx swells, no eardrum vibrates. Yet if I swing my attention onto my inner speech, I'm aware of it *sounding* in a very thin version of my own tone of voice. I catch myself in its silent sound, a paradox audible only to me. We don't, though, seem to have much of a vocabulary, an odd lack, for this everyday sensation. On what, then, does my conviction of the tonality of my inward voice depend; do I have a sort of *inner ear* designed to pick up this voice which owns nothing by way of articulation? For I can detect my usual accents and the timbre of my voice as soon as I try to overhear myself by trapping the faint sonority of my inner words. But they are audible, if that's the adjective, only in a depleted form which keeps some faint colouration but is far less resonant in the ear than when I'm speaking aloud. (Well, of course! Still, if my inner speech is less loud to me, that isn't just because it's not uttered.) It's as if an inner ear is alert to my inner voice, although what happens isn't exactly an instance of *hearing* my own voice speaking. So when I think I can overhear my own inner speech, what do I mean? This silent speech is an apparent oxymoron. Is it more of an ear-voice, which detects it at the same time as it issues it? But I do have the feeling of hearing something, in the same way that I can run a tune audibly through my head, yet without humming it even silently. Or I want to say that I "hear" it; there's no exact verb for this peculiar kind of hearing something which isn't actually sounded, and which evades any measurement of articulation. Yet a kind of hearing it surely is. (Riley 2004: 58–9)

I have quoted the passage at such length because it seems to mime some of the ruminative rhythms of inner vocality itself, in its saltations, lingerings and coilings back on itself, marked by swivel words like 'for', 'still', 'or' and 'yet'. This is text that keeps surprising itself as, and into, sound.

How are we to sound out this internal sonorousness? What are its qualities and effects? Subvocalisation does not seem to get it, since this relates only to the subliminal quasi-production of sound. And inner hearsay inhabits and requires a complex space, a space in which one will always be in at least two places at once, spaced out, since one will always be in – no, one will always in fact *be* – a scenario. For where there is something as-if heard, there must one as-if hearing. And it is anyway not at all clear that when I hear something in the ordinary external way, I hear it at a particular 'point of audition', though my position in space will certainly create the conditions of what I hear. But when I hear something, I hear it both from where I am and from where I assume it is.

I want to propose that this reading voice is not vestigial but virtual, not diminished but disseminated. What matters is not the channelling or vocal acting out of the text in the reader's own voice, but the creation of an auditorium or *arena of internal articulations*. The inner space of the inward voice is a production, a staging, a topographic projection. In reality, this space is not really inside anything or anywhere inside. It is just not outside. Innerness is an approximation to the particular kind of pantopicality, or atopicality, of the voice that has absconded from space, or instituted another kind of 'space' entirely.

'Take care of the sense, and the sounds will take care of themselves', the Duchess advises Alice (Carroll 1976: 121). Let me return to a point I made in passing a little earlier, namely the coincidence in the French word *sens* between sense and direction. The distinction between sounded and silent reading is a distinction between words that have an order or direction – a 'drift' as we might say in English – and words arranged with a looser or more mutable sense of direction. Sound belongs in essence to consequential and irreversible time, while the eye inhabits a much jumpier, complex and recursive kind of space, a space that allows for a certain amount of lateral, back-and-forth play, a jumping of the tracks, as opposed to a line that is simply played out.

We are accustomed to characterise this as a difference between the linear and the non-linear, though this forgets that the eye, too, has to move from one place to another and can never be in more than one place at once, though the speed at which it performs these actions may sometimes persuade us that it can. The reading eye scans the space of the page as the eye surveys a landscape. Its movements approximate to what Michel Serres has characterised as the movement of the maze or the labyrinth, the making out of complex volumes from linear movements.

> We inherit our idea of the labyrinth from a tragic and pessimistic tradition, in which it signifies death, despair, madness. However, the maze is in fact the best model for allowing moving bodies to pass through while at the same time retracing their steps as much as possible; it gives the best odds to finite journeys with unstructured itineraries. Mazes maximize feedback. . . . Let us seek the best way of creating the most feedback loops possible on an unstructured and short itinerary. Mazes provide us with this maximization. Excellent reception, here is the best possible resonator, the beginnings of consciousness. (Serres 2008: 143)

Serres multiplies in his writing many versions of this mazelike convolution – the scribbling flight of a fly, the chancy dance of a single point in a volume of kneaded dough, the intricate folding of proteins or the mapping out of the phase-space of iterative functions – but, at the point in *The Five Senses* at which the passage I have just quoted occurs, it is the structure of the ear that best exemplifies the capacity of the maze to hold up and fold sound on itself. Serres materialises in the architecture of the ear the two-sidedness of the hearing apparatus, that it both transmits and receives sound in terms of the complex structure of the ear:

> Sound is transmitted here in non-linear fashion, travelling from hardest to softest; here, at each stage, it submits to loops, circuits or feedback. The box receives the captive energy, organizes the repetition anticipated by the prefix, it traps noise, sound and message, makes them circulate quickly, brings them to rest, makes them vibrate in themselves for themselves, and through these circular movements transforms transmission into reception, resolving the contradiction that besets hearing. (Serres 2008, 143)

The fact that inflected languages give a sonic index of the function of a word in a sentence, so that words have their spin, posture or orientation inscribed in them, is oddly enough what allows them to develop complex cross-fades and counter-rhythms through the interruption of expected word order. One of the paradoxes of the development of language is that, as silent reading has become more and more the norm, so uninflected forms have also tended to replace inflected forms, which is to say, the structure of sentences has become more and more dependent upon word order and therefore the continuous emission and emergence of the sound stream.

The increasing commonness of silent reading is to be regarded, therefore, not as the simple turning down of sound, but as the creation of a more complex space of inner resounding. Augustine's reflections on Ambrose may give us some help here, for Augustine distinguishes many more bodily components to the reading practice than we tend to. There are not just the eye, ear and tongue, but also the 'cor', the heart. Not only this, but the mouth is in operation in more ways than one. Augustine tells us that one of the effects of Ambrose's inaccessibility was that he was not able to discern anything of Ambrose's own spiritual struggles, or of 'how savory joys that mouth hidden in his heart fed upon in thy Bread' (*occultum os eius, quod erat in corde eius, quam sapida gaudia de pane tuo ruminaret*) (Augustine 1912: 1.272–3). Alberto Manguel has drawn attention to the commonness of the association between reading, chewing, swallowing and ingesting (Manguel 1996: 170–3). But the analogies between reading and eating are not simple. In one sense it is the ear that seems most gullible, the most like a mouth, the most obedient. Ezekiel describes a spiritual voice entering into him which commands:

> son of man, hear what I say unto thee; be not thou rebellious like that rebellious house: open thy mouth and eat what I give thee.
> And when I looked, behold, an hand was put forth into me; and, lo, a roll of a book was therein;

> And he spread it before me; and it was written within and without; and
> there was written therein lamentations, and mourning, and woe.
> And he said unto me, Son of man, eat that thou findest; eat this roll, and
> go, speak unto the house of Israel (Ezekiel 2.8–10–3.1)

But only the starving person bolts things down whole. There is, in eating as
there is in the ingestion of reading, rumination, dallying, delaying, delectation,
tasting and turning over.

Silent reading opens up a quasi-sonorous space in which sound is lifted
out of the linearity of the sound stream, seeming to allow it to turn back on
itself. Only in the last century and a half have we begun to develop phonographic technologies that have allowed the actualisation of the conditions of
this inner auditorium, in which sound is capable of being suspended,
repeated, reversed, turned back on and fed back into itself. But the book,
at least the form of it that developed out of the scroll, provides the model and
promise of this re-sounding space. The book, and all its ways of reflecting on
or adverting to itself – with footnotes, headings, indices and their hyper-
textual enlargements – instantiates the phonomorphic furniture of the inner
auditorium. This is not a passage from sound stream to paper space, but an
integration of sound and space in a complex new amalgam, for which there
is no simple or consistent visual or sonorous correlative. We do, however,
have a word that participates in all the dimensions that are here convened:
the ideas of the book, of space and of the pressure of sound swell together in
the word 'volume'.

The space of literature might be regarded as attempting to approximate
to the condition of this white voice or sound space. There are few writers
who have gone further in this direction than Samuel Beckett, whom Riley
describes as 'the arch inscriber of inner speech on the page' (Riley 2004: 95).
Many of Beckett's texts ask us to listen, or to imagine listening, to streams of
words and voices that are themselves said to be internal murmurings or
overhearings. Their space is the strained, uncertain listening space evoked
by Moran, as he tries to decide which of two names for the obscure being
who is the subject of his pursuit and report is right:

> Of these two names, Molloy and Mollose, the second seemed to me perhaps
> the more correct. But barely. What I heard, in my soul I suppose, where the
> acoustics are so bad, was a first syllable, Mol, very clear, followed almost at
> once by a second, very thick, as though gobbled by the first, and which might
> have been oy as it might have been ose, or one, or even oc. (Beckett 1973: 113)

Where *Malone Dies* dwells on the awkward, elaborate paraphernalia of the
writing process, as Malone describes in detail the pages of his notebook and

the diminishing stub of his pencil, the speaker in *The Unnamable* is at a loss to explain how it is that his writing is coming about: 'How, in such conditions, can I write, to consider only the manual aspect of that bitter folly? I don't know. I could know. But I shall not know. Not this time. It is I who write, who cannot raise my hand from my knee' (Beckett 1973: 303).

The Unnamable digs out and inhabits a terra incognita between script and voice. It is as though a nagging, nattering internal voice were being automatically transcribed, but without ever quite achieving the fixity tradi-tionally attached to script, so the words seem to flicker and wriggle. There is din and babble everywhere, even as the speaker tells us repeatedly of his deafness and his straining to hear the very words to which he is giving utterance. He is, like the soul in Andrew Marvell's 'Dialogue of the Soul and the Body', 'Deaf with the drumming of an Ear' (Marvell 1971: 1.21). The speaker of *The Unnamable* talks at one point of his fear of sound, in which the voice to which we are paying heed alternately blends with and splits from the sounds to which it is hearkening:

> fear of sound, fear of sounds, all sounds, more or less, more or less fear, all sounds, there's only one, continuous, day and night, what is it, it's steps coming and going, it's voices speaking for a moment, it's bodies groping their way, it's the air, it's things, it's the air among the things, that's enough, that I seek, like it, no, not like it, like me, in my own way, what am I saying, after my fashion, that I seek, what do I seek now, what it is, it must be that, it can only be that, what it is, what it can be, what what can be, what I seek, no, what I hear, now it comes back to me, all back to me, they say I seek what it is I hear, I hear them, now it comes back to me, what it can possibly be, and where it can possibly come from, since all is silent here, and the walls thick, and how I manage, without feeling an ear on me, or a head, or a body, or a soul. (Beckett 1973: 391)

Perhaps the strange, oscillating space imagined by the speaker of *The Unnamable* is a space procured precisely by this sighted sound and sounded sight. It is an attempt both to see and hear this white architecture of vocality.

There is a deeply engrained tendency to read the passage from orality to print as a retreat from the body. For Julia Kristeva, the entry into the world of writing enjoins a move from the mother's body, the locale of the chora, in which the infant is simply the place of intersection of drives, impulses and sounds, to a world of signs, in which words are pale substitutes for what they signify (Kristeva 1984: 25–9). This reproduces the well-known logocentric prejudice that ties speech to the presence of a speaking body and print to its absence. To see the coming of writing as a silencing implies that this retreat of sound is also an abrogation of the body as such. Laura Mandell has recently read the marks of orality in Wordsworth's writing as a partial retrieval of this lost maternal body:

> The symbiotic relation to the mother's body is not altogether foregone but persists in sound and beat: linguistic material is its sublimate. Dancing and reading aloud can bring about a partial return to symbiosis, to a sense that one's body is merged with the materiality around it. The mother's body is resurrected in sound. (Mandell 2007: 77)

But this is an oddly cramped notion of embodiment. Written signs, after all, are perfectly material, fully bodily. So one cannot gloss muteness as disembodiment in itself. This makes it seem odd for 'body' to cluster on the sonorous side of things, and for silent signs to seem in contrast so bleached of body, though it is hard to ignore or think past the sensory economy that enjoins this way of distributing things. But sounds are no more or less significatory in themselves than marks. Indeed, there is good reason to suggest that the signifying function arises earlier in sounds than in visible objects, that sounds become the signs or promise of presence, not to say, in the baby's own cry, the means of procuring it, rather than presence itself. It is true that a piece of paper with the word 'water' on it will not slake my thirst, but it is not as if croaking the word 'water' will do any better, even though there is something that suggests to me that the latter might pull off the trick. Kristeva's body of sound, the chora, is in fact a different kind of body – not so much a body in space, as the body of space. The sound space evoked by the literary text is not privative, but saturated, interpenetrating, multisensical.

Modern technologies potentiate and pluralise the strange condition that is already instanced and inhabited by literary writing. This is not silence, not the living voice parched and eviscerated into the flatness of speech, and not therefore the defeat or retreat of sound. For the condition of literature has been for centuries the promise of a phonographic order of what during the nineteenth century came to be called 'visible speech', of sound propagating into, and out of, visible and material inscriptions. The invention of the phonograph produced vigorous dreams of a transcodable world, of a world scored with sonorous signatures, in which everything represented something that could be 'played'. In his 1919 prose piece 'Primal Sound', Rilke (2001) imagined a device that could play the grooves and seams of the skull as a phonograph follows the grooves of a record and bring to hearing its implicit voice. Ours is not a world of silenced sound, but rather one of sonorised appearances. The phonographic order we have entered is one in which sound is not restricted to that which is heard. What would be the most striking feature of modern life for somebody arriving from the fifteenth century? Surely it would be the cacophony of written language, extending even to human bodies: have human beings ever worn writing as emphatically and ecstatically as today, with our badges, labels, slogans and blazons? There is no better emblem of this emblematising, this mobilisation of writing by bodies, and bodies by writing, than Joyce's sandwich-board men in *Ulysses*.

> A procession of whitesmocked sandwichmen marched slowly towards him along the gutter, scarlet sashes across their boards. Bargains. Like that priest they are this morning: we have sinned: we have suffered. He read the scarlet letters on their five tall white hats: H. E. L. Y. S. Wisdom Hely's. Y lagging behind drew a chunk of bread from under his foreboard, crammed it into his mouth and munched as he walked. Our staple food. Three bob a day, walking along the gutters, street after street. Just keep skin and bone together, bread and skilly ... He crossed Westmoreland street when apostrophe S had plodded by. (Joyce: 1986: 127)

Literature does not silence sound: it auditises the field of the visible. It opens up larger and more variable spaces of reprieve from the distinct orders of the visual-spatial and the oral-temporal. These spaces may not be bodily in the blunderingly crude sense that we affix to that term: that is, they may not be subject to the usual restriction of unshareable space and irreversible time. But that is only one view of what a body is and does. Bodies are also affectings, as Spinoza and, following him, Gilles Deleuze, argue (Deleuze and Guattari 1987: xvi). A body is the sum total of what it may effect and affect. The body is a field of potentials and exposures, which is always therefore ahead or aside of itself. Seen in this way, the paradoxical kind of sound-body suggested by literary works, and pressed to a certain kind of limit by the work of Beckett, is a kind of white body corresponding to that proposed by Serres, a body that can in principle inflect itself in all postures, positions, directions, and possibilities, and which 'fills its space equally: high as much as low, right as much as left, it abandons preferences and determinations, its memberships, and knows the better how to do so because it has often crossed the old white river. Here it is, a completed body' (Serres 1997: 24–5).

Corresponding to this white body would be something that we might call a white voice, on the analogy of the whiteness of white light or white noise, that includes all possible frequencies. Such a voice has minimal colour, taste or locative twang; it is, so to speak, vocality itself, without the distinguishing grain that would tie it to a particular space, time, or body. It is a necessity of Beckett's writing that the white voice seems faint, but its faintness really booms with phonic ghosts. Miss Carmichael in

Beckett's abandoned play of 1937, *Human Wishes*, bullied by the blind Mrs Williams who demands that she act as amanuensis for her roared *obiter dicta*, and who accuses her of not writing down her words as instructed, replies with thin defiance: 'I write very quiet. Very quiet I write, and very fine' (Beckett 1983: 158).

CHAPTER 8

Slow Going

The stage directions for Beckett's television play *Ghost Trio* specify that the door leading off the room to a tunnel stage right and the window to stage left should be 'imperceptibly ajar', an instruction that gave the set designer for the first production agonies of scruple (Beckett 1986: 408). This stage direction might suggest an exquisite variation on the whiskery old gag: 'When can't you tell that a door is not a door? When it's imperceptibly ajar'. What this direction means in fact is that the door will turn out later to have been imperceptibly ajar, when it is able to be opened without turning a knob or releasing a catch. This is the aspect of slowness that interests me most of all in Beckett's work; the slowness of things happening, as it is put in *The Lost Ones*, 'by insensible degrees' (Beckett 1984: 163). No other writer has joined his writing so unflinchingly to the rhythm and duration of insensible elapse, to the ordinary mystery of what Beckett in his notes for *Happy Days* on Winnie's forgetfulness calls the 'incomprehensible transport' from one moment to another, the inability either to coincide with the passing of time, or to be able to arrest it (Knowlson 1985: 150). Again and again I will have to keep coming back to this point, in the face of my own attempts to make slowness apprehensible and comprehensible. An academic paper is one of many devices we have for gathering up time and making a narrative artefact of it. Narratives are well equipped to offer a simulacrum of this quality of temporal passage because they not only represent the fact of time passing, they also themselves extend through time in their telling. They take time, as we say. But this will always turn out to have been a ruse, a way of turning aside from the actual conditions of time passing, which remain definitive for any narrative, but unlegislatable by it. What I mean to try to get at, but will be content to have managed merely to get amidst, is the experience of going slowly, of slow going.

Let me attempt to distinguish the two: going slowly and slow going. Going slowly has a good reputation. It can connote care, attentiveness and a fullness of response, a refusal to be rushed past or hustled aside from one's purpose. Going slowly is at the heart of that process of delaying, holding back from immediate gratification, which is the foundation of selfhood and of culture – the toleration of frustration in the interests of a greater yield of pleasure or value further down the line. Going slowly has traditionally been associated with the possibility of being able to be, as opposed to the modern forms of becoming. This kind of slowness has traditionally meant the examined life; it has meant culture itself. The impulse to slow down, to linger, loiter or retard is there throughout Beckett's work: for example, in the section of *Company* that follows the movement of a second hand around a watch-face (Beckett 1989: 47–8). It is there, too, in those recommendations to pause or hold back, which are found throughout that text: 'Leave it at that . . . Imagine warily' (Beckett 1989: 20, 38). Slow and steady wins the race. Going slowly ought to give us time to keep pace with our lives, ought to allow us to watch our step, to hear the feet however faint they fall. Slowness has the reputation of allowing us to take control over our lives, to take our time or be there, as we impenetrably say, in the moment.

In the condition I am going to keep on calling slow going, however, there can be no convergence of the one who undergoes and the one who perceives the time of elapsing. There can be no deliberation. We cannot live at the rate at which we nevertheless must live; we cannot live in the time that it will over and over again turn out that we were all along living out. Life, and the pivotal moments of a life, the moments after which nothing was ever the same again, will all in the end be, in the concluding words of Beckett's play *That Time*, 'come and gone in no time' (Beckett 1986: 395). 'No time' here seems to mean not only 'in the blink of an eye' but also something like my slow going; the immeasurable, unexperienceable drift of accretion and degradation, the insensible process that one cannot live slowly enough to live wholly knowingly, because then one would be getting ahead of oneself, living more quickly than the process that lives itself out in our living. Going slowly is something we attempt to do to time; slow going is what time does to us, through us. 'Whether or not we use it, it goes / And leaves what something hidden from us chose' (Larkin 1988: 153).

This word 'going' is itself often at the intersection of the two kinds of duration. Going slowly implies a kind of going on: persistence, or progress. Slow going will always turn out to have been a going out. Beckett's work allows, even seems to require, some acknowledgement of this slow going. But it does not see round the question of its own slowness, is not in charge of the meaning of its slowness. It does not thematise its slow going, or when it does, it cannot itself any more be or be undergoing the process of slow going (except of course, and necessarily, unknowingly). Slowly going on, in a way that will be more than a slowing down, will turn out to have been 'darkward bound' (Beckett 1984: 163), a slow and sure going out. We cannot apply a measure to this movement of slow going because it is itself the only scale against which to measure the refusals and remissions of elapsing time of which the hectic interval of human life is composed.

The spatial sublime of magnitude has been converted in our era to a temporal sublime of speed. Speed accomplishes the attenuation of mass and extended substance. The rule seems to be, the smaller, the faster. Early modernity marvelled at itself in the haughty substance of the Great Eastern; later modernity sees its image, or rather loses sight of it, in the imperceptible, in the nano-engineered processor based on a single molecule. Samuel Beckett participates in this miniaturisation; instead of epics and monuments (*A la recherché du temps perdu*, *Finnegans Wake*), Beckett scaled down. But miniaturisation is not accompanied by lightness and speed in Beckett's work. He is in fact the most important inaugurator of a mode of aesthetic defection from speed. It seems to be precisely the uninterpretability of slowness that has made it so important in the art of that – what is the wrong word exactly? – rearguard, that avant-garde which, finding itself humiliatingly outstripped by a culture in which acceleration has become the dominant value, began to look for ways of turning from speed or promptness or punctuality; an art that wanted to try to stop being on time; hence musical minimalism, and especially the beautiful excruciation of Steve Reich's phase-experiments; and the rent, discontinuous fabric of the work of John Cage and Morton Feldman; the interest in processes of slow decomposition in the work of Helen Chadwick, Andy Goldsworthy, and Damien Hirst and the confrontation with slowness of Michael Snow's *Wavelength* (1967). Slowness is not representable because it is the presence of the decay of presence. Representation is an effect of punctuality, or promptness, of the ravelling or puckering of time. Slowness testifies to asynchrony, a failure to meet up or come together. Speed is inflammatory, infectious. It calls me into its condition, chiding and chivvying, pulling me out of my time into its more than time, time raised to the power of time. It calls me into its synchronicity, holding a promise that I will be able not only to accomplish particular purposes more quickly, but also to beat speed, to be at one with what breaks exultantly with mere being, to be merged with its ecstatic going out from the mere condition of going on. Speed is not merely ecstatic because it throws us out of ourselves; it also offers the prospect of a mode of being in that condition of being beside ourselves. Slow going is always the failure to be there, to have been there, in our own midst, in the condition of slow going that will have been going on, as we so composedly say, all the time.

This is why speed seems to offer itself as a hunger for a kind of terminal velocity: we know that the speed of light is the fastest that anything in our observable universe can go. Slowness is indeterminable, since in order to know the absolute limit of slowness, we would need to know how long the universe is going to last. The terminal rate of slowness would then be that of some singular event which unfolded continuously and occurred only once in the course of that entire history. Slowness is of course relative. Slowness is slow by comparison with the right speed, or relative to expected or desired promptness or despatch; relaxed slowness is relative to hurry or pressure to speed up. We mistake the experience of slowness as a simple negative measure; if only things could go more quickly, in the queue, on the end of the line, during pain or unhappiness. But slow going is not quite this. It is the experience of a loss of temporal relativity; when things are going slowly, the scale of measurement itself begins to elongate, to attenuate, to dissolve. The extreme sense of measure, the inhuman measuredness of much of Beckett's work, its quality of calculated slowness, is itself perhaps a protest against the erosion of measure that begins when slowness gathers. It is a go-slow protest against the process of slowly going. For even to explicate slowness is of course to speed it up, to save one the necessity in future of going through it all again, so intolerably slowly. It is to summarise. Two words repeatedly scratch that itch to economy, the desire for summary in Beckett's work: 'so on'. These words answer the need to pucker up the agony of unrelieved elapse into something calculable and roughly predictable, that may then be dispensed with: 'So on infinitely until towards the unthinkable end if this notion is maintained' (Beckett 1984: 177).

A brief respite: where are we in this paper? Somewhere near the beginning, to be sure, but already with intimations of what it will be like to be in the middle, and where we are going to be by the end. As I sit typing these words, I am both before and ahead of this moment (this moment being in point of fact 6.25 AM on Friday 25 September). Actually it is not; I decided to tell you the time at which I wrote these words a minute or so after I had actually written them. In fact, I can tell you exactly when the thought occurred to me to go back to what I had already written and record the time I had written it, because I made a note of it. It was just after having typed the phrase (wait, I'm just popping to the end of the paragraph to find it again, OK, I'm back) 'what was then envisaged as the first sentences'. These words were first written two minutes later at about 6.27. So, by the time we get to that phrase it will be about 6.27, though in fact as I write these words (these actual words 'these words'), it is already 6.32. So, then, let us finally strike out towards the past that this parenthesis has now strewn in its own path: I asked where are we in this paper? I have a pretty good idea of how I will get to this point and what will succeed it (actually I have stopped the clock several times in order to visit what was then envisaged as the first sentences, and to play around with what I have in mind as its end).

In all of this, I have been substituting temporal ordering for temporal duration. But none of these games of anticipation and recall could come about or have any meaning except by virtue of the fundamental condition, as unseizable as it is unfleeable, of elapsing. No matter how my writing limps or sprints, compresses or relaxes, no matter what complex origami I effect on the sequence of its composition, time will have passed, quickly or slowly, quickly and slowly. I cannot get in step with this elapsing for which I am always too fast or slow, and which is neither the time of writing, nor the time of reading. All I can do, and cannot anyway but do, is to disclose it as the geologically mobile ground of all my lurches of protention and retention. I wanted, sitting at my desk, to predict what the speed of that passing might be, but I could not. Its condition of taking place is its horizon of possibility, an horizon that, no matter how I struggle to watch myself, to write the time in which my writing (and then, when I gave this paper, my speaking, and then again, as I marked the paper up for the web, and now, again, as I revise that version for print publication, my writing again), to get in step with the time of my speech, I cannot get myself into the field of my chronic vision, any more than Winnie in *Happy Days* can see her own face. I seem always to be out of step with the time that not only passes, but passes away, passes away from and through me, even though I am its sole measure.

Jean-François Lyotard reflects on the difficulty of conceiving what he calls a phenomenology of elementary time. Like Beckett, he is interested in trying to grasp what it would be like simply to be, in time, without any attempt to grasp, hold, or reserve the experience for later use or contemplation. The French word *maintenant*, he says, recalls to us 'how much maintenance there is in the least instant' (Lyotard 1990: 159). Lyotard goes on to suggest that time must be apprehended, which is to say minimally represented, or held in memory, in order to be experienced:

> The constitution of the present instant . . . already demands a retention, even a minimal one, of various elements together, their 'constitution', precisely. This microscopic synthesis is already necessary for the slightest appearing. For plunging into the pure manifold and letting oneself be carried along by it would allow nothing to appear to consciousness, nor to disappear from it for that matter, appearing not even taking 'place'. This place is due to a synthesis, that of apprehension, which as it were hems the edges of the pure flow and makes discontinuous the pure continuum of the flow while making

continue the pure discontinuity of its supposed elements. In short the river
needs a bank if it is to flow. An immobile observatory to make the movement
apparent. (Lyotard 1990: 159)

One could reverse that final judgement: Lyotard says we need to pinch time
to perceive its passage. We need to put our hand into the current, to feel its
onward pressure from the resulting turbulence. There needs to be something
nontemporal inserted into the flow of time for temporality to come into
being. But we might as well say that the hand recognises that it is stationary
only because there is passage, because of the difficulty of holding its position
against the current. We can only ever stop time because of its passage. The
static observatory does not create the passage; the passage creates the possibility of the observatory that can never be in the right place at the right time.
I spent some considerable time in a book I wrote a long time ago reflecting
on the ways in which Beckett gathered, folded over and resynthesized time,
especially in the trilogy (Connor 1988). I was tempted then to see atemporal
repetition as a triumph over the tyrannical fantasy of present time or linear
passage. The book and the precipitate person who wrote it were both in the
grip of a Bergsonian attitude towards time, which had perhaps transmitted
itself through the work of that most loyal of Bergsonians, Gilles Deleuze.
Bergsonian was my desire to track and preserve the building continuities
and the unarrestable accumulations and recurrences of time in Beckett's work.
When no time is wholly distinct from any other time, there is, to be sure, no
static presence, but time nevertheless seems to form an ideal plenitude. I am
committing myself now to apprehend the force in Beckett's work of what
could be called a dissociative rather than an accretive duration, of the tense
we could call the present discontinuous; the ordinary, fundamental, terrifying
topple of time's slow foot into the next moment, the *disfazione* (unfolding,
unworking, working out, falling out, dissolution, decomposition) of sheer
elapse that never resolves into anything as dramatic and determinate as
collapse or relapse, the pitiless passing away, in soft and imperceptible
torrent, that passes understanding.
    When Lyotard says, commenting on his evocation of the synthesising
apprehension of time, 'you see that we have got into phenomenology'
(Lyotard 1990: 159), he is reminding us of the ways in which phenomenology
has helped to explicate the ecstatic nature of temporality, the way in which
the comportment to a future and the relation to a past plucks at the
instantaneous present, thus both dividing being from itself and giving it
its emergent unity in division. 'I project myself toward the Future in order
to merge there with what I lack; that is, with that which, if synthetically

added to my Present would make me be what I am', writes Sartre (1984: 127). Living in time thus draws us both out of and into ourselves. We are all, and all of the time, in and out of time, our inability to be thoroughly in time our way of belonging to it. Such ecstatic projections of being into becoming, however, depend upon speed, by which I mean upon variations in speed; to be ahead of yourself is to go faster than you are in fact going. Even to slow things down is really to live faster than one is living: since, to slow down, to apply the brakes on living, one must get ahead of oneself, take the measure of one's headlong plunge into futurity, in order to rein it in and hold it back.

Speed and slowness have new possibilities and poignancies in a world of storable and reproducible time-media, such as film and music, which allow us simultaneously to preserve stretches of time (we may never know the tempo of Mozart's symphonies, but we know exactly the speed at which Billie Whitelaw performed *Not I*) and to manipulate these recorded stretches, speeding them up and slowing them down. In fact, recording is a kind of master-mechanism for Beckett's work in prose and drama after the trilogy because recording allows a certain kind of play between actual and possible speeds and durations. Recording allows one both to reproduce and to change the speed of a playback. It suggests the possibility of going both faster and more slowly: Krapp winding through to the place he wants in his tapes and, once there, lingering on it in fond, unbelonging longing. This possibility is enacted in what Krapp does with the word that embodies this possibility, the word 'spool'. There is no better picturing in Beckett's work of the regular process of at once going on and going out than the spool of tape unreeling itself at the end of *Krapp's Last Tape*. As the tape is played, it is transferred from the left-hand spool to the right. The more one has gathered on the right, the less remains on the left. Going on can only be accomplished by going out, winding on by reeling off. After all the complex envelopings and pocketings of times within times, all the topological loopings together of past and present in *Krapp's Last Tape*, the play tries to expose us to the pure elapsing of moments. The unspooling tape is Beckett's answer to the retentive, accretive rhythm of the *fort/da*. In these moments of unspooling, we seem to be brought into the immediate experience of something going on, of a time both losing momentum and gathering it as it runs out.

Of course, this is not in reality pure exposure to elapsing. It is a painful interval of slowness that interrupts the continuum of ordinary time, delays the return to non-theatrical time that will come at the end of the perform-ance. It is at once the collapse of representation (nothing is here being represented except what is in actual fact happening, the slow reeling away of the seconds) and a kind of staging of time, which is to say the introduction of a complication, or turbulence, into slow going. A pinch of time is taken up between finger and thumb, though we recognise that time has not merely been taken, but also taken up, in this experience of being exposed to the pure elapsing of time only after it has finished.

One of the most striking responses in Beckett's work to this apprehension of elapse is in the attempt to control and determine its own speed, the aim being partly to resist the corrosive effects of pure passage, to shape duration into rhythm, and partly to ensure that the work has a chance of staying as close as possible to a pure and unmediated process of taking place. The issue that preoccupied Beckett most of all in his direction was not character-isation, or setting, or even tone, but speed of delivery. The director has an opportunity to synchronise the time of the work with the time of its performance that is not available to the writer of prose, or the writer of drama whose works are primarily read rather than seen.

The literalising of temporal ecstasis has become the norm for us, in a world in which the dream of a permanent now is carried by the collapsing together of live transmission and recording, and the maintenance of the *maintenant* through technologies that ensure nothing slips out of date and everything is for ever. Our capacity to inhabit a permanent, undecaying instantaneousness is the mark of the otherworldliness of our world. Beckett's convoluted temporalities, in which nothing is ever over and done with, everything can recur or be revived, and in which past, present and future are looped inextricably together, anticipate and mirror the refusal of narrative typical of this world. Narrative is always phenomenologically conditioned by the fact that it occupies and is exposed to 'real time', and therefore must always cope with the danger of interruptedness, with the possibility, which it can never fully legislate, that reading can be broken off, or broken into by other concerns (boredom, hunger, sexual desire, death). To cope with the contemporary culture of interruptions, narrative has generated its own inter-ruptive syntax, taking the condition of its exposure to temporal contingency and making it a necessary part of its being. Thus hypertext, while seeming to surrender itself to the discontinuities introduced into the reading by the choices of the reader, in fact weaves interruptedness into its own fabric, turning chance into choice, and making accident its own.

Beckett's prose fiction anticipates our contemporary world of staged or hyper-represented time – a world in which duration, the condition of living on, of lasting out, has been turned into a problem of temporal ordering. The world of hypertext is a world of generalised time shift – of plastic, reversible, reconfigurable time. If hypertext, anticipated as it is by the temporal convolutions of writers such as Proust, Joyce and Beckett himself, is an attempt to find in discontinuity a higher, more stable form of continuity, then the opening of Beckett's work out of this continuity into the condition of slow going represents a breaking open of discontinuity itself; not the breaking of the familiar continuity of time by the familiar kinds of modernist and postmodernist discontinuity and temporal paradox, but the rupture of interruption by the principle of continuous elapsing.

Beckett's prose fiction attempts at once to score or to stage time, and to expose itself to this disarticulating continuity of elapse. In Beckett's work, these temporal agonistics centre upon punctuation. There are, we may say, four epochs of punctuation in that work. There is the classical or traditional epoch, in which all the resources of punctuation are used. This extends from *Dream of Fair to Middling Women* to *Murphy*. With *Watt* comes Beckett's discovery of the extraordinary capacities of the comma, to create a kind of counterpoint between the sheer going on of the sentence, with no awareness of its likely end, and the interruptions, resumptions and folding over that the comma gives. It is in *The Unnamable* and *Texts for Nothing* that the capacities of the comma, to breach and bridge, to arrest and accelerate, are taken to the limit. It is the comma above all that is the vehicle of Beckett's attempt to encounter and inhabit the condition of elementary duration, and to synchronise itself with its own (not ever really its own, that is going to be the point) time of taking place:

> Ah, says I, punctually, if only I could say. There's a way out there, there's a way out somewhere, then all would be said, it would be the first step on the long travellable road, destination tomb, to be trod without a word, tramp tramp, little heavy irrevocable steps, down the long tunnels at first, then under the mortal skies, through the days and nights, faster and faster, no, slower and slower, for obvious reasons, and at the same time faster and faster, for other obvious reasons, or the same, obvious in a different way, or in the same way, but at a different moment of time, a moment earlier, a moment later, or at the same moment, there is no such thing, there would be no such thing, I recapitulate, impossible. (Beckett 1984: 101)

Walking and telling are always closely connected in Beckett's work, and this passage tells a brief story of a story told through the taking of steps. If only, the narrator says, there could be a first step, a first word, in the direction of a destination, then the whole thing, the whole journey, the whole story, would become destined, available to be travelled and told. The narrator would like there to be a way out of time through the storying of time, through the projection of a perspective according to which the first of a sequence of steps could be visible as, and known in advance to be, the first.

If a particular punctual moment could be seen in this way, it might be possible to match the time of the telling to the time of the passage told of. Indeed the passage that unbuds from this apprehension magically begins to deliver the very sense of measure or metre that the narrator requires: 'faster and faster, no, slower and slower, for obvious reasons, and at the same time faster and faster, for other obvious reasons, or the same, obvious in a different way, or in the same way' (Beckett 1984: 101). Beckett seems to have drawn the time told and the time of the telling into simultaneity; but the telling is always out of step with what it tells. When the narrative pulls itself up with that first 'no' ('faster and faster, no, slower and slower'), is it because it has got ahead of itself, or because it is lagging behind itself? Something pulls the narrative back, requiring it to acknowledge that what seems like acceleration is in fact deceleration, and then that both of them are effects of perspective. The reader is invited to move at the same pace as the words, measuring slowness and speed against each other. The same moment can be experienced as both slow and fast because it is always possible to view the moment from the perspective of before and after (with so many steps already taken, each new step will seem painfully slow; with so few left to take, it will seem sickeningly fast). What allows the weaving of this rhythmic ecstasy is a necessary averting from the elementary elapsing that is always, like the tortoise in the fable, too slow either to be outstripped or caught up with. 'The same moment, there is no such thing, there would be no such thing, I recapitulate, impossible' (Beckett 1984: 101). In the tiny gap between the alternative readings 'I recapitulate that it is impossible' and 'it is impossible for me to recapitulate' lies all the force of time's negligible, ineluctable passage, for which narrative will always have been too quick and too slow (Beckett 1984: 101). The narrative prefers to show us this non-coincidence rather than to tell us of it, but it cannot show it except by its very inability to show it, by its disclosure of the time that will slowly have built, or wasted, as the narrative is taking place. No matter how Beckett's elementary narratives attempt to live in and live out the tense of the present discontinuous, that time can never be got into the narrative.

The epoch of the comma is followed, most notably in *How It Is* and the 'cylinder pieces' and short residua of the 1960s and 1970s, by a suppression of all punctuation but the full stop (not even this is available in *How It Is*), accompanied progressively by the withering away of predicative forms. It may seem as though the attempt here is to deliver us to a static manifold, in which before and after are arbitrary and interchangeable. Instead of telling a story, *Lessness*, for example, simply alternates the ideas that some narrative movement might remain in prospect ('In the sand no hold one step more in the endlessness he will make it' [Beckett 1984: 155]) and that the very possibility of change, or there ever having been change, has been abolished: 'Never but this changelessness dream the passing hour. Never was but grey air timeless no sound figment the passing light' (Beckett 1984: 155). In the title of the French version of the work, *Sans*, the condition presented in the text is named as an elementary privation, an atemporal condition of being without. In the English title, *Lessness*, by contrast, there is a much stronger tincture of temporality, in the hint of progressive passing away or reduction, the process of getting less or what *Worstward Ho* will call 'leastening' (Beckett 1989: 118). For, even if we imagine *Lessness* (the only text in which Beckett consciously employed chance procedures in the composition process) as an entirely unwilled and mechanical process that simply plays through its permutations, the text must always in fact be being read as not for human eyes, by human eyes, within a horizon of unfolding or elapsing time. The reading of *Lessness* will always require a certain ordeal, the labour of subduing human time to the inhuman time of its verbal permutations.

The feeling that many have of an opening out or flowering in *Nohow On*, the so-called second trilogy formed by *Company*, *Ill Seen Ill Said* and *Worstward Ho*, in particular, is due very largely to the resuscitation of syntax, and especially of the verb, and the consequent relief at the possibility of knitting together the gaps that yawn and claw in earlier work: 'And now here, what now here, one enormous second, as in Paradise, and the mind slow, slow, nearly stopped ... The words too, slow, slow, the subject dies before it comes to the verb' (Beckett 1984: 75–6).

The question of punctuation is in a sense itself thematized in *The Lost Ones*, Beckett's definitive evocation of the condition of slow going. What is it that is most inhuman about *The Lost Ones*? Surely it is the absence of any events. What we are given is a process in the frequentative mode. Nothing that we see, or hear reported, of life in the cylinder is actually happening, or has definitely happened on a particular occasion. Everything has happened in just the same way, and will continue to happen in just the same way as it is now surmised to be happening. There are no absolute, unique or once-and-for-all events. Everything, it appears, can be undone or qualified. What counts is only the slow going, slow going on, slow going out, of the cylinder and the report that could be given of it, seen in the long run. At the same time, narrative strains to come into being, strains to congeal into punctual moments, the unequivocal first and last moments in a putative sequence. We know that there must be such moments in any sequence. There must be a first tiny tremor in the earth that produces the earthquake, a first uncountermanded malignity from which the fatal carcinoma blooms. These events are absolutely punctual, epochal, marking an absolute break from what has come before, and a microscopic initiation of an enormous and irrevocable change. But they can never be known in themselves, they have no here and now, since their meaning is inundated by what they portend or, in the case of last events, begin to conclude. They are events that will have been the first and will have been the last, seen from the perspective that both belongs and does not belong to them. The narrative is held together by the tension between the merely stochastic nature of the phenomena and our desire for there to have been a definable beginning and end: was it that time, or was it another time?

The Lost Ones is the most explicitly scientific work of a writer who we know (from a notebook kept in the early 1930s, and now in the University of Reading Beckett Archive) familiarised himself in early life with certain developments in contemporary physics. It is a work that painfully brings together the unrepresentable dimension of entropic decay, the process whereby, in a closed thermodynamic system, the random differences of speed and location, which make the energy of the molecules available for work, will inevitably tend to equalise, leaving the system inert and function-less. In one kind of model, the universe is no more than such a closed thermodynamic system. Not only is it bound to end in time, the fact of time only has meaning in terms of the slow approach to the condition of heat death. As is well known, James Clerk Maxwell posited a universe consisting of two chambers, connected only by a trapdoor. He imagined a being or demon who, merely by operating the trapdoor to separate positively charged particles from negative, would preserve infinitely the capacity of the system to generate electrical potential, and therefore work. Human beings have cast themselves in the role of that demon; as the alien element in the system that makes it possible negentropically to turn the current of time upstream. Humanity is a clot or valve in the expiration of time. The demon presence in *The Lost Ones* is the narrating voice, or even, since as usual we are in a hurry here, narrative itself, which is at once the unconscious and unjudging witness of the phenomena of the cylinder, and the agency that, by positing purpose, movement and outcome in the cylinder, seems to hold back the movement of time towards the ending of time, seems to bend pure succession into a swirl of persistence, a kind of rhythm or temporal shape other than that of coming apart. It is narrative itself that constitutes what Ilya Prigogine has called a 'dissipative structure' in the otherwise chaotic succession of events (Prigogine 1968: 1695).

In one crucial episode, the narrating consciousness postulates the idea of a way out of the cylinder. The second law of thermodynamics applies only to closed thermodynamic systems. If a new source of energy could be introduced into the system, or the system revealed as a subsystem of some larger system, the inexorable progress towards decay could be retarded. If there could exist a way out of the cylinder, then there would be the possibility of some new source of life and variation in it, something to hold together its slow unravelling.

> From time immemorial rumour has it or better still the rumour is abroad that there exists a way out. Those who no longer believe so are not immune from believing so again in accordance with the notion requiring as long as it holds that here all should die but in so gradual and to put it plainly so fluctuant a manner as to escape the notice even of a visitor. Regarding the nature of this way out and of its location two opinions divide without opposing all those still loyal to that old belief. One school swears by a secret passage branching from one of the tunnels and leading in the words of the poet to nature's sanctuaries. The other dreams of a trapdoor hidden in the hub of the ceiling giving access to a flue at the end of which the sun and other stars would still be shining. Conversion is frequent either way and such a one who at a given moment would hear of nothing but the tunnel may well a moment later hear of nothing but the trapdoor and a moment later still give himself the lie again. The fact remains none the less that of the two persuasions the former is declining in favour of the latter but in a manner so desultory and slow and of course with so little effect on the comportment of either sect that to perceive it one must be in the secret of the gods. (Beckett 1984: 162)

The narrative both forces and forbids itself to see to the end of life in the cylinder, speculating obstinately about the progressive unfolding of events while reminding itself constantly that ideas about the ending of things in the cylinder are notions and hypotheses rather than fact or even reliable inference. The slowness of the cylinder's going and the cleaving of the act of narrative witness to its elementary phenomena are so absolute as to disallow any precipitate hurrying to a conclusion – until, that is, the final paragraph, which Beckett added some years after having abandoned the text as apparently unfinishable. This paragraph suddenly projects us far into the future of the cylinder, to the point where everything may be about to come to rest, after one last encounter between a searcher and the object of his enquiry, the eyes of a long-since vanquished and immobile woman:

> There he opens then his eyes this last of all if a man and some time later threads his way to the first among the vanquished so often taken for a guide. On his knees he parts the heavy hair and raises the unresisting head. Once devoured the face thus laid bare the eyes at a touch of the thumbs open without demur. In those calm wastes he lets his wander till they are the first

to close and the head relinquished falls back into its place. He himself after a pause impossible to time finds at last his place and pose whereupon dark descends and at the same instant the temperature comes to rest not far from freezing point. (Beckett 1984: 178)

This is the only determinate event in the whole of *The Lost Ones*. Something has at last happened that cannot, it appears, be reversed or undone by subsequent events; but that thing that has at last happened is the last thing of all to happen, ever. It is the moment at which narrative begins, the moment at which the possible becomes actual. It is brought into being by an act of violent grace, the sudden acceleration away from the sheer condition of imperceptible slow going in the cylinder. The reality of the cylinder, its slow going, remains unrepresentable, except by abandoning the attempt to represent it. Like the story of a human life, the end of the story of the cylinder will always have to have been either too early or too late. The only time that counts will be beyond its power to tell.

The story goes that, watching technicians testing the image quality of *Quad*, the most hectic and raucous piece that he ever wrote, for reception by monochrome receivers, and running the tape through in slow motion, Beckett had the idea of a sequel that would be 'ten thousand years later' (Knowlson 1996: 593). Seeing the hectic bustle of the performance he had already recorded transformed into this laboured shuffle, suggested to Beckett a fast-forward to a time when everything would have nearly run down. As a result, he wrote *Quad II*, a slow, dim coda to *Quad*. The thing that has always surprised me about this story is Beckett's surprise at his own discovery. How could he not have realised that the stuttering hurry of the choreographic system he had set up in *Quad* would have exactly the same outcome as in the cylinder of *The Lost Ones*? How could he not have anticipated from the beginning the idea of a slow decay of the system he had set up, just as in *Play*, for which he suggests an exact repeat in performance, only slower and more diminished in energy? One answer might be simply that, amid all the complex repetitions, the loopings together of beginning and end, that make of Beckett's work a kind of dynamic entirety, there is a dimension of unknowingness, of being merely amidst the process of going on, that cannot finally be retarded or accelerated. There are knowledge, memory, struggle and resistance, not to mention the miniature convulsions of time caused by laughter; but there is no accumulation of these goods in the midst of the unpausing going on and going out.

The Lost Ones may perhaps be taken as a proleptic summary of the whole of Beckett's work, considered as a system closed upon itself, and therefore inexorably, but by insensible degrees, proceeding towards exhaustion and saturation. If the entire effect of that work is to act as a kind of interval, a turbulent suspension in the senseless and insensible unspooling of things in general, it also acknowledges that unfolding, that unrepresentable background from which turbulence derives its energy, and which it may be, in the end, its larger end to have assisted.

Narrative has sometimes found in our era a vocation to synchronise itself with the time that it can neither command nor countermand, a vocation that has a particular sharpness when we have devised so many ways of turning the irreversibility of time's passage into story time. It is in their dealings with slow going that Beckett's writing and other arts and artists of the dilatory get closest to coinciding with the time their stories take. And what have we been about here, rereading and replaying that work so obsessively? Passing the time, which would have passed anyway.

PART III

Worlds

CHAPTER 9

Beckett's Low Church

Nobody, at this time of day, could miss the abundant signs and tokens of belief in Beckett's work, which have been thoroughly tracked and ticketed by a succession of writers. The most comprehensive by far of these concordancers is Mary Bryden. Introducing her devotional detector to every nook not only of Beckett's published works, but also of his letters and unpublished manuscripts, Bryden's book *Samuel Beckett and the Idea of God* (1997) shows just how thronged Beckett's work is with the bric-à-brac of religious belief, practice and sentiment – saints, priests, hymns, prayers, psalms, qualms, knotty points of doctrine and more crucifixions per square foot than *Spartacus*. Increasingly, it seems, the question to be asked of religion in Beckett's work is not 'what religion is there in Beckett?', but rather 'what is all this religion doing in Beckett?' – or even 'what are we to do with all this religion in Beckett?' So insistent is the presence of religious matters and allusions in Beckett's work that assertions like those of Spyridoula Athanasopoulou-Kypriou, that Beckett is opposed to all forms of 'metaphysical quest' and aims to help people to accept reality in all its absurdity and thereby allow 'peace, dignity and freedom to enter in their souls' (Athanasopoulou-Kypriou 2000: 48), seem archaic and scarcely credible, even though her view is one for which I feel considerable sympathy.

We can perhaps characterise readings of religion in Beckett in three ways. Early readers of Beckett were at pains to bring to light such religious references, seeing in them a compensation for the savage 'existential' bleakness of Beckett's world and work. Religious belief here is said to be hidden, tenuous, perhaps infinitely deferred, yet, once intimated, unmistakable. Perhaps representative of these approaches is Colin Duckworth, who, observing that 'Beckett constantly denies God and yet is obsessed by God', follows Jean Onimus in maintaining that 'God is absent *in* Beckett's work and world, but not absent *from* it' (Onimus 1968: 75; Duckworth 2000: 138, 135). Lance St. John Butler acknowledges what he calls the 'sarcastic-ironic-blasphemous' element that is prominent in many of the references to religion in Beckett's early work, but finds an unironic solemnity in later religious references, leaving religion 'a raw, sore place where salvation, hope and comfort are on offer in a way that, if true, would overwhelm Beckett's world with a heartbreaking joy' (Butler 1992: 180–1). Such approaches attempt to show that Beckett's world and Beckett's works are not, despite appearances, or not quite yet, beyond belief.

A second line of argument, which has sometimes been deployed in rivalry with or contradiction to this, reads all the religious references in Beckett as merely an elaborate apparatus of sardonic denial or denunciation. According to this line of argument, God crops up throughout Beckett's work in order for it to be demonstrated decisively yet never quite conclusively that he is not there: 'First dirty, then make clean' is the formula offered in *The Unnamable* (Beckett 1973: 302). In this sense, religious feeling and belief are on a level with all the other shreds and patches of customary life that survive in Beckett's world, in order to provide a kind of comic energy of collapse – and the bigger, like God, they come, the louder and more ignominiously they fall. Like the goods gathered for the potlatch, religion, on this view, is just another vanity to feed the bonfire. This view is typified by Hersh Zeifman, who concludes that '[i]nstead of providing support for a Christian interpretation, the presence of biblical imagery in the plays serves rather to undermine such an interpretation through ironic counterpoint' (Zeifman 1975: 93). This is in fact the default reading to be found almost throughout Bryden's *Samuel Beckett and the Idea of God*. It takes a more melancholic form in arguments like that of John Pilling that Beckett is a 'mystic without God' (Pilling 1976: 138), that Beckett's work retains the scenery and properties of theological, or even mystical tradition, in order to make the absconding or eviction of the divine tenant the more bitterly or ridiculously evident.

A third mode of reading the question of religion in Beckett began to emerge in the 1980s, and has become ever more vigorous in recent years, for reasons which I will consider a little more explicitly later. This approach distinguishes the religious from the mystical in Beckett's work, finding in Beckett's comic antipathy to established forms of religious belief a mystical atheology, or *via negativa*, which either parallels or frankly recapitulates the apophatic tradition. Apophasis names the attempt to arrive at knowledge of the divine through negations of all the things that the divine is not, which is to say pretty much anything you could bring to mind or tongue. This line of argument really begins with Hélène Baldwin, whose *Samuel Beckett's Real Silence* (1981) maintains that '[t]he progressive stripping-down of the self which takes place in so many of Beckett's works is not just a search for self, but in fact the "negative way" of mysticism, whose object is to break the bonds of time and place and find what Eliot calls the still center of the turning world' (Baldwin 1981: 6). Beckett's works, therefore, 'analogically represent the negative way' (Baldwin 1981: 155). Baldwin's claims are extended and particularised by Marius Buning, with particular reference to the figure of the thirteenth-century mystic Meister Eckhart, especially his principles of 'detachment' ('*Gelassenheit*'), dissimilarity or 'self-naughting' and 'break-through' ('*Durchbruch*') into nothingness. Buning sees the TV play *Nacht und Träume* as Beckett's 'furthest (allegorical) journey into nowhere and into nothing, which is at the same time everywhere and everything' (Buning 1990: 140).

So let it be supposed that there are three strains of the religious in criticism of Beckett. The first is cryptic belief – where the belief, though straightforward and even orthodox in form, is nevertheless fugitive and uncertain. This kind of religious belief remains what it is or traditionally has been, but almost terminally diminished, like so many other things in Beckett. Then there is repudiated belief, in which religion is there to be sighed over, signed off, or sent up. Finally, there is the religion beyond belief. In this form of belief, belief is actually beside the point. The very form of religious negation is what guarantees it as religious. It is not just that Beckett never definitively has done with religion; it is that this never-having-done, the 'leastmost all' (Beckett 1989: 119) of the dwindling that can 'never to naught be brought' (Beckett 1989: 118), as the jingle of *Worstward Ho* has it, itself becomes definitive.

An apparently more secular – and also more sectarian – version of this argument is brought forward by those who find in Beckett a Protestant sensibility powerfully at work despite, or perhaps even because of, Beckett's religious scepticism. Declan Kiberd gives us a roll-call of Protestant qualities to be found in Beckett, finding him 'the first since Swift to confront head-on the great drama of the puritan conscience, tackling such themes as work and reward, anxious self-scrutiny, the need for self-reliance and the distrust of artifice and even art' (Kiberd 1985: 122). One might object that the Protestant work ethic seems strangely lacking in the bedridden Beckett of the 1930s, but Kiberd finds even in Beckett's most indolent heroes a strangely puritanical absolutism, in 'the desire for self-sufficiency in the world of pure mind', and argues that '[f]or the Protestant ethic of work, he has substituted the Puritan ethic of relentless self-exploration' (Kiberd 1985: 124, 129). This line of argument has recently been taken further by Sinéad Mooney, who decodes Beckett's Protestantism in a more politicised manner:

> It is this Irish Protestant sense of the marginal and excluded, the spiritually-hyphenated, the less-than-complete assent to an identity, a coercive cultural

heritage, a literary tradition perceived as unmediated pressure rather than incitement, which provides, so to speak, the bedrock for Beckett's henceforth increasingly puritan probing of the quintessentially Protestant activities of examination of conscience, autobiography and iconoclasm. (Mooney 2000: 225)

This way of arguing seems to cut in two directions at once. On the one hand, it seems to drain the theology out of Protestantism, which then becomes culturised, and no more than the name of a generalised self-reliance and disaffection with institutionalised belief. On the other hand, continuing to identify such disaffection as 'Protestant' maintains the bond with that from which the protesting sensibility might wish to abscind, not to mention assuming the inescapable necessity of the sectarian alternative, as neatly expressed in the joke about the newcomer to Belfast, who, when asked his religion, replies that he is a Jew, to be met with the impatient rejoinder: 'Yes, but do you mean a Catholic Jew or a Protestant Jew?'

The difficulty of making any definitive break with religion parallels the difficulty for the artist of making a definitive break with represented subject or 'occasion', of which Beckett speaks in his *Three Dialogues With Georges Duthuit* – indeed, Beckett himself makes clear the analogy between the aesthetic and the religious:

> I know that all that is required now, in order to bring even this horrible matter to an acceptable conclusion, is to make of this submission, this admission, this fidelity to failure, a new occasion, a new term of relation ... No more ingenious method could be devised for restoring him, safe and sound, to the bosom of Saint Luke. (Beckett 1970c: 125, 121–2)

The very forms of Beckett's unbelief are said to be those of a believer rather than an unbeliever. His belief is constituted as doubt, which is a mode of belief, rather than incredulity. Indeed, Beckett has become a centrepiece of attempts to recapture for religion or render as religious the experience of religious doubt, or doubt about religion. Perhaps this can be seen as the effort to give Beckett's work a distinctive content, to reduce it or lift it to a series of propositions *about*. Beckett's failure, disinclination, or refusal to believe is turned into an interesting relation to belief, rather than being allowed to be an absence of relation to belief. Too often, the feeling that in Beckett 'uncertainty is always raised to a metaphysical power', as James Wood has put it, leads precipitately and illegitimately to the assumption that there is indeed a kind of metaphysics of uncertainty in Beckett (Wood 1999: 276). In *Language Mysticism*, Shira Wolosky proposed a Beckett whose work 'repeatedly recalls the discourse of theology' and of which 'the premises and practices of negative theology act as a generative condition' (Wolosky 1995: 91, 93). And yet, she insists, the failure of language to achieve immaculate negation, to arrive at nothingness, makes Beckett a 'counter-mystic' (Wolosky 1995: 90). The problem is that Wolosky simply affirms that Beckett's is a negative theology without the theology – that never arrives at mystical unity or emptiness. This may be counter-mystical in the sense in which mysticism has hitherto been understood, but it is of little utility against the kinds of claim that are currently made on behalf of radical negation of the Beckettian kind (and perhaps partly because of the Beckettian example), namely that a theology or a mysticism that never comes home, 'safe as the saying is and sound' (Beckett 1989: 77) is in fact the truest mysticism, that the theology that is absolutely bereft of God is the only possible theology.

Perhaps the problem of what to do with the matter of belief in Beckett is a localised version of the problem, if that is what it is precisely, of the return or refusal to be evaporated, of religion in the heart of the most radical and sceptical forms of philosophical thought. For this way of taking Beckett's refusal of religion, namely, as a religious refusal, as a believer's disbelief, associates Beckett with the mysterious but unmistakable drift with certain strains of radical critical theory towards theology. More particularly, it links with the marked strain of the apophatic within what has been called the 'theological turn' in contemporary literary and cultural theory, which has been tracked in collections such as Robert P. Sharlemann's *Negation and Theology* (1992), Harold Coward and Toby Foshay's *Derrida and Negative Theology* (1992) and Ilse N. Bulhof and Laurens ten Kate's *Flight of the Gods* (2000). Not for many a long year, one may surmise, has the name of pseudo–Dionysius the Areopagite been on the lips of so many.

In what follows, my definition of religion and religious will need to include more than just the belief in supernatural beings. My definition of religious thought requires only that it be radically unworldly, that it depend on beliefs that are out of this world. Another name for this kind of belief is magical thinking, since it will often, and perhaps even most often, depend upon an accessory belief, or faith, in the powers of thought to make the world in its own image, even and especially when the manifest content of that thinking affirms the limits of language. It involves what is known as 'the power of belief', which is the belief, or will-to-believe, that belief has power.

Believing On

Before proceeding to the consideration of this rhyme between readings of Beckett and some wider currents in contemporary thought, I want to pause

to lay out some thoughts about the nature of religious belief, and its relation
to other kinds of belief.

For us, believing has become a matter of believing *that* rather than believing
in. Belief derives from *be-leven* and cognate forms like Old English *belyfan*
and West Saxon *gelyfan*. These in turn derive from Germanic *ga-laubjan*
('hold dear, love') from an Indo-European base *leubh-* (like, love, desire).
This makes sense of the expression to 'believe on', which was more common
than 'believe in' during the fifteenth century, as well as earlier expressions
that have also had their day, like 'believing into' and 'believing on to'. As so
often, the preposition carries the freight of the proposition. Belief in this
sense is much closer to the idea of love to which it is etymologically related
than to the question of truth.

The usage that is primary today is belief in the truth of a proposition
or body of doctrine or, as the OED has it, in 'the genuineness, virtue, or
efficacy of a principle, institution, or practice'. 'Believing in' something, in
the sense of believing in the truth of its existence, is also a later development.
To believe something has for some time meant to accord it credit or grant it
veracity. It introduces a hiccup or flutter into belief, making every statement
of belief a statement about another statement. 'I believe that the earth is
round' is henceforth a telescoping of the proposition 'I believe that statement
"The earth is round" is a true statement'. Once belief enters into discourse,
then discourse, in the literal sense of a running back and forth – *dis-currere* –
enters into it.

The mediation involved in believing that something or other is true
rather than, as we tellingly say, trusting implicitly in its truth, which is to say
never raising or reflecting on it as a question of truth or falsity, always
threatens a sort of fracture. Once one affirms the truth of a belief, once one
affirms a belief in a truth, one has entered the jurisdiction of the dubitable,
of that which one may henceforth take leave to doubt. The difference is
coiled up, spirochaete-like, in the expression 'I love you'. In response to the
statement 'I love you', one may say 'your love is not true', but this is a
different thing from saying 'That (that is, the statement that you love me) is
not true'. The one is a matter of fidelity, the other of sincerity. The opposite
of truth is falsity, while the opposite of fidelity is betrayal. This is why being
an infidel is so much more drastic than being an unbeliever. Unbelief is a
matter for remedial persuasion, since it suggests that one may yet be brought
to believe, while infidelity is a matter for punishment or pardon, suggesting
as it does an act of betrayal or unfaithfulness that has already occurred.

Enunciating his own kind of epistemological credo, former U.S. Secretary
of Defense Donald Rumsfeld instructed us that there are known knowns

(things we know we know), known unknowns (things we know we don't know), and unknown unknowns (things we don't know we don't know) (Department of Defense 2002). One of these unknown unknowns is the missing corner of what is in fact an epistemological quadrangle. For are there not also *unknown knowns*, things we do not know that we know? Belief is perhaps in this corner.

There are two kinds of unnegotiable belief, which is to say beliefs that are intransigent to reason because they are not predicative beliefs. One is what we might call *infracredential belief*, or belief that has not come to explicitness as a predication. This characterises the way in which many forms of institutionalised belief are held by its adherents; it is the kind of faith that has never been questioned because it has not yet risen to the level of propositional truth. It may perhaps be, as Slavoj Žižek has suggested, that 'the direct belief in a truth that is subjectively fully assumed ("Here I stand!") is a modern phenomenon, in contrast to traditional beliefs-through-distance, like politeness or rituals' (Žižek 2003: 6). Infracredential belief becomes evident in what we call fundamentalism, but it also changes its nature, for fundamentalism will tend fatally to pin belief to a text or a series of formalised articles of belief. Now its strength, namely its willingness to assert its faith in the mode of credo, or absolute belief, is its weakness. Fundamentalism is brittle, or can always become so, because its adherents and its antagonists are required to know and affirm so clearly what it would mean no longer to believe, that it makes unbelief so eminently thinkable. Theirs is now a matter of known rather than unknown knowns, which makes fundamentalists, in Žižek's terms, modern rather than premodern. Fundamentalism has always begun to see round itself, hence its hysterical obsession with the infidel or the fallen. Arguments about belief often disguise this fault-line that runs through the question of belief. Religious belief attempts to approximate to the condition of faith without credence, of a belief that has no need to pass through propositions. And yet no religion can exist for long without a formalised statement of beliefs, which immediately opens a gulf between belief-in-action, or acting-in-the-belief-that, or acting-as-though-you-believed and the act of affirming belief, wherein, as we have seen, falls the shadow. Perhaps no religion has had more difficulty in negotiating this movement from the realm of faith into credence than Christianity, precisely because it stakes so much on the ritual of professing faith, the 'credo'.

Then there is *ultracredential belief*, that is to say, belief in which all possible predications have been dissolved or rendered undecidable, leaving only the form or force of belief, in the absence of any content. As we will soon see, this is the form taken by the more theological forms of deconstructive thinking.

Accordingly, there might also be said to be two ways of being beyond belief. One involves the withdrawal or withering of credence from propositions or doctrines to which it had previously been attached. Another involves the leaving behind of that mode of according belief, and returning to a mode of *believing on*, a mode of no longer knowing what one knows. In this condition, one is in belief as one is in love. The form of argument known as fideism, for example, makes a positive virtue of the disconnection of faith from credence. It finds its canonical exposition in Tertullian's *De Carne Christo*:

> crucifixus est dei filius: non pudet, quia pudendum est. et mortuus est dei filius: prorsus credibile est, quia ineptum est. et sepultus resurrexit: certum est, quia impossibile. (Tertullian 1956: 18)

> [The Son of God was crucified: there is no shame, because it is shameful. And the Son of God died: it is wholly credible, because it is ridiculous. And, buried, He rose again: it is certain, because impossible.] (my translation)

Blaise Pascal argued a version of this in his *Pensées*:

> Who then will blame Christians for being unable to give rational grounds for their belief, professing as they do a religion for which they cannot give rational grounds? They declare that it is a folly, *stultitiam*, in expounding it to the world, and then you complain that they do not prove it. If they did prove it they would not be keeping their word. It is by being without proof that they show they are not without sense. (Pascal 1995: 122)

Apophatics

Fideism finds a curious parallel in the religious turn taken by late deconstruction. From its beginnings, deconstruction has been accused of being a form of 'negative theology'. And, from early on, Derrida has defended himself against this charge by arguing that deconstruction is more radical than negative theology, since negative theology finds a kind of frame or terminus in the idea of God, the point of negative theology being, if only in some unthinkable end, to arrive at an understanding of God. The problem with traditional negative theology, for Derrida, is precisely that it is never really negative: it operates ultimately as 'the name of a way of truth', characterised by a 'desire to say and rejoin what is proper to God' (Derrida 1995, 69), meaning that 'the generative movement of the discourse of God is only a phase of positive ontotheology' (Derrida 1976: 337n.37). By contrast, deconstruction, *différance*, aporia, the trace, the gift, and the rest of the rattling caravanserai of *différance*'s 'vice-existers', ensures its own survival in the very non-arrival of God. 'Theological' seems an odd term for this, since the absolute, eternal deferral of the decidability of the existence of God is God itself.

Theologically minded readers of Derrida have had to find ways to cope with, or sidestep, Derrida's early remarks that '*Différance* is not theological, not even in the order of the most negative of negative theologies' (Derrida 1982, 6). One way to do this is indicated by Hugh Rayment-Pickard, when he writes that '[t]he point of these refutations and deconstructions is to clear the path not for a new kind of negative theology – still less a new positive theology – but a theology of impossibility' (Rayment-Pickard 2003: 126). The suggestion is that, for Derrida 'aporia itself would constitute the basis of an "other" theology which is neither positive nor negative, between the life and death of God' (Rayment-Pickard 2003: 130). 'Language has started without us, in us and before us. This is what theology calls God', Derrida has murkily affirmed (Derrida 1989: 29).

There is no more enthusiastic exponent of Derrida's 'generalised apophatics' (the 'enthusiast' being literally the one who has a god in him) than John D. Caputo, whose *The Prayers and Tears of Jacques Derrida* is an energetic, exhilarating, infinitely elastic series of variations upon Derrida's 'apophatico-apocalyptico-quasi-atheistic messianic' religion (Caputo 1997: 41, xxviii). Caputo captures very well the voluptuous hunger that runs through Derrida's work and writing:

> There is in Derrida what one might call a certain overreaching, trespassing aspiration, what I have been calling here, all along, a dream, or a desire, a restlessness, a passion for the impossible, a panting for something to come. . . . [T]here is in Derrida, in deconstruction, a longing and sighing, a weeping and praying, a dream and a desire, for something non-determinable, un-foreseeable, beyond the actual and the possible, beyond the horizon of possibility, beyond the scope of what we can sensibly imagine. (Caputo 1997: 333)

This is a weak thought amplifying itself into unlimited power – a kind of acrobatic apophatics, or omn-impotence. If infracredential belief is both manifested and put at risk in what we call fundamentalism, this intimate opposite of fundamentalism may be called repressive anti-foundationalism. It is repressive because it does not allow any kind of outside or differentiation. Every disagreement with or refusal of religion will find itself enfolded in the nebulous embrace of this theology without God that has bought up all the shares in atheism. Like Murphy's mind, such anti-foundationalism has 'excluded nothing that it did not itself contain' (Beckett 2003: 63). The inability, or is it perhaps refusal, to tolerate either decisive affirmation or decisive negation that is enacted through the trilogy and reaches its apogee in *The Unnamable* and *Texts for Nothing*, a condition that Beckett names as the purgatorial (Beckett 1983: 33), forms a close parallel with this mode of never-quite-negative theology that does not want to help itself turn into a theology of the never-quite-negative.

Absolution

There is another modality of religious thought, which is even more aggressively emptied of content. This is to be found, not in the work of Emmanuel Levinas and Derrida, but in the work of Alain Badiou, Slavoj Žižek and Giorgio Agamben. As it happens, this work has come to cohere upon a single figure, Saint Paul, whose writings are traditionally held to embody a shift from a Jewish to a Greek, a Judaic to a Christian dispensation, and has routinely been blamed for the formalisation of Christian revelation into oppressive doctrine ('Give me back the Berlin Wall, give me Stalin and Saint Paul / I've seen the future, brother, it is murder', as Leonard Cohen sings [Cohen 1992].) This may account in part for the emphasis in this work, not on the (unknowable) divinity as Father, but on the revolutionary irruption of the Son. The ineffable absolute, the absoluteness of its ineffability, here becomes the unassimilable event of revelation. (We will have to continue for quite a while yet to put up with these 'in-'s and 'un-'s.) And yet there will prove to be striking rhymes between the apophatic and the evental.

In marked contrast to the divinity-bibbing agnosticism of Derrida, which is religiose because of its condition as religious excess, a religious exceeding of religion, Alain Badiou insists that his interest in Saint Paul is that of a militant atheist, stating unambiguously at the beginning of his *Saint Paul: The Foundation of Universalism*, that '[f]or me, truth be told, Paul is not an apostle or a saint. I care nothing for the Good News he declares, or the cult dedicated to him' (Badiou 2003b: 1). Badiou's interest in Paul is as one who bears witness to the event of Christ's life and, more particularly, his death and resurrection. The concept of the event is at the centre of Badiou's philosophy. He means by an event the sudden, disruptive arrival of a truth. But truth, for Badiou, is not a property of propositions and has nothing to do with the common-or-garden concurrence between statements and states of affairs. Truth occurs rarely, and is always apprehended, when it is, in the form of radical strangeness or indigestibility by previously existing dispensations of thought. So truth is defined by its novelty, which one might think makes it difficult to distinguish from what others might regard as error or falsehood. But it is precisely because of their unassimilability that the truths announced in events can lay claim to being universal, though also utterly unique, or irreducible to previously existing frames of understanding. This means that truth-events are both singular and universal. A truth is singular, because '[i]t is neither structural, nor axiomatic, nor legal. No available generality can account for it, nor structure the subject who claims to follow in its wake. Consequently, there cannot be a law of truth' (Badiou 2003b: 14). But it is also universal, and for the same reason, namely because it 'is *diagonal* relative to every communitarian subset; it neither claims authority from, nor (this is obviously the most delicate point) constitutes any identity. It is offered to all, or addressed to everyone, without a condition of belonging being able to limit this offer, or this address' (Badiou 2003b: 14). But, as so often with Badiou, this universalism is exclusive rather than inclusive. The universal comes about, not because every community of belief is included, but because every limiting community is excluded: 'the fidelity to such an event exists only through the termination of communitarian particularisms and the determination of a subject-of-truth who indistinguishes the One and the "for all"' (Badiou 2003b: 108).

Truth-events of this kind are not simply offered up to, or available for, inspection and adoption by subjects. For Badiou, subjects are actually requisitioned, or called into being by events. One can scarcely make a choice, informed or not, to follow the implications of an event, since there is no subject worthy of the name before the fidelity to the event. The subject is not the one who makes the choice of cleaving to the event; it is the not having a choice. This subject not only is founded upon an untimely ripping of the event out of the continuum of history, but itself takes the form of a continuing or extended rupture:

> [A]n eventual rupture always constitutes its subject in the divided form of a 'not . . . but', and that *it is precisely this form that bears the universal.* For the 'not' is the potential dissolution of closed particularities (whose name is 'law'), while the 'but' indicates the task, the faithful labor, in which the subjects of the process opened up by the event (whose name is 'grace') are the coworkers. (Badiou 2003: 63–4)

Another name for the 'event' is what Paul, distinguishing the new dispensation from the old, is 'grace', which 'is neither a bequest, nor a tradition, nor a teaching. It is a supernumerary relative to all this and presents itself as pure givenness' (Badiou 2003b: 63).

For this reason, 'proceeding from the event delivers no law, no form of mastery, be it that of the wise man or the prophet' (Badiou 2003b: 42). It is like nothing on earth. If you want to know what kind of thing an event is, you need to think of something that you can't possibly think of, an exercise that would tax the capacities even of Lewis Carroll's White Queen. You can recognise an event (or, pretty much always, can't) because there is no way to name or describe it, or not in existing language: the event 'is of such a character as to render the philosophical logos incapable of declaring it . . . For established languages, it is inadmissible because it is genuinely unnamable' (Badiou 2003b: 46). The language that Paul is driven to invent, we may read with some surprise, is one 'wherein folly, scandal, and weakness supplant knowing reason, order and power, and wherein non-being is the only legitimizable affirmation of being' (Badiou 2003b: 47). Given all this negativity, it is not surprising that what Badiou calls 'the Christ-event' can be interpreted as the beginning of negative theology, for

> [o]ne must, in Paul's logic, go as far as to say that *the Christ-event testifies that God is not the god of Being, is not Being.* Paul prescribes an anticipatory critique of what Heidegger calls onto-theology, wherein God is thought as supreme being, and hence as the measure for what being as such is capable of. (Badiou 2003b: 47)

Badiou's reading of Saint Paul has provided the core of Žižek's remarkable attempt to harness what he sees as the radical force of Christianity for revolutionary politics. Žižek is much more explicit than Badiou about the clean break that his politics would make with the Levinasian ethic of alterity, as it is expressed both in deconstructive messianism, and in weaker, blurrier form, in liberal tolerance for the other.

Žižek insists that his is a materialist reading of the radicality of Christianity, though it is hard to square this with the gloss he offers on Pauline grace through Lacan's conception of the access of the Holy Spirit as the rupturing effect of the symbolic order – 'the Holy Spirit stands for the symbolic order as that which cancels (or, rather, suspends) the entire domain of "life". . . When we locate ourselves within the Holy Spirit, we are transubstantiated, we enter another life beyond the biological one' (Žižek 2003: 10). For this reason, and once again like Badiou before him, Žižek stresses Paul's lack of interest in the life of Jesus, the miracles, the parables. Just as Lenin betrayed Marx into actuality, so Paul, the after-comer who was not part of Christ's apostolic inner circle, '"betrayed" Christ by not caring about his idiosyncrasies, by ruthlessly reducing him to the fundamentals, with no patience for his wisdom, miracles, and similar paraphernalia' (Žižek

2003: 10). In contrast to the quietism of Buddhism, and the alterity that contemporary postmodernists sentimentally admire in Judaism (mistakenly, in Žižek's view), Paul is, quite simply, Lenin, who makes the revolution actual (Žižek 2003: 9), and Christianity is to be identified with 'authentic revolutionary liberation'. This 'is much more directly identified with violence – it is violence as such (the violent gesture of discarding, of establishing a difference, of drawing a line of separation)' (Žižek 2003: 10). Christianity is important for revolutionary politics, not because of any ethical correspondence between Christian belief and revolutionary principles, but because of a purely formal correspondence in the nature of the violent act that inaugurates them: 'Christian love is a violent passion to introduce a Difference, a gap in the order of being, to privilege and elevate some object at the expense of others' (Žižek 2003: 33).

At first sight, the event is at completely the other end of the scale from the Derridean process. Derridean religiosity represents the extreme of a form of implicative thought. The force of its denial and denegation is directed against any form of entirety, exclusiveness or isolated self-sufficiency, in which nothing is ever quite itself or exactly other to itself. The Badiouan event resembles Derridean apophasis in that it is defined wholly through negation. But where Derridean aporia propagates and tends towards apophatic saturation, the Badiouan event is scarce, exotic, difficult to detect and harder to cleave to. The absolute exceptionality of the event denies all inclusiveness or implication. Events don't just happen to be hard for law, language, or reason to get hold of; they are definitionally so. The event is 'a-cosmic and illegal, refusing integration into any totality and signaling nothing' (Badiou 2003b: 42).

The religiosity of Badiou and Žižek expresses itself primarily in the desire for absolutes, as opposed to the 'absolute absence of the Absolute' that Beckett found in Joyce (Beckett 1983: 33). As opposed to a contingent mooning after absolutes that somebody of my disposition can fall into in milky moments – wouldn't it be nice if there were an absolute end to hunger, absolute freedom for everybody, absolute justice, but, hey, what can you do? – theirs is an absolute craving for the absolute, meaning that nothing but an absolute will do, and unless there is an absolute, there will in fact be absolutely nothing. They share the conviction that only absolute change could be real change, and, without absolute change, everything must inevitably remain absolutely the same. This suggests an important distinction from Derrida's religion, which indulges and encourages a kind of voluntarist totalism, which employs the principles of suspension and deferral to ensure that everything is in part invoked by everything else. Derrida's is a mysticism of the All. By contrast, religion provides for Badiou and Žižek the fantasy of the absolute break, the absolute subtraction from, and transcendence of the order of the given, for what is given can only be the law, the State, Capital, and so on.

What the two religiosities have in common is the refusal of worldedness, which is to say, of finitude (contingency, multiplicity, fragmentation, mortality). In the case of Derrida, thought magically totalises the world, conjuring *pleroma* out of deferral. In the case of Badiou and Žižek, the refusal of the world is a refusal of connection or contamination, something like the 'attack on linking' theorised by Beckett's analyst W. R. Bion, and perhaps suggested in part by his experiences with Beckett (Bion 1993). The finitude of 'the world' now increasingly presents itself in the form of the hyper-connectedness that ensures that nothing can be absolute, autonomous, sole or whole, because there is nothing that does not have everything to do with everything else. This is what the austere principle of the event is designed to disclose and refuse. Seen through the scorching eyes of the political mystic, the world appears merely as base remainder, a Beckettian landscape of cinder and clinker.

We should, I think, acknowledge that Beckett allows himself the profound infinitism that characterises our present explosive moment of religion, that rapturous embrace of the impossible, the absolute, the unencompassable. There is a war in Beckett's works, between his impulse to finitude, his intense desire to find a way of being in the world, and the ways out into the absolute that he allows himself – the relaxing of the vigilance that would prevent one naming the unnamable.

Exposure

There is a kind of arrogance involved in taking Beckett's way of the negative as a religious way. Even granted that Beckett's art may be regarded as a *via negativa*, and granted the striking parallels between his systematic project of undoing and that of mystical writers, there is no reason to assume that the end of the particular low road taken by Beckett is God, or 'the divine'. The illogic here goes: Beckett proceeds via negations; negative theology attempts to approach God via negations; therefore Beckett must be attempting to approach God. Actually, Derrida has given typically luxurious warrant to this view of what he calls 'the becoming-theological of all discourse' in his 'How To Avoid Speaking':

> From the moment a proposition takes a negative form, the negativity that manifests itself need only be pushed to the limit and it at least resembles an

apophatic theology. Every time I say: *X* is neither this nor that, neither the contrary of this nor of that, neither the simple neutralization of this nor of that with which it has *nothing in common*, being absolutely heterogeneous to or incommensurable with them, I would start to speak of God, under this name or another. God's name would then by the hyperbolic effect of that negativity or all negativity that is consistent in its discourse. God's name would suit everything that may not be broached, approached, or designated, except in an indirect and negative manner. Every negative sentence would already be haunted by God or by the name of God, the distinction between God and God's name opening up the very space of this enigma. If there is a work of negativity in discourse and predication, it will produce divinity. (Derrida 1989: 6)

One can see how Hent van Vries can claim that '[t]his is one way to affirm the continuing – and perhaps, ever more prominent and promising – conceptual, imaginative, argumentative and rhetorical resources of the religious and theological tradition, of its archive and its acts, its judgments and imaginings' (Vries 2005: 615–16). A set-up in which every under-mining is its own undermining, every refutation is the secret proof of what it seeks to do away with, is indeed Philip Larkin's 'quite unlosable game' (Larkin 1988: 167). Where Beckett does everything he can to maintain his incapacity to write *about*, here that incapacity to write about but only amid, is itself the occasion, the aboutness, the import, outcome or upshot of his work.

At his best, Beckett inhabits belief in the mode of exposure. Belief is always liable to the condition of being 'posited', set out in a form that would prompt credence or incredulousness. Beckett's work often deals in notions, propositions, data, in the strict sense of that which is given. 'That then is the proposition. To one on his back in the dark, a voice tells of a past' (Beckett 1989: 5). Getting, or keeping things going, is a matter of 'notions' being maintained. This gives the impression of a work developed, not out of belief, but out of self-conscious hypothesis and experiment. But in fact, these works rely upon an imperfectly possible faith in that which is merely given as possible. Beckett works in hypothesis, which literally means what stands beneath, or understanding. Of course, because there is no reason to believe, because this is a belief beyond or without reason, so equally there is no reason to prefer any one form of belief over another. Perhaps this is what we are likely to find in Beckett: that there is the impulse or the gesture of unreasoning belief, without a particular or determined content. Belief has a way in Beckett of suddenly being precipitated out of the act of narrating alone. 'Yes, it was an orange Pomeranian, the less I think of it the more certain I am' (Beckett 1973: 12).

This exposure to the nature and consequences of belief is part of the condition of finitude that Beckett can never wholly set aside or let alone, the condition precisely of never being able to account for oneself, because one may always at any moment be betrayed into such accounting. It is, however, also true that Beckett's exposure can become a self-protective routine, a shield against exposure, just as masochistic self-shaming can be brandished or deployed as a defence against the hypervisibility of shame.

And it is just this kind of apophatic routine that makes Beckett's work come to resemble and probably provide some considerable comfort to the negative theology of some forms of modern critical theory. Beckett's work sometimes comes close to the arrogant or anxious intransigence that, far from being a mode of the 'nohow on', is a self-propagation because it has taken itself so far beyond predicable belief as to constitute a kind of authoritarian inviolability, an immunity of the ineffable. The lexicon of the illimitable that expresses itself in so many positive forms of excess in critical theory has passed across into a religious discourse that secures all the traditional forms of prestige of metaphysics in the mode of a negative, or, rather, of a deferred or conditional negative, a negative that will never allow itself to resolve into positive negativity.

This pride in being laid low is a familiar predicament in the history of religion, which has seen so many efforts at disestablishment, whether among Montanists, Diggers, Levellers, Shakers, Quakers, so liable to found schools of belief and find followings. It is in this sense that the 'dirty low-down Low Church Protestant high-brow' (Beckett 1970b: 184) has helped form a kind of low church, a church sustaining itself in abasement raised to the condition of indemnified self-assurance.

Beckett's work finds its unfolding between imposed and exposed belief. By imposed belief, I mean belief that comes unbelievably from the outside, and is therefore relatively easy to dispose of. *Texts for Nothing* perhaps gives us the handy-dandy of belief and unbelief in its most concentrated form. Much of the text is taken up with the work of unbelieving, the effort to effect unconsent in the face of implausible beliefs – 'It's they murmur my name, speak to me of me, speak of a me, let them go and speak of it to others, who will not believe them either, or who will believe them too' (Beckett 1984, 87) – or with the denunciation of the impulse to believe attributed to his keepers or internal locutors – 'Vile words to make me believe I'm here, and that I had a head, and a voice, a head believing this, then that' (Beckett 1984: 107) But the *Texts for Nothing* are also corrugated by the will-to-credulity: 'I had it told to me evening after evening, the same old story I knew by heart and couldn't believe' (Beckett 1984: 74). Rather than being simply imposed upon him, the voice in *Texts for Nothing* is in a continuing condition of exposure to his belief, and need for belief. 'From an Abandoned Work' provides two striking examples of the intemperate power of belief to erupt into the work, discovered, with a kind of delight, after the fact:

> Ah my father and mother, to think they are probably in paradise, they were so good. Let me go to hell, that's all I ask, and go on cursing them there, and them look down and hear me, that might take some of the shine off their bliss. Yes, I believe all their blather about the life to come, it cheers me up, and unhappiness like mine, there's no annihilating that. (Beckett 1984: 133)

An even more plausible moment of involuntarily recovered belief, which cannot quite be dismissed as credulity, occurs a few lines later. 'A ton of worms in an acre, that is a wonderful thought, a ton of worms, I believe it. Where did I get it, from a dream, or a book read in a nook when a boy, or word overheard as I went along, or in me all along and kept under until it could bring me joy' (Beckett 1984: 134). Indeed, the very determination not to believe, the will-to-incredulity often finds itself ring-a-rosying with the items of belief: 'Organs, a without, it's easy to imagine, a god, it's unavoidable, you imagine them, it's easy, the worst is dulled, you doze away, an instant. Yes, God, fomenter of calm, I never believed, not a second' (Beckett 1973: 307).

Perhaps the most sober and most slowly dissipated eruption of belief is the pseudo-religious discussion of the belief in 'a way out' among the denizens of the cylinder in *The Lost Ones*. The first thing we learn about the belief is that it fluctuates, but with a sort of permanently recurring rhythm: 'From time immemorial rumour has it or better still the notion is abroad that there exists a way out. Those who no longer believe so are not immune from believing so again in accordance with the notion requiring as long as it holds that here all should die but in so gradual and to put it plainly so fluctuant a manner as to escape the notice even of a visitor' (Beckett 1984: 162–3). The belief also gives rise to sectarian rivalry, rendered with mock-scholarly solemnity as though they were the terms of a medieval disquisition:

> Regarding the nature of this way out and of its location two opinions divide without opposing all those still loyal to that old belief. One school swears by a secret passage branching from one of the tunnels and leading in the words of the poet to nature's sanctuaries. The other dreams of a trapdoor hidden in the hub of the ceiling giving access to a flue at the end of which the sun and other stars would still be shining. (Beckett 1984: 163)

Once again, this division is as it were multiplied through fluctuation, as members of the two parties of belief repeatedly change affiliation: 'Conversion is frequent either way and such a one who at a given moment would hear of nothing but the tunnel may well a moment later hear of nothing but the trapdoor and a moment later still give himself the lie again' (Beckett 1984: 163).

Gradually, however, a kind of logical trajectory seems to emerge from the arbitrary fluctuations: 'The fact remains none the less that of the two persuasions the former is declining in favour of the latter but in a manner so desultory and slow and of course with so little effect on the comportment of either sect that to perceive it one must be in the secret of the gods' (Beckett 1984: 162). The last phrase neatly encapsulates the credential fissure, for it either means having the omniscience of divine beings' or 'having the all-seeing point of view of those seated in the gods, i.e. the gallery. Nevertheless, and though we have earlier been assured that 'it is doubtful that such a one exists', the conviction grows that there is a logic, and even a providence, in this shift from belief in a way out via the tunnels to a way out through the roof.

> For those who believe in a way out possible of access as via a tunnel it would be and even without any thought of putting it to account may be tempted by its quest. Whereas the partisans of the trapdoor are spared this demon by the fact that the hub of the ceiling is out of reach. Thus by insensible degrees the way out transfers from the tunnel to the ceiling prior to never having been. (Beckett 1984: 163)

Belief here seems to be governed by self-interest; better a belief in something safely impossible, a belief on which it would not be possible to act, than a testable belief that, once tested, would in the end inevitably lead one to despair, even if that is what is going to happen anyway. The passage ends with a remarkable, tender salute to the helpless determination of the cylindrees to continue in 'possession of their belief (and the grammar allows the possession to go both ways round) right up to the putative end of their world: 'So much for a first aperçu of this credence so singular in itself and by reason of the loyalty it inspires in the hearts of so many possessed. Its fatuous little light will be assuredly the last to leave them always assuming they are darkward bound' (Beckett 1984: 163).

The Derridean and the Badiouan modes of the religious are lent credence by two distinct modes of writing in Beckett, the omnimpotence of the Derridean mode that sustains and succours itself through the indefinite holding at bay of belief, and the austere vigilance of Badiou, on the *qui vive* for some principle that would transcend the whole believing business. The Derridean mode of opulently maximised denegation comes to a head in *The Unnamable* and *Texts for Nothing*, whereas the Badiouan mode of vigilant parsimony is visible in later, sterner texts like *Worstward Ho* and *Stirrings Still*. Badiou is far from simply wrong, I think, to make out in Beckett's work a hankering for the event that would set at naught the twistings of 'no's knife in yes's wound' (Beckett 1984: 115), and nor is Andrew Gibson (2006) wrong in his efforts to reorientate our reading of Beckett in Badiou's cold, bleak light.

But, in the end, or at least for a good part of the way leading to it, Beckett is possessed by a need that exerts little traction on either Derrida or Badiou, namely the desire to have been of this world, sufficiently so, at least, to be able credibly to take leave of it. This fundamental worldliness entails a sad, glad giving over of the omnipotence of thought practised by all forms of theology, and especially the two opinions, of generalised apophasis and austere fidelity to the event, that divide without opposing those still loyal to that old belief.

CHAPTER 10

The Loutishness of Learning

Et In Academia Ego

For as long as I can remember, I have been irritated by the word 'academia', used to describe the professional sphere I inhabit. There is something so wilfully ridiculous and wish-fulfilling about the notion of academic life as constituting a kind of looking-glass land, or fantasy republic – a kind of Ruritania of the mind. Of course, this idea of the academy has a long history. Though its contemporary meaning is very distinct from its historical meanings, the aroma of that long history is an important component in its modern definition. The original academy was the plot of land in which Plato took up residence, and was so named because it was the property of one Academus. As a result, the word came to mean a place of learning, or more metaphorically, a philosophical school of thought, especially one marked by extreme scepticism. From the end of the seventeenth century, the word was applied to a particular kind of institution, whose role was not so much instruction as cultivation and preservation of national forms of culture. From the seventeenth century onwards, an 'English Academy' was frequently mooted, but the term referred mostly to an institution, based on the French model, that would reform and regularise the English language (Monroe 1910). Eventually, the English Academy function was performed, in a descriptive rather than a prescriptive manner, by the Oxford English Dictionary project. The Royal Irish Academy was described in 1835 as 'a society of men under whose sanction and auspices . . . antiquities might be investigated, and the fugitive productions of genius, in other departments of literature, cherished and preserved' (Anon 1835, 120).

Over the course of the nineteenth century, the idea of the academy took up residence more and more in the university, as universities, especially in the United States, expanded their reach and function. By 1904, it was possible for R. S. Woodward, in an address on the opening of the new academic year in Columbia University, to enumerate some of the distinctive features of the modern university. He emphasised that the university no longer fulfilled the conserving and cultivating function of the academy, in that it owed less allegiance to the arts and historical achievements of a particular nation:

> The modern American university has broken to a large extent with custom and tradition. It is an institution characterized by intellectual agitation, by adjustment and readjustment, by construction and reconstruction, the end of which is not yet in sight. This complex organization is the resultant of the more or less conflicting educational activities of our times. It is a resultant due in part to world-wide influences; it expresses a generalized academic ideal. (Woodward 1905, 42)

Woodward focussed on the range and complex internal differentiation of the modern university:

> Little surprise is manifested at the close juxtaposition of a professor of metallurgy and a professor of metaphysics, and it has actually been demonstrated that professors of poetry and professors of physics can dwell in peaceful activity under the same roof. Here too the ten or a dozen faculties and the various student bodies mingle and intermingle in a spirit of cooperation and mutual regard almost unknown outside and hitherto little known within, the academic world. (Woodward 1905, 42)

Woodward also identified an important new feature of the modern academic institution, namely, its distinctive mixture of closure and openness. The university is both powerfully integrated, and yet also more open to knowledge as such.

> [T]he domain of this atmosphere is not bounded by academic walls. It is not a limited medium within, but is actually a part of, the unlimited medium of the intellectual world; for the modern university has broken also with custom and tradition in allying itself closely with the external world of thought. (Woodward 1905, 42)

Woodward points here to the most distinctive and defining anomaly of the modern academy; that is, 'the academy' no longer refers to a particular institution, or a particular tradition or set of allegiances – Platonic philosophy, French language and culture, or Irish antiquities. It refers to an entire academic culture, concentrated in and typified by universities, yet also extending well beyond them. So 'the academy' no longer means a particular kind of withdrawal, signified by a particular place, but rather a particular kind of noplace, a floating republic. It is constitutionally suspended between the actuality of particular kinds of institution and the complex, if embattled dream of an ideal. It is for this reason that the academic is made up of much fantasy and projection.

During the twentieth century, the idea and the actuality of the academic have both amplified and pulled against each other. Universities have become a central part of the economies of leading and developing nations. Their teaching and, in science and engineering, their research functions have demanded huge amounts of investment and have themselves sometimes generated significant economic returns. As universities have become ever more integrated into their societies, so they have proclaimed, as it seems, ever more insistently, their need for autonomy, especially in the form of academic freedom. A search on the word 'academic' in any database of academic writing will find more articles with the phrase 'academic freedom' in their titles than any other pairing. The university is defined by this tension between intellectual autonomy and economic function. We are accustomed to see this as a recent development, but we find a writer in 1955 complaining that '[e]ducation has become big business, and business has become the touchstone for educational practices' (Kattsoff 1955, 313).

Of course, the academy has also made a business out of minding its own business – renewing and prolonging itself in its own self-reflections, and reflections, like this one, on its own self-reflectiveness. The heated debates within the humanities and social sciences about the political function or not of academic writing are often conducted as variations of this theme.

The rise of what is called the academy during the twentieth century has been the consolidation of what one might think to be a disabling contradiction, though it ought to have become clear long before now that there is nothing in the least disabling about it. This is the contradiction between the pure ideals of academic freedom, unconstrained critique and pure research, and the economic and political demands of those who plan, manage and finance, and also those who attack, exploit and wreck, academic institutions. Only radical heteronomy, the fact that universities are so bound into the complex requirements of education and economic planning, can underwrite the kind of autonomy that academics want to believe they should have.

More Essential Work

Modern art and literature have been deeply impacted by the parallel growth of the institutions of explication and transmission formed by the academy. The most important and influential mediator between literary culture and what would become known as academic culture was T. S. Eliot. Like many other writers in the twentieth century, Eliot made a conscious choice to be a writer instead of an academic – the most likely berth to begin with being a department of philosophy rather than literature. But the choice was not straightforward, nor was it in any sense conclusive for Eliot. He arrived in London in 1914 as the holder of a Sheldon Travelling Fellowship from Harvard, and went up to Merton College in the autumn of 1914. Following his marriage and move to London in 1915, Eliot turned to teaching, supplemented by such reviewing as he could get, to support himself and his new wife, Vivien. He taught for a term at High Wycombe Grammar School and then at Highgate School, where one of his pupils was John Betjeman. Eliot then applied to the Oxford University Extension Delegacy, who hired him to give a course of lectures (in Yorkshire) in 1916 on French literature. In 1916, he applied for work with the University of London Extension Board and was taken on to teach a course on English literature in Southall, which he did until early 1917. At the same time, he continued working on his dissertation on F. H. Bradley, which was submitted to Harvard in April 1916. He repeated the Southall course later in 1917. He also taught courses on Victorian literature and Elizabethan literature for the London County Council, at the County Secondary School in Sydenham, during 1917 and 1918. The audience for the latter dwindled from twenty-four to ten because of things like influenza and what Eliot described as 'death, removal and more essential work' (quoted in Schuchard 1974: 297 n2). He seems to have taken the lectures seriously, but was also somewhat dismissive of his students. He regretted the fact that his Ilkley audience was 'mostly ladies' (quoted in Schuchard 1974: 1664) and that, while it 'did not wish mere entertainment ... [it] was not prepared for study' (quoted in Schuchard 1974: 168). In 'The Function of Criticism', five years after he finished lecturing, he offered the following advice:

> I have had some experience of Extension lecturing, and I have found only two ways of leading any pupils to like anything with the right liking: to present them with a selection of the simpler kinds of facts about a work – its conditions, its setting, its genesis – or else to spring the work on them in such a way that they were not prepared to be prejudiced against it. (Eliot 1958: 32)

In March 1917, Eliot had also joined the Colonial and Foreign Department of Lloyds Bank in Cornhill. So for the next several years, he was leading, not just the double life of the poet and banker, but a triple life as poet, banker, and academic.

Eliot's reputation was secured simultaneously as a poet and a critic. Most decisive of all was his influence on the discipline of English studies as it was forming in Cambridge. This had begun even before the fame that came with the publication of *The Waste Land*. The young I. A. Richards read the volume *Ara Vos Prec*, a collection of Eliot's verse up to 1920, and went to meet Eliot at Lloyds Bank to try to persuade him to take up a position in the Cambridge teaching faculty (Ackroyd 1984, 99). When *The Waste Land* did appear, it was taken up not so much by the literary world as by undergraduates. In 1926, Eliot gave the Clark Lectures at Cambridge, on the Metaphysical poets, and was persuaded to apply for a fellowship at All Souls, though it seems that, in the end, the Fellows took fright when they read Eliot's most recent volume of poetry (Ackroyd 1984, 157).

Eliot's career provides a remarkable example of a writer who was at once artist and self-explicator. Eliot's critical views, on the necessity of difficulty in poetry, on the struggle between modern chaos and poetic order, on the relations between the primitive and the modern, and the impersonality of modern art, formed the methods and perspectives used to read his work. Richards' practical criticism, designed to elicit and display the 'intricately-wrought composure' (Richards 2001: 27) of poems that created structure out of tension, was almost tailor-made to fit Eliot's poetry, and Eliot remained the most representative example of modernist writing. Wyndham Lewis summed up the symbiosis between Eliot and Cambridge critical method acidly but acutely in suggesting that, if you were to ask Eliot for guidance about his work, he would be likely to reply 'I am sorry, I am entirely unable to answer you. I have not the least idea. It is not to *me* that you must address such questions. Go rather and address yourself to my partner, Mr I.A. Richards. He is not very reliable, but he probably knows more about it than I do' (quoted in Ackroyd 1984, 220). Altogether, one may readily agree with Ackroyd that Eliot provides an example of 'a poet setting the context and the principles for the description and critical evaluation of his own work' (Ackroyd 1984, 177). And yet Eliot seemed able to perform this dual function only by anticipating and enacting in himself the relation of noncoincident convergence that has characterised the relations between art and academic criticism. One part of Eliot, the authoritative lecturer, the judicious critic, and the institutionaliser of modernism as editor at Faber, was involved in developing the literature to the second degree that would become an indispensable bridge between artistic culture and society in the second half of the twentieth century. The other half seemed to exist in a state of permanent fugue, resisting any communication with or acknowledgement of his academic self. Hence the strange oscillation within Eliot's criticism between a classical respect for form, impersonality and the careful and knowing negotiation of complex tensions, and the frequent assertions of the unknowable and unanalysable roots of the poetic impulse. It was necessary that the poet both know and not know what he was doing, though neither knowing nor unknowing were quite satisfactory or sufficient. Eliot moved between the characteristic modern alternatives of explicitation and mystification.

Bright Boy of the Class

If we are to judge by the final sentences of *Anna Livia Plurabelle*, the figure cut by the young Samuel Beckett in the Joyce circle was that of a brilliant, if slightly bumptious scholar. The put-down of the uppity young Protestant swot that suddenly appears in Joyce's text – 'Latin me that, my trinity scholard, out of eure sanscreed into oure eryan!' (Joyce 1975: 215) – is given its sting by the fact that Beckett had been involved in translating part of this section of the *Wake* into French: Beckett in fact quoted the sentences that immediately precede this one in his 'Dante . . . Bruno . Vico .. Joyce', but broke the quotation off just before it (Beckett 1983: 29). The portmanteau idea of the 'scholard', or dullard scholar, captures well the dunciad quality of much of Beckett's learned wit at learning's expense. Indeed, the very history of the word 'dunce' – originally a term of respect for a follower of Duns Scotus – displays a nice Beckettian declension. The denunciation of the dunce has a poignant self-application in the case of Beckett that it does not have in other writers, and is necessarily delivered with more of a forked tongue.

I think that where, for Joyce, the apparatus of scholarship was the arbitrary and disposable institutional envelope of learning, for Beckett, the two remained anxiously entangled with each other. The Schoolroom scene in *Finnegans Wake* II.ii is the work of one who can richly exploit the infantile comedy of the schoolroom because it is so far from him, or all the elements of it are equidistant. It is easy to see the similarity of the marginal annotations of the textbook, forming a trinity of Shem and Shaun to left and right, with Issy's comments in the footnotes, to the joyous ramifications of reverie and obscenity that rioted quietly in the medieval scriptorium. We can contrast this with the inquisition of Louit in Becket's *Watt*, which is a magnificent example, sad and savage at once, of the kind of mauling of the academic order of things that only the apostate can effect. Perhaps, in a variant on the Wildean formula, this is the rage of Caliban at not seeing himself on the class list. Though battles of books abound in Joyce's work, the academic feudings and altercations are rendered with a kind of equanimity, and therefore a sort of even-handed amicability, that is not to be found in Beckett. For Beckett, there is always the sour ache of reproach, that he was not able to live up to his own academic self-ideal, and that the academic life was equally unable to live up to his ideal of it. Joyce, all this goes to say, is a gaily, gaudily postgraduate writer; Beckett is stuck in the remedial form, doggedly cramming for the retake.

It is far from an exact analogy, but one might perhaps say that scholarship has something of the same status for Beckett as Catholicism does for Joyce. Joyce remained 'supersaturated' by Catholicism, even after he seemed to have left its articles of faith and observance far behind. Beckett remained orientated and impregnated by an academic habitus long after he seemed to have broken with it (no doubt Joyce, in the crudely sectarian mood into which he could very occasionally descend, would say that there was nothing to break with in Protestantism). And yet, the academy exerted its pull even on Joyce. He spent a little time in 1920 teaching English at the University of Trieste. It is an extraordinary thought that, even at the moment of his apotheosis, following the publication of *Finnegans Wake*, Joyce was so strapped for cash that he was considering teaching. Beckett discovered for him that the University of Cape Town needed a lecturer in Italian – this might perhaps have been the same post that Beckett himself had applied for in 1937 (Beckett 2009: 523–8) – though Joyce decided against applying when he heard how violent the thunderstorms could be in South Africa (Gluck 1979: 39).

The struggles to be and say that absorb Beckett are regularly represented as struggles to learn and know. Through the length and breadth of Beckett's writing, the pretentiousness and vanity of scholarship are routinely mocked. In *Malone Dies*, Saposcat toils ineffectually to become the academic high-flyer his parents wish for. Called upon to think, *Waiting for Godot*'s Lucky produces a panic-stammering, Touretteish outpouring of vacuous philosophical jargon. In characterising the relation between *The Unnamable*'s Mahood and the 'college of tyrants' who struggle to impart to him the lessons of how to have been a human being, Beckett glosses his own condition as a writer, in which pedagogy is always at issue:

> [T]hey gave me to understand I was making progress. Well done, sonny, that will be all for today, run along now back to your dark and see you tomorrow. And there I am, with my white beard, sitting among the children, babbling, cringing from the rod. I'll die in the lower third, bowed down with years and impositions, four foot tall again, like when I had a future, bare-legged in my old black pinafore, wetting my drawers. Pupil Mahood, for the twenty-five thousandth time, what is a mammal? And I'll fall down dead, worn out by the rudiments. (Beckett 1973: 339)

The voice of *The Unnamable* speaks of the pensum that, as alternately dunce and 'bright boy of the class' (Beckett 1973: 380), he is required to learn

and discharge, as though he were simultaneously preparing for and partic-
ipating in an infernal, interminable viva voce examination. In *Watt*, the
peristaltic passage of Mr Knott's servants into, through and out of his service
is a little like a college's intake and output of successive cohorts of students.
The heads in *Play* resemble a row of schoolchildren blurting out their
answers as the eye of the teacher lights on them. *How It Is* seems to give
us a narrator caught in a pedagogic *ménage à trois*, struggling to inflict his
cruel instruction on Pim, as he himself strives to repeat his own lesson.
A letter written by Beckett to Barbara Bray in 1960, during the composition
of *Comment c'est*, notes the link between 'Pim mud & Portora playing fields'
(Cordingley 2012: 536). These scholastic associations may be given extra
bite by the fact that it was while in the early stages of floundering in the
imaginary mire of *Comment c'est* in February 1959 that Beckett received, and
accepted, the offer of a D.Litt from Trinity College. Beckett was capable of
enjoying the chime between the *comment c'est* of the novel he had in hand
and the fact that the degree was conferred at what he referred to as 'the
Commencements farce' (meaning the Summer Commencements cere-
mony) in July (Knowlson 1996, 465). Cordingley also persuasively suggests
that the masochistic dynamics of self-translation involve Beckett in an
'internalized pedagogical sadism' (Cordingley 2012: 512). The notion briefly
bubbles up late in Beckett's writing life, in the reference in *Ill Seen Ill Said* to
the observing eye which is 'on centennial leave from where tears freeze'
(Beckett 1989: 72), the term oddly recasting Dante's frozen hell as an academic
institution from which only occasional sabbaticals can be wrung. For
Beckett, the examined life is decidedly not worth living.

　　The conflicted desire for the academic life, crossed by the desire to leave
off desiring to desire it, seems for Beckett to have been bound up in part
with his relation to his (not very academic) father. The speaker in 'From an
Abandoned Work' assures us, 'Fortunately my father died when I was a boy,
otherwise I might have been a professor, he had set his heart on it. A very fair
scholar I was too, no thought but a great memory' (Beckett 1984: 131). It
seems to me to be possible that Beckett feared that the truth was the
opposite of this; Knowlson suggests that the greatest anxiety he had about
resigning his Trinity fellowship in 1931 was the disappointment it would
mean for his father (Knowlson 1996: 142), who died eighteen months later,
seemingly bringing to a pitch the intense physical and mental distress that
led Beckett to psychoanalysis. Part of Beckett may have thought that, far
from being saved from an academic career by the death of his father, his
spurning of the chance of such a career may have hastened his father's death,
or at least darkened his last year of life. Beckett seems to have read up on

psychology, perhaps self-defensively, before and during his psychotherapy with W. R. Bion, as though in preparation for some kind of formal disputation rather than a consultation.

Beckett's academic anxiety also precipitated two poems that address Beckett's sense of displacement in and from the academy, represented for him by Trinity College. The first, more well-known piece is 'Gnome', which Beckett may have sent in a letter of January 1932 (Beckett 2009: 107), but which was first published in 1934:

> Spend the years of learning squandering
> Courage for the years of wandering
> Through a world politely turning
> From the loutishness of learning.   (Beckett 2012: 55)

Loutishness is a striking term to use for the posturing emptiness of learning. Beckett may recall it in the name of his mendacious Ernest Louit in *Watt*, who, it is implied, has never undertaken at all the expedition to the west of Ireland for which he extracts funds from the college, but rather trained up Thomas Nackybal to play the part of the prodigious Gaelic mathematician he claims to have discovered. To be loutish is to be crude, unrefined and blundering, as well as merely unlearned. The term runs together the clumsiness of the bumpkin with the stupidity of the unschooled. Arthur Golding twins 'the lerned and the lout' in his 1567 translation of Ovid's *Metamorphoses* (Ovid 1567, sig. A3v). Beckett's use of the term reflects his strong sense of the betrayal of academic or intellectual distinction amid the trivialities of the academy, and of his association of class and spiritual distinction with academic distinction. What seems to have enraged him most of all was the vulgarity of the academic life – academics should simply not be as slovenly and self-serving as they are.

The term 'loutishness' aptly replays the duality contained in the poem's title. A gnome is defined by the OED as 'a short pithy statement of a general truth; a proverb, maxim, aphorism, or apophthegm'. But a gnome is also a squat, dwarflike inhabitant of the lower earth. The root *gno-* means to know, and yields words like gnostic, prognosis and diagnosis. But Beckett may also have in mind the strange fascination of the word 'gnomon' for the young boy in Joyce's story 'The Sisters'. A gnomon is defined in Euclid as the remainder of a parallelogram after the removal of a similar parallelogram containing one of its corners, and Bernard Benstock (1988) reads the gnomon as a figure for omission itself, seeing *Dubliners* as 'gnomonic' throughout. Beckett's 'Gnome' seems similarly orphaned from its predication, with the dull euphonies of its gerunds and the incongruously jogalong lilt of its feminine endings failing to parse that opening 'spend', which is as grammatically enigmatic as it is seemingly emphatic. Is it a sardonic imperative – 'Go ahead, you may as well spend those years squandering your courage'? Or is it the bitten-off end of a lament or protest – 'What misery, to spend the years of learning squandering courage'? The poem is both neatly folded on itself and missing its essential point or payoff, and so spools out frictionlessly in mid-air.

On 10 May 1934, Beckett sent what seems to be a companion quatrain to Nuala Costello:

> Up he went & in he passed
> & down he came with such endeavour
> As he shall rue until at last
> He rematriculate for ever. (Beckett 2009, 209)

Beckett implicitly linked the two poems with the remark 'I grow gnomic. It is the last phase' (Beckett 2009, 209). To matriculate is to enrol, or be incorporated into an institution, which Beckett here associated with a less than bounteous alma mater. Here, the word 'rematriculate' connects the academic process of going up, passing through and coming down to bodily processes, of birth, defecation and other kinds of academic and corporal expulsion, in a way that looks forward to the trilogy, and to the caca and poo that are spasmodically induced in Lucky's 'Acacacacademy of Anthropopopometry' (Beckett 1986, 41). To rematriculate here means, in the expression Malone ventures, to be 'given birth to . . . into death' (Beckett 1973: 285), to be taken back into the womb of unbeing. Beckett may have remembered this when he was himself rematriculated, or received back into the womb of Trinity, in 1959. Beckett's account to Con Leventhal of his horror at having to accept the degree is full of a characteristic ambivalence regarding the academic world:

> I shall accept the honour if it is offered to me. I don't underestimate it, nor pretend I am not greatly moved, but I have a holy horror of such things and it is not easy for me. If I were a scholar or a man of letters it might be different. But what in God's name have doctoracy and literature to do with work like mine? However there it is, right or wrong I'll go through with it if they ask me. (Knowlson 1996, 465)

I think Knowlson is right to suggest that Beckett saw this as a making of peace, or at least the striking of a truce, both with the college he had deserted – albeit, if Anthony Cronin is to be believed, taking with him a college master key (Cronin 1997, 165) – and the bright future that he had denied his parents (Knowlson 1996, 465). A further reassimilation was Beckett's donation of large amounts of unpublished materials to Trinity before and after his death.

Anathema

Academic fantasy hums with fear, rage and envy. It is above all anathema
and the associated affect of contempt that characterises Beckett's relation to
academic life. Beckett is caught up in this in his own denunciations of the
academic disposition, many of which occur in his own sporadic, conflicted
attempts at critical writing. Sometimes, as in the episode of Louit's inquisition in *Watt*, the denunciation is numbed by a kind of melancholy
absurdity. At other times, it is much more fiercely sardonic, as for example
at the beginning of 'Peintres de l'Empêchement':

> I have said everything I had to say about the painting of the Van Velde
> brothers in the last number of Cahiers d'Art (unless there has been another
> one since then). I have nothing to add to what I said there. It was little, it was
> too much, and I have nothing to add to it. Fortunately it is not a matter of
> saying what has not yet been said, but of saying again, as often as possible in
> the most reduced space, what has already been said. Otherwise one disturbs
> the connoisseurs. That to start with. And modern painting is already
> disturbing enough in itself without one wanting to render it still more
> disturbing by saying sometimes that it is perhaps this thing and sometimes
> that it is perhaps that. One would then give oneself unnecessary trouble. And
> one is already troubled enough, of necessity, and not only by modern
> painting, without wanting to give oneself any more trouble, by trying to
> say what has not been said, to one's knowledge. (Beckett 1983: 133, my
> translation)

The text rolls ingeniously and with apparent affability on, spinning out the
joke that to carry on saying nothing is better than risking saying something
new, while all the time allowing the pressure of contempt for habitual and
received opinions to accumulate beneath the patient reasonableness:

> For in affirming something and cleaving to it, through thick and thin, one
> may end up forming for oneself an opinion on practically everything, a good
> solid opinion, capable of lasting a lifetime ... [B]y affirming, with firmness,
> one fine day, of modern painting, and then again affirming on the next day
> and on the next and every day, that it is this thing and this thing only, then in
> the space of ten or twelve years, one will know what modern painting is,
> perhaps even well enough to enlighten one's friends, without having had to
> spend the best part of one's leisure time in those so-called galleries, narrow,
> cluttered and badly-lit, using one's eyes. This is to say that one will know
> everything there is to know according to the accepted formula, which is the
> summit of all science. To know what you mean, therein lies wisdom. And the
> best way of knowing what you mean, is to mean the same thing, patiently,
> every day, and thus to familiarise oneself with the customary formulae, amid
> all the shifting sands. (Beckett 1984, 133–4)

Siegfried Unseld, the director of Suhrkamp press, relates an episode that illustrates Beckett's impatience with the *Times Literary Supplement*–like impermeability of the academic. Unseld had arranged a reception in Beckett's honour in Frankfurt in 1961, at which Theodor Adorno was to speak. Beckett had had lunch with Adorno earlier, and had politely declined Adorno's suggestion that the name of Hamm in *Endgame* derived from Hamlet. Adorno persisted, provoking some anger in Beckett. When Adorno spoke at the reception that evening, he repeated the suggestion, prompting Beckett to whisper into the ear of his host 'This is the progress of science that professors can proceed with their errors!' (quoted in Knowlson 1996, 479). The danger, for the exacting young man that Beckett was, always lay, as he put it in the first sentence he ever published, 'in the neatness of identifications' (Beckett 1983: 19), in 'solution clapped on problem like a snuffer on a candle' (Beckett 1983: 92).

But the assault upon factitious and formulaic certainties is at odds with some of the tendencies of Beckett's own earliest forays into critical and scholarly writing, which are nothing if not opinionated. Beckett sneers, snipes and dismisses as arrogantly as any sedately ensconced Regius Chair. Beckett's minting of opinion in response to Ezra Pound's judgements, in a review of 1934, is characteristically arbitrary, mandarin, self-regarding and dogmatic:

> Strange that such *sen de trobar* as Mr Pound's should not vibrate to Rimbaud's ironical Hugoisms, also that it should succumb to Gourmont's *Litanies de la Rose* (transcribed in full). There is no mention of Apollinaire, whose *Chanson du Mal Aimé* seems to me worth the whole of the best of Merril, Moréas, Vielé-Griffin, Spire, Régnier, Jammes (all quoted, the last copiously) put together. (Beckett 1983: 78)

Another remarkable, but little-remarked feature of Beckett's critical style in his writing of the 1930s is its crustacean antiqueness (and in this it resembles other modernist writer-critics, such as Pound and Wyndham Lewis). His is a language of smirking self-exhibition, of highly wrought phrase-making, creased and corrugated by snarling self-disgust. It is a sort of poisoned belle-lettrism, a connoisseurship turned convulsively and self-mutilatingly on itself. It is entirely unlike the plainer, more professionalised, technicised critical diction that had begun to be developed among university critics like I. A. Richards and William Empson from the early 1920s onwards, a critical writing that attempted to take the measure of its literary object rather than wrangling or straining to effect sacramental mingling with it.

Beckett's critical writing during the 1930s, in the difficult period following his break from Trinity, bristles with the conflict between different manners of writing. On the one hand, there are the apparently painstaking abstractions and philosophical technicalities: 'The identification of immediate with past experience, the recurrence of past action or reaction in the present, amounts to a participation between the ideal and the real, imagination and direct apprehension, symbol and substance' (Beckett 1970c, 74). On the other hand, there are the throw-away jokes that suggest a kind of scornful disgust with the whole business of explication and discrimination. Beckett wrote in nervous self-defence to Thomas MacGreevy of his *Proust* that it seemed 'very grey & disgustingly juvenile – pompous almost – angry at the best . . . I feel dissociated from my Proust – as though it did not belong to me, ready of course to get any credit that's going but – genuinely, I think – more interested than irritated at the prospect of the nose-pickers' disgust' (Beckett 2009, 65). A month later, Beckett wrote a grateful letter in response to MacGreevy's praise of the book, but acknowledging that it was more about him than its apparent object: 'I feel it tied somehow on to Proust, on to his tail board, with odds & ends of words, like bundles of grass jack in the boxing under a kite. Not that I care. I don't want to be a professor (its almost a pleasure to contemplate the mess of this job)' (Beckett 2009, 72). There is much comedy to relish in Beckett's evocations of the academic, but this ridicule is closely allied to ire, even when it seems to be diffusing it. Beckett takes revenge on the academic disposition in sarcastic sniggers and quips, though he was also bored and disgusted by his own frippery, and appalled by how much it had in it of the cynical academic self-satisfaction he loathed. Much turns on the word 'quip'. In May 1931, Beckett wrote to MacGreevy of his sense of the 'futility of the translation' of *Anna Livia Plurabelle*, adding, 'I can't believe he doesn't see through the translation himself, its horrible quip atmosphere & vulgarity' (Beckett 2009, 78). The word also occurs in a November 1930 letter in which Beckett complains of the combined influences of college and home:

> This life is terrible and I dont understand how it can be endured. Quip – that most foul malady – Scandal & KINDNESS. The eternally invariable for- mulae of cheap quip and semi-obscene entirely contemptible potin chez Ruddy & in the Common Room Club, and Kindness here at home, pumped into me at high pressure. I am getting my rooms (Fry's) ready at the top of 39. Perhaps things will be better when I get in there. But the Ruddy vico seems to be a dead end. If I could merely listen to him talking philosophy or Motin & the Précieux, things would be easy. But all his old anti-isms are flourishing and I am tired of them: you know what they are – priests and soldiers & the Romantics – mainly. And then the enduring & unendurable QUIP, far worse than the Giraudoux astuce. I like Ruddy toujours and very

much as you know, but how am I to give him that impression when he quiptificates in the midst of his adorers. (Beckett 2009, 48–9)

Beckett's frustration seems to come together with the judgement that 'every day here *vulgarises* ones hostility and turns anger into irritation & petulance' (Beckett 2009, 49). The 'here' is technically Beckett's family home in Cooldrinagh, but seems to encompass Trinity too. Beckett had not forgotten his sense of the vulgarity of 'quiptification' fifteen years later when translating *L'Innommable*, in which he resolves, 'Yes, now I've forgotten who Worm is, where he is, what he's like, I'll begin to be he. Anything rather than these college quips' (Beckett 1973: 351).

Altogether, Beckett's critical writing conveys the sense of a peculiarly knotted kind of performance, a strangulated effort to sing in academic tune, on which much of the trilogy and especially *The Unnamable* might be seen as a bitter, teeth-gritting commentary. Academic writing seems to have provided Beckett with the model of a violent ventriloquism, the force-feeding and forced evacuation of words and opinions not his own, that runs through *The Unnamable*, *Texts for Nothing* and *How It Is*. But here Beckett seems to fuel his contempt for the loutishness of learning with the very habit of angry condemnation that disgusted him. It is not the least, and is among the most unlovely, of the loutish habits that Beckett clung to in his long retreat from the academic life.

Erudition

Nobody could ever accuse Beckett of wearing his learning lightly. Where Joyce was an unabashed pilferer and pillager of ideas and arguments, Beckett wrapped his allusions up in an air of patrician mystery. Where Joyce's writing honestly invokes and invites the ingenuity of the crossword-solver, at one point even invoking the name of Beckett in his encouragements to the perplexed reader – 'Bethicket me for a stump of a beech if I have the poultriest notion what the farest it all means' (Joyce 1975: 112), Beckett's erudition is intended to mock and lock out 'the great crossword public' (Beckett 1983: 92).

Ruby Cohn describes the Beckett who wrote 'Gnome' as 'this erstwhile academic who would spend years whittling down his erudition' (Cohn 2001: 66). Beckett's notebooks help us appreciate the surprising amount of effort he put into whittling it up. Matthew Feldman says that the notebooks Beckett compiled between 1932 and 1938 show him 'progressively pulling up the ladder of knowledge in order to destroy erudition from above' (Feldman 2006, 149). Well, I am not sure how many rungs Feldman still thinks there were in Beckett's *scala scientiae*, but his own investigations, leading the way for many others, seem to make it clear how much of the Indian rope trick was involved in the ascent to his windswept eyrie of unknowing. What is amazing is how the myth of Beckett's erudition continues to prosper in the face of the obvious fact of his embarrassing dependence upon cribs and bluffer's guides. Feldman observes, accurately, and helpfully, that the study of the notebooks shows that Beckett studied very few philosophers in the original (and probably studied even fewer psychologists in this way). Instead, 'he sought to understand the tradition of philosophy *qua* systematic thought' (Feldman 2006: 149). By this, Feldman clearly means that Beckett spent a long time copying out passages from general guides like John Burnet's *Greek Philosophy*, Archibald Alexander's *A Short History of Philosophy* and Wilhelm Windelband's *A History of Philosophy*, none of them very up to date or even at the time particularly highly regarded. Feldman concludes that '[t]he relevance of synoptic texts to Beckett's art clearly and significantly points away from an immersion in particular ideas, thinkers or modes of thought, to more general interests in the development of various European intellectual trends' (Feldman 2006, 149). It would be a justification at once lofty and nifty for an undergraduate, who had been detected basing his opinions and assertions on pilferings from survey rather than primary set texts, to claim that he was more interested in philosophy '*qua* systematic thought' rather than actual philosophers.

The word 'erudite' has undergone an interesting shift since it entered English in the fifteenth century. Coming from Latin 'eruditus', meaning taken out of a rude or uninstructed condition, it originally meant educated or well instructed; erudition usually meant the process of instruction, as applied to others – so 'the erudition of the young' would mean simply the instruction or education of the young. During the seventeenth century, the word started to be used to mean the condition of acquired learning rather than the process of imparting it, and slowly began to take on the slight connotations of pomposity, mystification and self-regard that it can have today. The OED suggests that the adjective 'erudite' is 'now somewhat rare exc. in sarcastic use'. This seems to me to overstate it a bit, but 'erudite' has certainly drifted closer to words like 'recondite' and 'esoteric'. Certainly, Beckett's erudition has more than a little of this exhibitionist occultism. I would say that, despite his efforts at times to force himself to acquire systematic knowledge, Beckett was a collector of orts, anomalies and out-crops, which, brandished as they were in his early writing, served admirably to hint at a hinterland of systematic and integrated scholarship. while also suggesting by the very casualness of the way in which they were tossed out that nothing as comically plodding as conscious and systematic study, of 'erudition' in the honest old sense, had gone into their acquisition. At times, it is almost as though Beckett were deliberately preventing himself from seeing the larger picture, lest he come to resemble the kind of 'gentle skimmer' he wanted so to despise. So he became a snapper-up of unconsidered trifles instead. 'I bought the Origin of Species yesterday for 6d and never read such badly written catlap', he wrote to MacGreevy in 1932. 'I only remember one thing: *blue-eyed cats are always deaf* (correlation of variations)' (Beckett 2009, 111).

Of course, Beckett may have spent a considerable amount of time reading and thinking about the material he read, but not nearly as much as an average undergraduate might be expected to, and none of it could come near to constituting erudition. But then, let us be fair, this is not Beckett's own aim or claim, or at least ceases to be after the 1930s. Beckett has not in the least cheated us, or even himself. However, the evidence of the note-books risks cheating academic writers on Beckett of their imago of the learned author, one who, in denouncing learning, is their fantasy twin, in that he has not merely turned from philosophy, but has turned philosoph-ically from it: that 'Beckett was a scholar who (despite his protestations of ignorance and bafflement) continued to wear his learning in almost every-thing he wrote' (Abbott 1996, 173), or that 'Beckett's meticulously culti-vated protestations of ignorance were deeply learned' (Feldman 2006, 20). The academic fantasy, of Beckett's secret cleaving to the academic in his secession from it, tugs in several directions.

Academic Fantasy

For Beckett, the academic life remained saturated by fantasy – saturated by the fantasies of those in it, but also by his own projected fantasies of it. Not only that, Beckett's work, and its critical afterlife, embody and relay a certain professional discomposure that the academy and the academic entertains with regard to itself. I would like the phrase 'academic fantasy' to harbour a number of different identifications and desires, and so, just in case it doesn't, let me say now what they are.

There is, first of all, the fantasy of being an academic, the fantasy, doubtless naïve, but still potent and far from contemptible, of having the kind of knowledge and wisdom and integrity that professors are supposed to have. I saw a bumper sticker once in America that read 'I want to be the kind of person my dog thinks I am'. Perhaps people spend so long toiling to be academics and then, once they are, striving for ever greater glory and success, on the long ladder from freshman to emeritus, in order to give substance to their pretence to themselves that they are the kind of person that they think other people think a professor is.

Or that they wish other people thought a professor was, for there is also the no less tenacious fantasy of what academics are popularly supposed in fact to be like: vain, envious, petulant, self-important, resentful, bullying, backbiting, devious, credulous, cupiditous, cowardly, egotistical, obstinate, obsessional, myopic, pettifogging, parochial and, in the sub-genre of academic detective fiction, homicidally sociopathic. Though academics groan about these clichés, they have their share in shoring them up, not least when they turn themselves to the writing of academic fiction.

But, added to these, there is the unsleepingly energetic dream-work of the academic himself or herself, internalising all of this and turning it to psycho-professional account in the mode of self-incrimination. Few have fingered this aggrandising self-belittlement better than Stanley Fish in his hilarious essay 'The Unbearable Ugliness of Volvos'. Fish writes here, as elsewhere in his work, about the methodical bad faith of a profession that dare not admit to the manifold privileges and gratifications it enjoys, for example, the growth during the 1970s and 1980s of the lecture and conference circuit, with its

> new sources of extra income, increased opportunities for domestic and foreign travel, easy access to national and international centers of research, an ever-growing list of stages on which to showcase one's talents, and a geometrical increase in the availability of the commodities for which academics yearn: attention, applause, fame, and, ultimately, adulation of a kind usually reserved for the icons of popular culture. (Fish 1994, 274)

Fish provides a series of aphorisms that summarise the ways in which academics masochistically manipulate their self-loathing into self-gratifying forms. The first two of these are: *'Academics like to feel morally culpable, especially in relation to those who would give anything to be in their place'* and *'Academics like to feel morally superior, which they manage by feeling morally culpable'* (Fish 1994, 277). Fish describes the way in which 'enfranchised academics, largely male, gazed with envy and strangely mediated desire at the disenfranchised, first at Jews, then at women, then at blacks, and then at Native Americans, and now at gays and Arabs' (Fish 1994, 277). He also points to the ways in which academics borrow from the real hostility towards academic life in popular culture (but is it quite as real as academics would like it to be?), since his aphorisms require 'a two-way commerce, victim and victimizer, trashers and trashees, each not only needing but desiring the other' (Fish 1994, 278). Thus, '[a]cademic-bashing has become the national spectator sport, and, predictably, some academics are among the best players' (Fish 1994, 278). Actually, this is not at all a new phenomenon. In an essay of 1955, Louis A. Katsoff remarked that '[t]he most amazing fact about contemporary liberal-arts programs in higher education is the amount and kind of self-examination going on. It is as if those who teach in liberal-arts programs had developed deep-rooted guilt feelings which they seek to alleviate by loud cries of "I have sinned" ' (Katsoff 1955, 311).

I called this methodical a moment ago, but I might perhaps as well have said methodist, since there is in it much of what used to be called the scrupulousness that characterised the clergymen with which Britain was so over-liberally supplied for several centuries, and who occupied more or less the same social niche as academics do now (indeed the requirement at Oxford and Cambridge for dons to be in holy orders made the coincidence actual rather than merely metaphorical). Scrupulousness means the excessive examination of one's conscience for real or imagined sins, mostly of omission, and its public form is self-righteous denunciation of others through one's own self-excoriating humility.

Indeed, the vast outpouring of sermons during the eighteenth century has parallels in the increasingly readerless publications that the academic profession nowadays uses for professional currency. If only the eighteenth century had had the internet, then every volume of sermons slaved over by a Suffolk curate, that, like Louit's dissertation 'The Mathematical Intuitions of the Visicelts', 'could not be of the slightest value to any person other than himself, and, eventually, humanity' (Beckett 1972: 171), could have been 'disseminated', as the research councils like to say, online, without the need for such prodigious sacrifice of Britain's fine woodlands.

There is a particularly fraught relationship between writers and academic critics of writing because they communicate and excommunicate in the same medium. I remember being struck as a teenager by a phrase used by George Steiner, a writer whom I read with dutiful avidity at the time:

> When he looks back, the critic sees a eunuch's shadow. Who would be a critic if he could be a writer? Who would hammer out the subtlest insight into Dostoevsky if he could weld an inch of the Karamazovs, or argue the poise of Lawrence if he could shape the free gust of life in *The Rainbow*? (Steiner 1967, 21)

Never at the time having read either of these writers (and never having succeeded, before or since, in feeling on, or even between my cheeks, that authentically Lawrentian afflatus), I nevertheless embraced my sweet-sour fate, joining in the fantasy of the literary academic that I was really just biding my time before emerging as the fully fledged 'creative' writer, possessed of a full set of generative organs, that I had secretly been incubating all along. After years of adherence, I at glad last gave up the idea that to be an academic critic is perforce to be a parasite, a hanger-on, a heel-tapper, a rag-picker, as though it were obvious that anyone who had any jizz in him would in the end start to write something real, which is to say, made-up, poetry, drama or, for preference (but why?) fiction. Having, late in the day, but still with some time left to profit from it, given up the grim destiny of being a Writer, it became possible for me to see what kind of writing I might be able to do. But I still remember what it was like to hug the delicious, desolating dream of my own impotence as a writer, and how gratifying it was to find in Beckett a writer whom I could assist and who could assist me in levitating impotence into a kind of omnipotence.

Beckett, his work and his commentators are skewered and traversed by these projections and hostilities. Beckett became an academic author in a way that Joyce expected to, but never quite did in his own lifetime. In fact, one might reflect on the formative humiliation it may have been for Beckett to make his debut as a published writer with an essay that was part of the PR exercise that was the *Exagmination Round His Factification for Incamination of Work in Progress* engineered by Joyce to establish academic credentials for his work. At the time the book was being prepared, under his direction, Joyce wrote to Valéry Larbaud, 'Depart from me ye bleaters, into everlasting sleep, which was prepared for Academicians and their agues!' (Ellmann 1982: 613). In 'Dante . . . Bruno . Vico .. Joyce', we can hear the gnashing of teeth as Beckett carries out his assignment to the letter, while doing every-thing he can to register his irritation at the job of explication that has been allotted to him and to leave his surly stain on it.

Joyce has certainly kept the professors busy in just the way he meant to, but he did not live into the era in which they would come knocking at his door begging audiences and testimonials as they did at Beckett's. Many of the remarks from which a Beckettian poetic might be constructed were produced as responses to the demand for authoritative guidance and expli-cation. Beckett seems to display a marked duality with regard to academics. On the one hand, there is his well-known hostility towards explication, or, as the Director in *Catastrophe* puts it, 'explicitation' (Beckett 1986, 459), a charge that seems to include in it the desire to protect the authentic art work from the cheapening and vulgarisation that would render it merely intelli-gible, and make it unnecessary really to encounter it. On the other hand, there is the fact of Beckett's impressive patience with and respect for the actual academics and scholars with whom he came into contact. This ambivalence may be a special instance of the split between Beckett's capacity for cruel and sneering rage and his horror at the thought of giving offence, a split which meant that he had sometimes to write letters of apology for his boorish or insensitive conduct. It may very well be that, for somebody of Beckett's temperament, the courtesy may be a modulation of the antagonism, a calmative screen that enables the contempt to be kept at full pressure.

Prior to his imperfectly executed policy of noncompliance with criticism, Beckett formed a kind of credo designed to keep his work clear of the avaricious clutches of the academy. This is the argument that, because art is of the order of the irrational, it has nothing to do with 'doctoracy' and the vulgar agonies of the dissertation. This creed seems first to emerge in *Proust*, and then to be articulated in splinters through the 1930s reviews, finally being informally formalised in the *Three Dialogues*. The claim for the irrationality of art is designed most of all to establish a kind of sovereignty by subtraction. Art is what is left after the work of explicitation and making clear has surrendered or receded. Not only is art ineffably untranslatable into any terms but its own, this undefinability is the only definition left of it. Poetry, Beckett writes in his review of Denis Devlin's *Intercessions* (almost as though he were denying the title of the collection) must be 'free to be derided (or not) on its own terms and not in those of the politicians, antiquaries (*Geleerte*) and zealots' (Beckett 1983: 91). What matters most about art is its inexplicabilty, its incomparability, its nonexchangeability with anything but itself. Hence Beckett's remark, after a quotation from Devlin, 'If I knew of any recent writing to compare with this I should not do so' (Beckett 1983: 93). For the Beckett of the 1930s, art is the name for radical immediacy – that which cannot be approximated, expropriated or unseated from itself, precisely because it has no self-subsistence. That, while ceasing to formulate this view publically, Beckett continued to hold stubbornly to it, is suggested by the translation he made in 1971 of the 'Hommage à Jack B. Yeats' which he had originally written for an exhibition of the painter's work in Paris in 1954. Where the French responds to the suggestion 'Border alors?' with the assertion that 'Sur ces images éperdument immédiates il n'y a ni place, ni temps, pour les exploits rassurants' (Beckett 1983: 148) [possible translation: 'Decoration then? There is neither place nor time in such sublime images for exercises of reassurance'], the English pins the question much more tightly to the question of explication: 'Gloss? In images of such breathless immediacy as these there is no occasion, no time given, no room left, for the lenitive of commentary' (Beckett 1983: 149). Beckett frequently has recourse to metaphors of alimentation or bodily incorporation to gloss the work of glossing, described in 'Dante . . . Bruno . Vico .. Joyce' as '[t]he rapid skimming and absorption of the scant cream of sense . . . made possible by what I may call a continuous process of copious intellectual salivation' (Beckett 1983: 26). Beckett was opposed to anything that eased the passage of art, whether inwards or outwards: 'May it stick in their anus', he wrote to George Reavey of the 'bolus' of *Echo's Bones* (Beckett 2009, 295). Hence his deliberately dyspeptic criticism, a criticism contrived to catch in its own craw.

Beckett's reluctance to cooperate with academics, or to cooperate too much with too many of them, can reasonably be defended as a reluctance to give a stamp of approval to interpretations that critics should be willing to assume responsibility for themselves – 'If people want to have headaches among the overtones, let them. And provide their own aspirin' (Harmon 1998, 24). Beckett wishes not to be forced to participate in the mediation of his own work, to become his own intercessor. But he felt the repeated necessity of interceding on behalf of the work precisely in order to protest and protect its incommensurability. Beckett is necessarily his own mediator, acting on behalf of his work's immediacy, often, as Bruno Clément has observed, within the work itself, in which 'there is . . . a voice resembling, to the point of their being mistaken for one another, the critical voice . . . Few, very few readers succeed in refusing a full and complete legitimacy to this metatextual voice of Beckett's texts, which denies them any pretension to stating the truth about the work in question' (Clément 2006, 199, 120).

Beckett must reluctantly have come to recognise that he was, if not an academic writer, then certainly an academics' writer, a writer whose work it would be implausible, even perhaps unthinkable, to subtract from the contexts of critical and scholarly explication that framed it. This is not just because of the loutishness of academic appropriation, but also because Beckett himself, inveterately vexed by academic longings and the vehicle of the vicarious longings of academics, found himself not altogether despite himself facilitating the work of academic self-inculpation. Beckett's suspicion of the exercise of academic explication ideally nourished the hermeneutics of suspicion on which academic criticism came to prosper from the 1970s onwards, impelled to some considerable degree by Beckett's own critical example. Beckett's mode of repelling all boarders came to provide an ideal point of identification for an academic self-ideal. Beckett's desertion of the academy validates the institutional phobia of institutions cultivated by academics. How true, the academic critic says, when confronted by Beckett's hostility to academicism; this is how loutish academics can be, as we, uniquely equipped as we are to reflect rigorously and unflinchingly on our own intellectual culpability, best know. Beckett and the academy are locked in a lascivious, Laocoon-like clinch, a cycle of dependence and resentment that constitutes a veritable anxiety of confluence.

There is a striking parallel between the great theme with which modernist writers and artists wrestled, namely the question of what kind of distinctiveness or autonomy art might be said to have in a world of commodities, consumption and corporate power, and the academy's self-reflections. What is more, the two are intertwined. Art and the academy are twins as well as antagonists. The autonomy and the sovereignty of the artist on the one hand and the academic on the other are maintained through a reciprocally defining distance; the artist is free of the encumbrances and accountabilities of the academic, and the academic is free of the unknowingness, that is, of the false freedom, of the artist.

The world of art and the world of learning are tangled together in a series of Laingian knots. Academia uses art and literature as an arena to consider its own struggles over autonomy. The artist-writer looks down on safely tenured academics, while envying their security and assured social status. At the same time, the artist-writer may despise the featherbedded unworldliness of the academic, regarding himself as having a much more authentic and immediate relationship with his or her reader. The artist-writer regards himself as the *Ding an sich*, the primary *materia aesthetica* on which academic criticism must feed, while resenting the tendency of criticism to develop more and more ways of operating in the absence of texts or authors.

Art and the academy furnish each other with the means to secure their respective forms of autonomy, that is, by each assuming or affirming its freedom from or exceeding of the other. But, for this same reason, each mistrusts and resents the other, as the proof of its own dependence, or less than absolute condition. The freedom of each is constrained by the fact that it is precisely a freedom from the other. Art requires the forms of mediation that the academy, among other agencies, supplies. The academy must sometimes reluctantly acknowledge its continuing need for forms of artistic object on which to operate.

Academic Politics

All this might be thought of as an argument regarding politics in a minor sense, bearing on the institutional politics of literature and the academy. Academic criticism has of course had a great deal to say about much larger, and apparently less introverted kinds of political investment and purchase than literary forms. I want to conclude by suggesting that in fact the particular form of familial rivalry that has developed between art and its accompanying academic institutions has also in fact formed and indeed limitingly deformed the understanding of the politics of literary art.

Although there are almost illimitable ways in which the political formations, implications and effects of literary and artistic works might be made out, in fact the political readings of literary works that have become normative in the last two or three decades fall into a very narrow and repetitious routine. The question to be asked is always some version of the following: how does this work consolidate or resist the operations of power? This question is itself precoded in terms of the power of the text either to affirm coherent and determinate meanings, or to disturb and perplex those meanings. The politics of texts are read, that is, in terms of a polarity between works that institutionalise meaning and works that in various ways elude, or prevent this kind of institutionalisation. How do these texts allow me to thematise their resistance to my powers of thematisation?

Two things might strike us about this way of thinking about politics. The first is how astonishingly romantic, not to say positively adolescent, it is to assume that the assertion and maintenance of fixity and limit are always on the side of political reaction, and the assertion of indeterminacy and radical change always to be seen as politically desirable. The rhetoric of academic politics continues to be locked into a Blakeian ethic of damning braces and blessing relaxes, and hopelessly mortgaged to the emancipatory fix. This view of things, leading to an unchallengeable lexicon of the illimitable, has grave difficulties in coping with both the forms of contemporary economic relations and the urgent demands of climate change. Generations of students and teachers continue to assure each other that the evil of capitalism consists in its constraining of the infinite potential for difference of human beings, unable to grasp or acknowledge that, if capitalism is to be identified with any single principle at all, it is that of mutability and indeterminacy. There seems no way to connect this politics of absolute indeterminacy to the forms of carefully deliberated limit that adapting to the depletion of natural resources and anthropogenic climate change will demand. There continues to be no way to conceive a left politics of limit.

The most recent example of this is the philosophy of the event, identified with Deleuze, Lyotard and, most frequently nowadays, Badiou. What matters more than anything else, Badiou insists, is that we should form a revolutionary subjectivity out of adherence to the event, defined as a kind of occurrence that resists all formalisation, resists all reduction to *doxa*, or positive knowledge.

The second is that it recapitulates in its form the *pas de deux* that is danced out by art and the academy, art insisting on its incapacity to be hemmed in by explication and academic readings instituting this very same value in their explications of the indeterminacy or exalted exceedings of art. The lexicon of the illimitable and the privilege of the event are the doxological refusal of doctrine, the institutionalised phobia of institutions. It is the image and the reflex of the non-coincident convergence, the rivalrous mimesis, acted out in the academic fantasy, between the academy and its fancied others, in which what is at stake is always the imaginary power of escaping the demands of power. If ethics may be defined as the deliberation of the good, and politics as the necessary coercion of the good, then this is a politics characterised by a refusal of coercion.

It can do no harm for me to recapitulate the three arguments I have been trying to get on their feet.

First, modern writers and artists on the one hand, and their academic explicators on the other, have had to develop a deep and defining relation of rivalrous mimicry with each other.

Second, the academic politics of this semi-amicable psychomachia involve a huge overemphasis on epistemology, or questions of knowing – in which ineffability, uninterpretability, cognitive indigestibility and irreducible otherness become sovereign principles, enabling both academic interpreter and artistic interpretee to affirm their autonomy from and through the other.

Third, the absorption in this specifically epistemological drama allows both academic and artist systematically to let academic politics (which is to say the politics of the sibling cultures of academic and artist) stand for actual politics – actual politics being dull, ugly, bungling and entirely indispensable, while academic politics are subtle, scrupulous, exacting, fascinating and exquisitely gratuitous.

Beckett and the World

Short of the World

The last words of *More Pricks Than Kicks*, Beckett's first volume of fiction to be published, conclude the diminuendo constituted by the gardener's reflections on the lifespan of roses with a dismissive shrug: 'So it goes in the world' (Beckett 1970b: 2004). The world, or its world, makes a fleeting, but piercing appearance in *Worstward Ho*, Beckett's last substantial piece of published prose, as the narrative is proposing to itself a series of accelerating abbreviations: 'From now one for the kneeling one. As from now two for the twain. . . . As from now three for the head' in order 'For to gain time. Time to lose. Gain time to lose. As the soul once. The world once' (Beckett 1989: 110). The allusion is dual – to John Dryden's *All For Love, or the World Well Lost* (1677) and to Mark 8.36: 'what shall it profit a man, if he shall gain the whole world, and lose his own soul?' (King James Version; see also Matthew 16.26). In his semi-summons of the phrase from Mark into his text, Beckett equalises its antithesis. Now it is not a matter of gaining or preserving one's soul ('that jakes' according to *Ill Seen Ill Said* [Beckett 1989: 96]) in preference to the world, but rather a garnering of both so that both may be 'well lost'. Where the 'so it goes' of *More Pricks Than Kicks* is sardonically offhand, 'the world once' has a gentler, more delicately decayed melancholy. It seems there was a world once, must have been perhaps, if it is now to be counted lost.

Human beings have spent millennia trying to live in the world, or trying to combat their willingness to eschew living in the world. Nearly every religion has tried to instil in its followers the precept that 'the world is too much with us', or we with the world. Quakers in particular developed the habit of referring to 'the world' as that which they have left behind or from which they set themselves apart: George Fox wrote *A Word to the People of the World* (1660) and Mary Anderdon wrote from Exeter prison a pamphlet entitled *A Word to the World* (1662), a title that was frequently used by Quakers, Baptists, and other religious sects. Beckett's work exhibits something of this constitutive maladjustment to the world, a maladjustment out of which a kind of world may itself be made.

If the world presents difficulties, then so does 'the world', the concept or idea of the world. One might easily say of the idea of the world what St Augustine said of time, namely that we understand it perfectly well as long as nobody asks us what it means (Augustine 1912: 2.239). Beckett's work is concerned not only with understanding the world, but also with understanding what might be called the world question: What makes a world? How can one live in the world? Where else could one live but in a world?

One of the few philosophers to have given sustained attention to the idea of world is Martin Heidegger. In chapter I.3 of *Being and Time* is a discussion of 'the worldhood of the world' that for Heidegger consists primarily in the assignedness of the world, which is always a world in-order-to or for-the-sake-of (*um etwas zu tun*), because '"for-the-sake-of" always pertains to the Being of *Dasein*, for which, in its Being, that very Being is essentially an *issue*' (Heidegger 1985: 116–17). Dasein is always a 'being-in-the-world' and never merely being as such, because it is the essential function or vocation of Dasein to make sense of the world, to disclose it as world.

When he returned to the question of worldhood in *The Fundamental Concepts of Metaphysics: World, Finitude, Solitude*, first given as a lecture course in 1929–30 at the University of Freiburg, Heidegger sought to make this argument clearer by establishing a distinction between those beings that merely consist of their world and those beings that are able to establish a relation to their world, and thereby bring it into being *as* a world. Heidegger distinguishes between the animal – his principal example is a lizard on a stone – who has an immediate or instinctive relation to the world, or rather to its world, and man who is open to the world 'as such'. He offers three theses that distinguish among stones, animals and men in terms of their relation to the world: '[1.] the stone (material object) is *worldless* [*weltlos*]; [2.] the animal is *poor in world* [*weltarm*]; [3.] man is *world-forming* [*weltbildend*]' (Heidegger 1995: 177). Animals, he writes, are absorbed, or captivated by their worlds, and thus unable to have a relation to them:

> We shall describe *the specific way in which the animal remains within itself* . . . the way in which the animal is absorbed in itself, and which makes possible behaviour of any and every kind, as *captivation*. The animal can only behave insofar as it is essentially captivated. . . . Captivation is the condition of possibility for the fact that, in accordance with its essence, the animal *behaves within an environment but never within a world*. (Heidegger 1995: 238–9)

The animal is not merely inert or insentient, like the stone: it has a kind of openness to what stimulates its action, but 'this possession of being-open is a not-having, and indeed a not-having of world – if the manifestness of beings as such does indeed belong to world' (Heidegger 1995: 270).

Heidegger derives much support for his thinking about the nature of the animal's world from the work of the Estonian biologist Jakob von Uexküll, who developed the notion that each animal exists not within the world as such, but rather in its own *Umwelt*, consisting only of the particular items of the world that have importance or significance for it. The most famous example is of *Ixodes ricinus*, or the European tick, which perches at the tip of a blade of grass waiting for a passing mammal to bump into it and dislodge it. Eyeless as it is, the world of the tick has only three components of significance: the odour of butyric acid that is contained in the sweat of all mammals; the skin characteristics of mammals (usually hairy and quite densely supplied with accessible blood vessels); and the temperature (typically 37°C) of the blood of mammals. The rest of the world's complexity leaves the tick utterly unimpressed, so much so in fact that, deprived of any of these prompts to action, a tick may remain in a state of suspended animation for many years. The European tick, as described so wonderfully by Uexküll (Uexküll and Kriszat 1992: 320–6), has travelled extremely widely in the hand luggage of European philosophers, appearing as it does in the work of Heidegger (1995), Deleuze and Guattari (1987), Serres (1982) and, most recently, Agamben (2004). Deleuze and Guattari find in the starveling ethology of the tick, bounded as it is by 'the optimal limit of the feast after which it dies, and the pessimal limit of the fast as it waits' an elementary kind of ethics (1987: 257), founded not so much on the nature of the organism in question – 'generic and specific characteristics, organs and functions, legs and snout', but on 'longitude and its relations, from latitude and its degrees. We know nothing about a body until we know what it can do, in other words, what its affects are, how they can or cannot enter into composition with other affects' (Deleuze and Guattari 1987: 256–7).

Heidegger helped himself to Uexküll's argument that the world of an animal consists of those things that captivate its action and attention. The term *Umwelt* usefully chimes with the two aspects which Heidegger had argued in chapter 3 of *Being and Time* constitute the 'worldhood of the world': first of all, the for-ness, or assignedness (the *um-zu*) of the world, and secondly, the fact that the ready-to-hand world is always constituted 'regionally', and 'the regional orientation of the multiplicity of places belonging to the ready-to-hand goes to make up the aroundness – the "round-about-us" [das Um-uns-herum] – of those entities which we encounter as closest environmentally' (Heidegger 1985: 136).

It is tempting to associate Heidegger's threefold distinction – man, animal and stone – with Malone's curriculum of the four, later three, stories he proposes to tell: 'I shall begin, that they may plague me no more, with the man and the woman. That will be the first story, there is not matter there for two. There will therefore be only three stories after all, that one, the one about the animal, then the one about the thing, a stone probably' (Beckett 1973: 182). It is very possible that Beckett knew enough of Heidegger's modes of locution to have a swipe at him, in having Molloy claim that the 'meaning of being' was beyond him (Beckett 1973: 39), especially as one of Beckett's friends at the Ecole Normale Supérieure was Jean Beaufret, whom Beckett later recalled as 'the Heidegger expert' (Knowlson 1996: 96). But, as Heidegger's lectures were not published until 1983, it is not safe to assume any direct allusion. However, there is another intriguing resonance between Heidegger and Beckett, in the idea of 'poverty in world'. In Beckett's *Three Dialogues With Georges Duthuit*, B. says, 'There is more than a difference of degree between being short, short of the world, short of self, and being without those esteemed commodities. The one is a predicament, the other not' (Beckett 1983: 143).

Little World

In his writing of the 1920s and 1930s, Beckett tries everything he can to assert a retreat from what Murphy calls the 'big world' into the 'little world', the fine and private place of the head. It would be easy to see this movement repeated through the ever-tighter constraints of the cylinder pieces, through to the oneiric spaces of *Nacht und Träume*, *Worstward Ho* and *Stirrings Still*. These acts of miniature mundation are anticipated towards the end of *The Unnamable*:

> make a place, a little world, it will be round, this time, it's not certain, low of ceiling, thick of wall, why low, why thick, I don't know, it isn't certain, it remains to be seen, all remains to be seen, a little world, try to find out what it's like, try and guess, put someone in it, seek someone in it, and what he's like, and how he manages, it won't be I, no matter, perhaps it will, perhaps it will be my world, possible coincidence (Beckett 1973: 409)

This strain in Beckett accords with an espousal of a more conventional aesthetic aim of making autonomous worlds within worlds, or worlds against the world – for example, where he praises Proust for the quality of his language, which, he says, 'makes no attempt to dissociate form from content. The one is the concretion of the other, the revelation of a world'

(Beckett 1970c: 88). The punchline of the 'Monde et le Pantalon' joke given to Nell in *Endgame* expresses neatly Beckett's preference for the well-wrought world of the work of art over the messiness of the actual world: ' "But my dear Sir, my dear Sir, look – [*disdainful gesture, disgustedly*] – at the world – [*pause*] – and look [*loving gesture, proudly*] – at my TROUSERS!" ' (Beckett 1986: 103). The defiant preference expressed in the *Three Dialogues* for being without the world over being short of world might also seem to accord with this opposition both to the big world and the big word 'world'.

But I would like to try to show in what follows that the condition of being *weltarm*, or short of world, is what constitutes the particular kind of worldliness of Beckett's work, which is a work, not so much of trying to escape from the world as of trying to find a way to have your being, or, better still, to have had your being, in it. My surmise is that Beckett alternates between the two kinds of world: the world as such, which is almost always notional and inaccessible, and the particular world within which the finitude or being-there of a particular being or state of being is constituted.

Beckett has a strong sense of what Heidegger might call 'worlding', the creation of worlds. But his characters and narrators live, not within 'the world' or worlds as such, but within *Umwelts* that they constitute from themselves, or that are constituted from themselves, not voluntarily, but unavoidably. As he wrote in *Proust:* 'Life is habit. Or rather life is a succession of habits, since the individual is a succession of individuals. . . . The creation of the world did not take place once and for all time, but takes place every day' (Beckett 1987: 18). In Beckett's narratives from the 1940s onwards, the world does not so much recede as become intermittent, fluctuating, spasmodic, liable both to seeming extinguishings and sudden insurgences. 'Just at the moment when the world is assembled at last, and it begins to dawn on me how I can leave it, all fades and disappears', we hear in *The Unnamable* (Beckett 1973: 336–7). Or in 'The Calmative': 'Little by little I got myself out and started walking with short steps among the trees, oh look, trees!' (Beckett 1984: 36). 'From an Abandoned Work' is particularly full of these intemperate flarings of world, in the vision of the narrator's mother, framed in her window, the vision of the white horse crossing his path, the pursuit by stoats.

The paradox of Beckett's writing is that, while he continues to try, or feint to try, to detach his characters from 'the world', or to limn various forms of 'little world' against the 'big world' of the *polis*, a copular form of being-there is always necessary for him. This 'there' is coeval with existence, in that it is what existence starts out from, in both the temporal and spatial sense. In *Worstward Ho*, the positing of 'a body', even one gratefully disencumbered with mind, instantly requires 'A place. Where none. For the body. To be in. Move in. Out of. Back into. No. No out. No back. Only in. Stay in. On in' (Beckett 1989: 101). The irreducible condition of existence in Beckett's writing is that one must always have what being one has 'in such a place, and in such a world', as he says of the characters in *Endgame* (Harmon 1998: 24).

It is in *The Unnamable* and even more tautly and paradoxically in *Texts for Nothing* that this production of the sense of world takes place. *Texts for Nothing* may be seen as a long, discontinuous meditation on the possible meanings of the words 'here' and 'there'. The here and the there are part of the fabric of a world that must always already be there; and yet this world also seems dubiously episodic. The *Texts for Nothing* are driven by the desire to find a way 'to have being and habitat' (Beckett 1984: 98), though the point of succeeding in being 'there' in the world is to be able to cease being there. But this assurance of place and time is not merely or continuously given, and the various speakers find themselves assailed by perplexities about the nature of their 'here' and 'now':

> I must be getting mixed, confusing here and there, now and then, just as I confused them then, the here of then, the then of here, with other spaces, other times, dimly discerned, but not more dimly than now, now that I'm here, if I'm here, and no longer there. (Beckett 1984: 102)

The speaker in *Text* V testifies, 'I don't know where I am' (Beckett 1984: 85). In *Text* VI, the speaker longs for location: 'I'd join them with a will if it could be here and now, how is it nothing is ever here and now? It's varied, my life is varied. I'll never get anywhere. I know, there is no one here, neither me nor anyone else' (Beckett 1984: 89). Sometimes the narration seems to give up on the project of world-making: 'Let there be no more talk of any creature, nor of a world to leave, nor of a world to reach, in order to have done, with worlds, with creatures' (Beckett 1984: 100–1).

And yet, for all the anxiety and fatigue involved in dreaming up both being and a world to be in, it is not possible to abolish them altogether, since 'being' is always in fact compound or embedded, a hyphenated 'being-here', or a 'being-there'. The resolution articulated at the end of *Text* X – 'I'll have gone on giving up, having had nothing, not being there' (Beckett 1984: 106) – is contradicted by the recognition that there is '[n]o point under such circumstances in saying I am somewhere else, someone else, such as I am I have all I need to hand, for to do what, I don't know, all I have to do' (Beckett 1984: 84). 'I'm here, that's all I know, and that it's still not me' (Beckett 1984: 81). 'What elsewhere can there be to this infinite here? . . . Yes, I'm here for ever' (Beckett 1984: 90).

This is to say, with Heidegger's help, and as others similarly assisted have said before me, that Sein, for Beckett, is always Da-sein. But we should also recognise that this kind of being-there does not add up to the project of worlding that Heidegger sees as immanent to Dasein. The two aspects of Uexküll's *Umwelt* that recommended themselves to Heidegger are disjoined: one is always within a world, that is 'um sich herum', but the 'um-zu' of that world is never guaranteed. The finitude of being in the world, being in some particular circumstance, some here or other, is perfectly compatible with indefiniteness: if one is out of place, it is always in some particular configuration.

Beckett's later works thematise this condition as that of the ghost, the figure who is both there and, as Amy claims in *Footfalls*, 'not there' (Beckett 1986: 43). But it should be remembered that the ghost has a curious relation to finitude, which means it is never entirely unearthly or out of this world. For ghosts, unlike gods and angels and sometimes demons, who have the gift of ubiquity, are traditionally tied to places, condemned for a certain time to walk the earth.

Earth

'What counts', we hear in *Text* IV, 'is to be in the world, the posture is immaterial, so long as one is on earth' (Beckett 1984: 84). As I just suggested, this is perhaps because to be 'on earth, come into the world' means that one is 'assured of getting out' (Beckett 1984: 98). Though 'world' and 'earth', 'monde' and 'terre', often consort together and can readily be substituted for each other, Beckett does seem to maintain a distinction between them.

Again, I want to make out a clarifying difference from Heidegger, who considers the relation between world and earth in his essay, 'The Origin of the Work of Art'. Heidegger sees in the work of art a strife between world and earth. He means by world and earth an openness and a closure, respectively. The world is always an opening or revealing, a showing of the nature of something, or bringing of it to its being. The earth, simply because it is that which is experienced, is concealing and self-concealing. 'The work moves the earth itself into the Open of a world and keeps it there. *The work lets the earth be an earth*' (Heidegger 1975: 46). One might say that the world is simply the disclosing of the closure of earth. The world produces the earth as earth, for 'To set forth the earth means to bring it into the Open as the self-secluding' (Heidegger 1975: 47).

> The world, in resting upon the earth, strives to surmount it. As self-opening it cannot endure anything closed. The earth, however, as sheltering and concealing, tends always to draw the world into itself and keep it there.
>
> The opposition of world and earth is a striving. (Heidegger 1975: 49)

Included among the many things Heidegger seems to want to mean by this striving is the contrariety of material and form. The earth, as 'the massiveness and heaviness of stone, . . . the firmness and pliancy of wood, . . . the hardness and luster of metal, . . . the lighting and darkening of color, . . . the clang of tone' (Heidegger 1975: 46), though subtending and supporting everything in the work of art, does not offer itself as an intelligible whole until it is lifted up into discernibility by that work. However, Heidegger strives to prevent this strife being understood in these simple terms, telling us, for example, that

> The world grounds itself on the earth, and earth juts through world. . . . In essential striving . . . the opponents raise each other into the self-assertion of their natures. . . . In the struggle, each opponent carries the other beyond itself. . . . The earth cannot dispense with the Open of the world if it itself is to appear as earth in the liberated surge of its self-seclusion. The world, again, cannot soar out of the earth's sight if, as the governing breadth and path of all essential destiny, it is to ground itself on a resolute foundation. (Heidegger 1975: 49)

In a certain sense, Beckett's practice might seem to shadow Heidegger's claims. When Beckett's narrators evoke the earth, it is to name something prox-imate, familiar, impending, but indistinct. The earth is often associated with the desire for merger or coalescence of identity. Molloy thinks of his ditch, '[h]ow joyfully I would vanish there, sinking deeper and deeper under the rains' (Beckett 1973: 27–8). The narrator of 'From an Abandoned Work' tells us that

> often now my murmur falters and dies and I weep for happiness as I go along and for love of this old earth that has carried me so long and whose uncomplainingness will soon be mine. Just under the surface I shall be, all together at first, then separate and drift, through all the earth. (Beckett 1984: 133–4)

Beckett's characters often seem literally to have a global or geomorphic awareness of the earth, as a sphere or 'earthball'. Molloy fixes the beginning of his journey to the middle of June through reflections on the hemisphere (Beckett 1973: 17), while the narrator of 'Enough' evokes an eternal spring-like mildness – 'As if the earth had come to rest in spring. I am thinking of our hemisphere' (Beckett 1984: 143). The planetaria inhabited or projected by the speaker in *The Unnamable* and the listener in *Company* attest to this kind of astronomical grasp of global spaces. If these speakers move in blind orbits, they are geostationary ones.

Beckett's earth is perhaps also to be seen as closed or secluded in Heidegger's sense, precisely in the way it withholds or withdraws itself from being constituted as 'world', 'a world' or 'the world'. It is in this sense that all Beckett's characters are local, parochial, regional. It is never the world as such, but always one or other version of 'my part of the world' (a phrase used twice by Molloy [Beckett 1973: 17, 51]) that is in question. But it is also true that the earth (and its correlative, the sky, which might be said to be a modality of earth) is open in another sense, namely that it is uncompleted, unordered and unbordered. So we have this odd sequence following Molloy's observation (itself repeatedly made through Beckett's work) of the lightening of the sky just before nightfall:

> This phenomenon, if I remember rightly, was characteristic of my region. Things are perhaps different today. Though I fail to see, never having left my region, what right I have to speak of its characteristics. No, I never escaped, and even the limits of my region were unknown to me. But I felt they were far away. But this feeling was based on nothing serious, it was a simple feeling. For if my region had ended no further than my feet could carry me, surely I would have felt it changing slowly. For regions do not suddenly end, as far as I know, but gradually merge into one another. And I never noticed anything of the kind, but however far I went, and in no matter what direction, it was always the same sky, always the same earth, precisely, day after day and night after night. (Beckett 1973: 65)

It is precisely because Molloy cannot be sure that he has ever escaped his 'region' that it becomes so vast, and potentially limitless: 'I preferred to abide by my simple feeling and its voice that said, Molloy, your region is vast, you have never left it and you never shall. And wheresoever you wander, within its distant limits, things will always be the same, precisely' (Beckett 1973: 65–6).

So Beckett's earth is both ineluctable and indefinable, extending beyond memory and experience, but also refusing to be levered or rounded out into anything like the condition of 'a world'. Where Heidegger sees the work of art as the struggle of world to lift earth up into openness, Beckett's work, whether of art or not, strives to keep open the discretion of earth, or earth's withholding of itself from world.

Worlding

Heidegger insists that the world 'is not the mere collection of the countable or uncountable, familiar and unfamiliar things that are just there'

(Heidegger 1975: 44). And yet it is also more than just the abstract idea of the world in general. Rather,

> the *world worlds*, and is more fully in being than the tangible and perceptible realm in which we believe ourselves to be at home. World is never an object that stands before us and can be seen. World is the ever-nonobjective to which we are subject as long as the paths of birth and death, blessing and curse keep us transported into Being. Wherever those decisions of our history that relate to our very being are made, are taken up and abandoned by us, go unrecognized and are rediscovered by new inquiry, there the world worlds. (Heidegger 1975: 44)

When we say 'globalization', we mean that world is more and more, and perhaps more and more pinchingly becoming one world. But perhaps we also name this strange sense that 'the world' is becoming more palpable than the 'actual' places and regions in which we may have our being. Heidegger's account of the worlding of the world (or, rather, more reflexively, the world 'worlding'), as a disclosing of the 'as-such' of the world, has recently been resumed and amplified in Michel Serres's account of what he calls 'hominescence', which consists of much more than the increased integration between different areas of the human world. Where animals of different species inhabit different and noncommunicating *Umwelts*, human beings are building a technological masterworld:

> If the ensemble of signals of all kinds is accessible as signs by the totality of living beings, our various devices tend to the reconstruction of this ensemble, like the sum of the habitats – our own, or each individual of our own – which each species carves out from its environment. Are we thus tending, at least asymptotically, towards a global reality, an integral of these spaces and times, the niches and durations of each species and by unifying them, to the beginning of integration? (Serres 2001: 145–6; my translation)

Serres proposes that we are some way advanced into the creation of what he calls a 'Biosom', which composes 'the complex, intersecting global space-time of the ensemble of all living creatures of this world' (Serres 2001: 147; my translation).

This involves much more than the joining together of places or the shrinking of gaps and distances. It involves the synchronisation of world time too. As Heidegger's rapt evocations of destiny suggest, the worlding or worlded world is temporal as well as spatial. The word 'world' in fact derives from a Germanic root *wer* = man, and *ald* = age, the primary signification therefore being 'the age of man'. World signifies, therefore, not a place, or environment, but a span of existence (the time of your life). It is doubtless

for this reason that the OED gives as the primary meaning of the word
'world' usages that emphasise this temporal sense, as man's present life, in
this world, as opposed to the world to come. That the idea of 'the world' has
always hitherto had some sense of the persistence of a form of being in time,
and therefore necessarily of limited duration, is suggested by the phrase
'world without end'. The world must be something that can come to an
end, as in Malone's rapt lunar vision of the 'Dead world, waterless, airless'
(Beckett 1973: 201), or the vision entertained by Molloy that seems to
anticipate it:

> a world collapsing endlessly, a frozen world, under a faint untroubled sky,
> enough to see by, yes, and frozen too. ... [H]ere nothing stirs, has ever
> stirred, will ever stir, except myself, who do not stir either, when I am there,
> but see and am seen. Yes, a world at an end, in spite of appearances, its end
> brought it forth, ending it began, is it clear enough? (Beckett 1973: 40)

We can, I think, posit a perverse conversation between Beckett's insistence
on considering the ends of man and man's contemplation of the fact that
'the world' is definitively, though certainly not irreversibly, entering its
condition as the 'the age of man'.

Something Out of Beckett

Some of the most dubious *obiter dicta* ascribed to Beckett appeared in
an obituary in the *Boston Globe*: '"There are no landmarks in my work,"
Mr. Beckett once said. "We are all adrift. We must invent a world in which
to survive, but even this invented world is pervaded by fear and guilt. Our
existence is hopeless"' (quoted in Campbell 1989: 67). These words have the
authentically naff ring of the manufactured quotation, foisted on and
extracted from the 'corpse-obliging' Beckett. But the idea of a distinctively
'Beckett world' is of course very strong. Reporting on the 1992 Beckett
Festival in The Hague, the *Samuel Beckett Stichtung* observed that 'From
1 to 16 April 1992 the city of The Hague was immersed in the world created
by Samuel Beckett' ('Samuel Beckett Festival and Symposium'). Other
reports during the centenary year of 2006 reflected on the conjunctions
and interferences between 'Beckett's world' and 'the world'. CBS News
offered a slightly more intriguing spin on this by remarking that '[t]he world
may have caught up with Beckett' ('Beckett Embraced By Native Land').
The rivalry between 'the world' and 'Beckett's world' becomes almost
sinister in Michael Hall's remark that '[i]n his centenary year, the spectre
of Beckett is more visible than ever, with events taking place around the

world to celebrate his work' (Hall 2006). Beckett seems to acknowledge his own relation to the 'Beckett world' in the reference, in an early draft of *That Time*, to someone who looks 'like something out of Beckett' (Beckett 1974: 2).

Curiously enough, the consolidation of the 'Beckett world', with its familiar landmarks, languages and local customs, has assisted rather than impeded the absorption of Beckett into the 'big world'. Beckett not only plays, but presumably also pays in capitals across the world, to audiences who have as strong a pre-understanding of what is to be expected from 'the world of Beckett' as readers of Dickens do of 'the world of Dickens' or Terry Pratchett fans do of *Discworld*. It would be foolish to pretend that the condition of becoming a 'world author' is unique to Beckett, or to search for the particular forms of universality that might account for the steadily increasing reach of his work. The amplification and ramification of his work and the idea of his work, the 'world' of his work, are just what we should expect. (Though let us not overstate this, either: 'Beckett' has nowhere near the global reach or tradability of an average gone-tomorrow model or film star. If Beckett is going global, then it is as a kind of 'global niche', a paradox that gets us to the heart of what we might mean by globalism today.)

Nor, by contrast, do I seek to encourage the work of enforced repatriation that is being undertaken by those who seek to assert the essential regionality of Beckett's work – its 'Irishness', its 'Protestantism', and so on. I think that, following the critical work being undertaken on Joyce's writing, by writers such as Emer Nolan and Andrew Gibson (however different they may be in their approaches), which seeks to weaken the consensus about Joyce's cosmopolitan modernism made by writers such as Richard Ellmann and Hugh Kenner and bring Joyce back home, we will see similar efforts to distort Beckett back into ethnic intelligibility. Indeed, the global and the local, the ahistorical and the atavistic, act in perfect consort here. Both Joyce and Beckett became the PR darlings of the Celtic Tiger, with its assertions of European Ireland, cosmopolitan Ireland – 'World Ireland'.

But the worlding of the world, the production of the world as such, finds a resistance and a complication in the work of Beckett. If Beckett's work needs to be seen as a kind of unworlding, a dyspeptic block to the project of Heideggerean worlding, then it may perhaps also be seen as a reflection of and on the nature of this worlding. Globalism means many things – among them the imposition on more and more of the world of risibly particularised and parochial notions of what the world should be. But, in political and philosophical terms, it might also be thought to name an incipient, but growing work of reflection on the same kind of questions that animate Beckett's peculiarly worldly work – the work he conducts on 'world'. Those questions include: What is a world? Can one live in such a thing? Or out of it? What worlds have there been, and what might there be? Can a world be made? Can one help making worlds? Of course, Beckett's work gives us no obvious guidance on such matters – why on earth or anywhere else should we expect such a thing? – but Beckett does instance for us a singular resolve to decline any grandiose worlding of the world, while also denying us and his work the consolation of ever being able to live out of this world.

CHAPTER 12

'On Such and Such a Day . . . In Such a World'

They told me I was everything. 'Tis a lie.   (*King Lear*)

Modern philosophy has become at once violently allergic and pathologically addicted to the question of limits in general and its own limits in particular. One might say that the exercise of modern philosophy, like the conduct of modern scientific enquiry, has been pre-eminently the overcoming of limits – limits of ignorance, confusion, incapacity. Since Nietzsche, philosophy has been a matter of strenuous exceeding and over-going. In contemporary philosophy, nothing succeeds like excess. The only way to do philosophy, especially if, as some in apocalyptic mood have wondered, philosophy may be near to being over, is to overdo it.

A philosophy of limit never quite arrives: it always becomes a melancholy or invigorating account of the limits of philosophy, which provokes the desire to exceed those limits or to engineer an asymptotic approach to the absolute limit. This means that the concept of limit comes to encode an immoderate urge to go to the edge of the known, the possible, the thinkable. This idea is implicit in the very word 'limit', which derives from the Latin 'limen', threshold, which implies that to go to the edge may always promise the possibility of going beyond – otherwise how would one know it was the edge? And yet, the 'liminology', the fact that, as David Wood has said, 'philosophy has an essential relation to the question of limits, and its own limits' (Wood 1990: xv) includes the queasy awareness that the desire of triumphantly overcoming limits is itself a cramping ambition, one that must therefore in its turn be overcome ('undercome', one might impossibly have to say).

Two Finitudes

What is meant by finitude? Finitude names that which is destined to end, rather than to endure – or, more accurately, it names the attempt to accommodate oneself to that necessity. The principal and overwhelming

form of finitude for Heidegger, from which many philosophical considerations of finitude take their point of departure, is the condition of *zum Tode
sein* or 'being-towards-death' that is a distinguishing feature of Dasein and
imparts its tension and tincture to the whole of life.

There are subsidiary forms of finitude, or being-towards-ending. As is
well known, or at least unignorable (which is not quite the same thing),
Beckett is drawn to the endingness of things in general. Where an ordinary
reader might wonder 'what happens next?', Beckett always defaults to the
question 'what happens last?' or 'how will the last thing of all happen'? It is
in this sense that Beckett is a secular, or vernacular, eschatologist, inclined
always to the ultimate outcome or upshot.

The finitude of mortality seems like an arbitrary, incomprehensible
violence to the cheerful ego that means to live for ever and goes on living
as though it thinks it will. But the finitude of death also offers an abatement
of empty time, the possibility of the sense of an ending in a world in which
nothing otherwise can ever finish becoming. The one kind of finitude
presents itself as a scandal and a disaster, the cankering of all human projects;
the other may present a hankering prospect of consummation. Beckett's
work compounds these two aspects of finitude in the use of interruption.
Beckett's finite world is always subject to interruption, which can, of course,
thwart the movement towards completion. But Beckett will sometimes
borrow the force of interruption, seeking to synchronise with it, for example,
with his fondness for unexpected or apparently arbitrary forms of breaking
off: 'Leave it at that' (Beckett 1989: 20); 'Molloy could stay, where he
happened to be' (Beckett 1973: 91).

A recurrent quibble in Beckett's work concerns the question of how
complete any apparent ending can be. That finitude does not always coincide
straightforwardly with mortality is made clear by the fact that death itself is
so indefinite in Beckett's work – one can suffer from being dead, but not
necessarily 'enough to bury' (Beckett 1973: 7). 'Over' (Beckett 1989: 11) is
among the most suspected words in Beckett. One might recall, too, the little
moment of perplexity that furrows Molloy's account of his difficulty in
getting his mother to understand the meaning of the four knocks he imparts
to her skull:

> She seemed to have lost, if not all notion of mensuration, at least the capacity
> of counting beyond two. It was too far for her. By the time she came to the
> fourth knock she imagined she was only at the second, the first two having
> been erased from her memory as completely as if they had never been felt,
> though I don't quite see how something never felt can be erased from the
> memory, and yet it is a common occurrence. (Beckett 1973: 18)

In order to be erased, in order for something to be there no more, it must once have been there, which always seems to the ember-anxious Beckett to come a miserable second to never having been there at all. This is a worry that ending may itself be limited, that it may not be definitive enough to cancel out the blot of having been, which may persist, unexpunged, unretractable and, perhaps worst of all, revivable.

So much, roughly speaking, for the finitude of mortality. This gets me into the vicinity of another idiom of finitude, which will in fact be the one on which I will be concentrating. This finitude means the inescapability of limit or restriction. The emphasis here is not on coming to an end, but on falling short, on deficiency rather than mortality. Finitude signifies a kind of privation in the heart of being, an awareness of the ever-present possibility of loss, and the looming necessity of death, which means that one is never 'quite there', as Beckett said of 'M' in *Footfalls*, and prevents one living wholly in the here and now. This aspect of finitude makes it hard to distinguish absolutely from indefiniteness. Finitude comes up short of the definite. This mode of finitude overlaps with that of temporal finitude, since, after all, death is often experienced or represented as just such a limit, or arbitrary curtailing. Finitude here means, not the certainty of coming to an end, but the certainty of ending unfinished, dying, as we all must, before our time, and consequently never being able to have, or inhabit, the time of our lives.

But if finitude means never quite being able to coincide with one's being here and now, it also means the inability to live anywhere else *but* in the here and now. Finitude means embeddedness, the impossibility of ever being otherwise than at a specific place and time, 'en situation', in a specific set of circumstances that cannot be discounted or set aside as merely incidental – 'the life of Monday or Tuesday', in Virginia Woolf's words (Woolf 1925: 189), which must nevertheless have been written on one day of the week or other. 'Death has not required us to keep a day free', says Beckett (Beckett 1970c: 17), reminding us nevertheless that there is a definite date in our diary assigned to death, as yet unknown to us, just as we first saw the light 'on such and such a day' (Beckett 1989: 8). As Philip Larkin madly asks in his poem 'Days': 'Where could we live but days?' The response he offers is loonier still: 'solving that question / Brings the priest and the doctor / In their long coats / Running over the fields' (Larkin 1988: 67).

Perhaps we might say that finitude names the coiled conjuncture of these two contrasting aspects: the lack or insufficiency that haunts being at its heart, and the irreducible excess of beastly circumstance in which we are always embedded.

Comedy is often implicated in thinking of and at limits. This is nicely illustrated by Beckett's allusion in *Malone Dies* to Jackson's parrot, which utters the words 'Nihil in intellectu' but refrains from or stops short before what Beckett calls 'the celebrated restriction' – 'quod non prius in sensu' (Beckett 1973: 218). The joke depends upon the fact that the bird seems to be saying, not that there is nothing in the mind that has not first been in the senses, but that there is nothing in the mind at all. Yet, because the bird is restricted, or restrains itself, from delivering the restriction, this leaves open the possibility that the mind might have unrestricted access to other things, things other than those which come to it through the senses (the idea of 'nothing', for example). But Beckett's account includes, by allusion at any rate, the restriction that the bird does not allow, inviting us to see the rhyme between what the bird does and doesn't say and the fact that it is a bird saying it (and so not really *saying* it at all). Parrots, and the philosophical popinjays who unthinkingly parrot slogans like this, may indeed have 'nihil in intellectu' – nothing in their minds at all, because everything they say will be a matter only, and exclusively, of the sensible, with nothing of the intelligible.

Comedy often arises from, or at least coincides with, this ironic interference of finitude and infinitude. This suggestion is assisted by Freud's diagnosis of the economic basis of the joke, which works by first establishing a restriction or inhibition and then relaxing its pressure: the joke works through the elasticity of the idea of finitude, the way in which the stress of finitude, when suddenly released, can seem to release a surplus of unbound energy – though never of course infinite energy, since jokes are as subject to the second law of thermodynamics as anything else. So we find Beckett offering us in *Murphy* a unique taxonomy of jokes, not in terms of their modes, objects or success, but in terms of their periods of expiry, yielding the distinction between jokes that had once been funny and jokes that had never been funny (Beckett 2003: 41).

I am helped to my intent with regard to Beckett's finitude by Jean-Luc Nancy's characterisation of what he calls 'finite thinking'. Finite thinking, for Nancy, is impoverished or disabled thinking – thinking as a kind of existence, thinking without ground or destination, the orientation towards a kind of 'sense' that could not hope to resume or reappropriate itself. Nancy calls it 'a being-to itself [that] no longer belongs to itself, no longer comes back to itself' (Nancy 2003, 8). So a finite thinking 'is one that, on each occasion, thinks the fact that it is unable to think what comes to it' (Nancy 2003: 15). Finitude here means incapacity to achieve completion, deficiency, shortfall – a singularity that refuses to be generalised, a *hic et nunc* never to be promoted to an anywhere or anywhen. There is no 'consolation or compensation' in this kind of finitude, writes Nancy (consolingly enough, one might feel): 'in finitude, there is no question of an "end," whether as a goal or as an accomplishment . . . it's merely a question of the suspension of sense, in-finite, each time replayed, re-opened, exposed, with a novelty so radical that it immediately fails' (Nancy 2003: 10). Going along with Nancy would give us readily enough the Beckett of intemperately renewed failure, of infinite suspension or deferral of finality – a Beckett who might therefore strike us as fishily congenial because too readily familiar.

This

If finitude means having to inhabit the inhibited condition of a self that does not come back to itself, Nancy also maintains that finitude means cleaving to the 'hic et nunc' of that which is not taken up into factitious infinitude. This seems curious: what kind of here and now can it be that cannot be grasped – not as the convergence of the grasper with the grasped, nor even perhaps as the convergence of a here with the now? A kind of its own: an experience of the unencompassability of the here and now that is possible of access only in the here and now. Only in the actuality of the moment can the irreducible passage – the moment mined with a motion – be grasped immediately, though this is to say, never on time, always prematurely or too late. Living in the moment is supposed to give intensity, decision or acceptance, depending, because it is supposed to relieve the mind of distractions – the protractions of the past and the attractions of the future. But those distractions are of course part of the finitude of living in time, part of the constitution of the fabled moment. So living in the moment must also include the experience of the nonappropriability of the moment. The only way to live in the moment is not to seek to grasp it, which is to say to miss it. One cannot both be in and have the here and now, because of the here and now's finitude, which is actual and indefinite. Indefinite, because unfinished and inappropriable by itself, as seems to be demonstrated by *Krapp's Last Tape*, when the old man (K3) listens to the ringing tones of the younger man he once was (K2) affirming that he has no need of anything now but the incandescent present: 'Perhaps my best years are gone. But I wouldn't want them back. Not with the fire in me now' (Beckett 1986: 223). K2 is limited, finite, in not knowing what he will become, as we, and the later Krapp (K3) will know it. Yet nobody else can inhabit this finitude as only K2 can (that is what finitude means); that is, nobody else can inhabit the uninhabitability of his now, precisely because his finitude is unfinished business until it is disclosed by the attention of K3 (or rather his inattention, since he is listening out for something much more important in his past). This is another reason why finitude can never be definitive. If K2 could have pulled it off, he would have achieved the kind of finite thinking that Nancy describes: one that 'on each occasion, thinks the fact that it is unable to think what comes to it' (Nancy 2003: 15). But he could only think this in general, in terms of an abstract preparedness for what the future may not bring, rather than any here-and-now finitude. Beckett does not merely seek to acknowledge finitude, he sometimes seems to want to appropriate it, to take its measure, to encompass it absolutely and without restriction (and so, *infinitely*). But the finitude of the here and now does not belong to it; it is a yet-to-come, proleptically belated here and now.

Beckett's master and semi-begetter Joyce also had a preoccupation with the capture of the indefinite definiteness of the here and now, which he called 'epiphany'. The Joycean idea of the epiphany involves the interfusion of the finite and the infinite, or an eruption of the eternal in the temporal, and his practice tends towards the attempt, not to show the godly in the momentary, as though a screen were suddenly made transparent to a blazing light behind it, as to show the radiance of the momentary itself, untransfigured, but lifted into itself. Duns Scotus's word for this is 'haecceitas', usually translated as 'thisness', the thing that defined what something was in itself, distinct from all others. But Beckett has a different sense of the *haec*; indeed, the very word seems to focus and carry his finitude. The last published work that Beckett ever wrote funnels down through this word, this thisness, which is now as far away from the unstinting apparition of being celebrated in Joyce and, before him, Gerard Manley Hopkins as it is possible to be. 'This' names that which is both unbearably proximate, so close at hand that all one needs to do to designate it is to point, and at the same time unnamable, too close, too inundatingly immediate for naming:

> folly seeing all this –
> this –
> what is the word –
> this this –
> this this here –
> all this this here –
> folly given all this –   (Beckett 2012: 228)

The original French version is even more insistent and yet, because of the relative abundance of demonstrative particles, gives the sense not so much of a kind of lockjaw or stuck groove, as of a frantic splintering under the extreme stress of ostension:

comment dire –
ceci –
ce ceci –
ceci-ci
tout ce ceci-ci   (Beckett 2012: 226)

Where the English allows us to hear a simple intensification in the repetition of 'this', the French 'ce ceci' gives us a doubled, reflexive 'this', in which the second 'this' is the object of the first, and for which an accurate rendering would be 'this thisness here'. 'This' must always name something immediately given in the actual or imagined vicinity of the speaker. And yet, precisely because the referent of 'this' is not contained in it, nor ever can be if 'this' is to retain its power to designate whatever lies at hand, to bring whatever it designates into the condition of the close-at-hand, 'this' will never be enough to name what it conjures. This, this 'this', the 'this this here' of 'What Is the Word?' provides a perfect résumé, or almost, of the condition of indefinite finitude.

I and some of my kind have devoted hours of long and more-or-less honest toil to showing the ways in which Beckett's work dissolves the claims of presence. Today, I feel more inclined to protest that what characterises Beckett's work is the effort to find his way to a presence, though a presence denuded of all determinations, its traditional, infinitive attributes – of permanence, essence, adequacy-to-self; a parched, patched, penurious presence.

Difficilis Facilis

My work is a matter of fundamental sounds (no joke intended) made as fully as possible and I accept responsibility for nothing else. If people want to have headaches among the overtones, let them. And provide their own aspirin. Hamm as stated, and Clov as stated, together stated *nec tecum nec sine te*, in such a place, and in such a world, that's all I can manage, more than I could. (Harmon 1998: 24)

This notorious statement, made by Beckett in a 1957 letter to Alan Schneider, has become a canonical nut that must ceremonially be cracked, an impediment ritually swerved around, like the dreaded centre of the square in *Quad*, if criticism of Beckett's work is to proceed, and it must, it must. But let us take note of what Beckett seems to be saying here. The first thing to note is that the 'as such' on which Beckett insists is insufficient, finite – it is 'all I can manage, more than I could' (and perhaps I am not alone in finding that 'could' oddly suspensive, as though it were a modal that lacked the word which would complete its sense – 'more than I could have hoped for', 'more than I could, once'?). It is sometimes assumed by the hopefully indolent that Beckett is saying that there is nothing for exegesis to do, that criticism and interpretation are useless and indulgent superfluities, adding complexity to a work that has no need of it because it is so simple, straightforward and self-interpreting. Our slackers are given succour in this view by the fact that, a moment earlier in the letter, Beckett has suggested that he and Schneider 'insist on the extreme simplicity of dramatic situation and issue. If that's not enough for them, and it obviously isn't, or they don't see it, it's plenty for us' (Harmon 1998: 46). Even here, there is difficulty. To allow the extreme simplicity of the words themselves, to let them be 'as stated', one would have to take care not to find anything to notice in the phrase 'extreme simplicity'; why not simple simplicity and leave it that – why the need to take simplicity to extremes, the need for simplicity to be 'plenty'? There is no simplicity that is truly single, with no wrinkle of implication in it.

And Beckett folds a bit of exegetical opportunity in what he writes. *Nec tecum nec sine te*, referring presumably to the impossibility for Hamm and Clov in *Endgame* to either live with or live without each other, requires annotation for one not completely incurious or naturally au fait with the epigrams of Martial: 'Difficilis facilis, iucundus acerbus es idem: / Nec tecum possum vivere, nec sine te', writes Martial to his Lesbia: 'You are difficult and easy, comfortable and rough / I cannot live with you, nor without you' (*Epigrams* XII, 46, Martial 1993: 3.126–7). In fact, Martial may himself borrow the phrase from Ovid's 'nec sine te nec tecum vivere possum' (*Amores* 3.11.39, Ovid 1987: I.214). The phrase has the seesaw that Beckett liked: 'Do not despair, one of the thieves was saved. Do not presume, one of the thieves was damned' (quoted in Ackerley and Gontarski 2004: 593); 'neither help nor hinder' (quoted in Bair 1978: 9). But it also names the predicament of conjoined contraries, in which opposites are inextricably implicated in each other. Beckett may well have thought that exegesis was folly, but this is not what he says here. *Nec tecum nec sine te* may also hint that, just as Beckett cannot work in the theatre without the help of a director, cast and crew, he cannot expect his work not to provoke exegesis, which he can therefore neither live with nor without. What he says here is that he refuses to be involved with critical interpretation, and takes no responsibility for easing its passage, and he says this precisely because such involvement would loosen the lock of the predicament he is attempting to state, both with extreme simplicity and 'as fully as possible'.

In short, Beckett's point is not primarily to criticise or discredit exegesis, but to keep it at a distance. In other words, this is not an attack on the practice of criticism, but an attack on its linking with whatever it is that he is doing, in forming the 'matter' of his work. For Beckett to become involved in exegesis would be for him to loosen the very tension of the non-relation that is his relation with criticism, simplifying the difficulty of the *nec tecum nec sine te*.

Beckett certainly at times nursed violent fantasies of giving the works to critics and other interpreters of his work who had gone to work on him – he wrote to Schneider a little later that he dreamed 'of all German directors of plays with perhaps one exception united in one with his back to the wall and me shooting a bullet into his balls every five minutes till he loses his taste for improving authors' (Harmon 1998: 59). But I think his austere apartness preserves the possibility of a certain kind of company. I once heard Sophie Calle speaking about her work at the Riverside Studios. Somebody from the audience asked a long, formidably thoughtful and intelligent question about the relations that might obtain between her work and theories of mourning and melancholia. The supplicant finished his epic enquiry by asking, 'So, do you think your work can be seen in these terms, or is it just me?' Sophie Calle considered and then replied: 'Yes, I think you're right. [*A beat.*] It's just you'. This apparently queenly swat generated the inevitable laughter, though I could detect no irritation or desire to humiliate in its tone. Sophie Calle was asking her interlocutor to take responsibility for his interpretation, was refusing to pretend to lift herself and him out of finitude, the condition of 'amidness' in the work she made, and whatever was to be made of it.

This is rough comfort and difficult ease indeed. The point of Beckett's finitude is to resist being drawn out (the literal meaning of *exegesis*) into validation, promotion, authorisation, exculpation, explication – into public relations. Perhaps this explains the 'incoercible absence of relation' (Beckett 1970c: 125) of which Beckett spoke, his disinclination to have a relation to himself or any other subject than being of or amid it – 'Je ne peux pas écrire *sur*' ('I cannot write *about*'), he wrote in 1949 to Georges Duthuit (Beckett 2011: 137). What is important for Beckett is finding a way of interested being, being *inter esse*, not the compound interest formed in the afterlife of explication. Beckett lived in a period in which the pressures to infinitise, to lubricate the issueless predicaments of finitude, had already begun to multiply massively. In his time, and ours, Beckett's work has been subject to huge amplification and enlargement, across genres, media, languages and cultures. He has been made the centrepiece of what might be called a contemporary aesthetics of the inexhaustible, which assumes the sovereign value of endless propagation and maintains a horror of any kind of limit. Beckett found himself, as part of his own historical finitude, having to invent, always anew, ever in the middle of the way, the means of his abstention from this infinitising.

The Progress of Alimentation

Perhaps the most obvious embodiment of the factitious infinite is the internet, whose claims to illimitability are often based upon the multiplicative power of its links, not only in the very large number of items that it makes accessible, but rather in the incalculably huge numbers of ways in which the items can link to each other. The internet presents a pseudo-infinity of relations, a literalisation of Henry James's insight in the preface to *Roderick Hudson* that '[r]eally, universally, relations stop nowhere' (James 1961: vii).

One of the ways in which, for all his easy assimilability to the interests of the internet, Beckett remains jaggedly indigestible is in the antagonism to linking. It is not too much to say that in Beckett there is a horror of universal association that matches the horror of eternal life. Perhaps the most obvious and difficult form of finitude in Beckett's work is its insistence on distinction, exception, apartness. A convenient method of disposing of this would be to suggest that it belongs to a neurotic and dominative desire to protect essence against accidence, where essence underpins the power of ruling minorities, traditional elites. But what are we to make of a finitude that will not relinquish the essence of accidence, the irreducibility of an essence reduced to that, to this, to 'this'?

W. R. Bion's essay 'Attacks on Linking' has frequently been brought to bear on the work of the writer he had analysed twenty years before. I have myself considered it in more detail than I have time or need to recapitulate here (Connor 2008). Bion follows Melanie Klein in seeing in certain schizophrenic patients a reversion or fixation at the stage of projective identification, during which the young child will tend to split off good and bad objects from one another – typically, the good and bad breast. Despite being split off, however, these fragments are still available to the subject to form a relation with, unless, as Bion believed might happen in certain psychotic conditions, that very remaining link is itself subject to angry denial and dissolution (Bion 1993: 107).

Beckett's attacks on linking do not have the Kleinian function of keeping good and bad safely quarantined from each other. Rather these attacks arise from a more obscure and general horror at the collapse of definitions, and the prospect it seems of opening a universal equivalence that is in fact a condition of maximum entropy. The problem is that the one who pushes the attack on linking to its limit, insisting on absolute non-correlation, is liable to turn instead to a kind of atomisation that is functionally indistinguishable from a world of universal equivalence. These two alternatives have gastronomic analogies. In *Watt*, maximal combinability is imaged in Mr Knott's stew made of all manner of good things; maximal non-relation is signified in the emetic or anorexic relationship to food – for example, in *More Pricks Than Kicks*, in the fiercely stinking cheese favoured by Belacqua Shuah, which seems to allow him to remain aggressively distinct from his food even as he consumes it (Beckett 1970b: 17).

There is no doubt that the recoil from links does at times reach phobic proportions for Beckett, but it does not necessarily preclude sociality or enjoin asocial or atomistic solitude. For Beckett, relation is only possible with distance and differentiation; everything else threatens incorporation or appropriation. As Heidegger somewhat grudgingly acknowledges, and Hans-Georg Gadamer more fundamentally insists, a primary form of human finitude is our *Mitsein*, or being-with-others:

> The genuine meaning of our finitude or our thrownness consists in the fact that we become aware, not only of our being historically conditioned, but especially of our being conditioned by the other. Precisely in our ethical relation to the other, it becomes clear to us how difficult it is to do justice to the demands of the other or even simply to become aware of them. The only way not to succumb to our finitude is to open ourselves to the other, to listen to the "thou" who stands before us. (Gadamer 2006: 29)

But this is no simple, self-evident, or merely given company. It is difficult ease: *nec tecum nec sine te.*

Unborderless

We are wont to think that the given, limited, actual world is what presses most stiflingly upon us, and that it requires strenuous exertion or careful vigilance to break the fascinating grip of facticity, in order that we can project ourselves into possibility, futurity, transcendence, infinity – or what Alain Badiou calls 'the happiness of a truthful arousal of the void' (Badiou 2003a: 36). Finiteness, we dream, is the merely given, infinity, that which is made or imagined in excess of the given. But it is in fact the realm of the given, or the so-called self-evident, that is most intractable to human thought. We find it almost impossible to grasp or coincide with this realm of the given, the incontinently renewable once-and-for-allness of every instant, the statute of limitations of every project. Our apprehension skeeters off the actual into whatever might prolong or retard it, making what shift we can, through fantasy, religion, literature, commerce, to remit its finitude.

I spent the first half of my sentient life pointing to everything in Beckett that seemed to qualify, complicate, defer or infinitise – all the near misses, failures of correspondence, 'vaguenings', temporisings, that seem to tend towards infinity – trying to loosen the adherence to finitude that haunts that work everywhere. My first book on Beckett attempted to negate the closure of repetition, prising open its fist to show the various forms of inexhaustibility that characterise Beckett's writing. That work, though necessary at one time, if only for me, now seems to me, in the light of an evasion, an attempt to turn unwisely tail from the exacting penury of the finite in Beckett's work. Nancy quotes a warning from Heidegger against this evasion: 'When being is posited as infinite, it is precisely then that it is determined. If it is posited as finite, it is then that its absence of ground is affirmed' (quoted in Nancy 2003: 9).

Among the many unique accomplishments alleged by human beings of themselves is their capacity to grasp the inescapability of their own deaths. On the contrary, the great human sickness is infinitude, the incapacity to seize finitude seriously and sustainedly. It is not just that we do not take seriously the 'one day' of abstract death; it is that we find it almost impossibly hard to apprehend the limited and finite nature of the lives we live every day, the fact that we can live only the life we can live, in such a place, in such a world. To say that Beckett's work constitutes a radical finitude is to say that it strives to permit itself the very least remission it can manage from this awareness of always having to live, move and have its being 'in such a world . . . on such and such a day' (Harmon 1998: 24), never in the world in general, or 'as such'. Beckett is, as Heidegger alleged animals were, 'poor in world' (Heidegger 1995: 177), poor in the worldhood of 'the world'.

Nancy names four ways in which finitude is disallowed, or deported, from itself: extermination, expropriation, simulation and technology. One might add to this the lexicon of the illimitable that has flourished in philosophy and criticism. This lexicon includes, but is not restricted to, jouissance, the semiotic, différance, the immaterial, the differend, flow, the impotential, desire and, of course – and the original perhaps of these many *noms de plume* – life. Against these, Nancy offers an ethics of finitude: 'Since the here and now is finitude, the inappropriability of sense, every appro-priation of the "here" by an "elsewhere," and of the "now" by an "afterward" (or by a "beforehand") is and does *evil*' (Nancy 2003: 19).

Some of the rare moments of saturated calm in Beckett's work come from this refusal of deported being, the acceptance of the only possible towards which all things hobble: 'There we are, there I am, that's enough' (Beckett 1986: 133). Nancy evokes an 'enjoyment – if the notion of enjoyment is not that of appropriation, but of a sense (in all the senses) which, here and now, does not come back to itself' (Nancy 2003: 21), which seems close to the 'happiness' seemingly glimpsed at the end of *Ill Seen Ill Said*, in which calm comes, not from satiety, but from its prospect, the momentary opening of the prospect of closing off:

> Farewell to farewell. Then in that perfect dark foreknell darling sound pip for end begun. First last moment. Grant only enough remain to devour all. Moment by glutton moment. Sky earth the whole kit and caboodle. Not another crumb of carrion left. Lick chops and basta. No. One moment more. One last. Grace to breathe that void. Know happiness. (Beckett 1989: 97)

Badiou sees rare moments like this as 'events' that serve both to dissolve and to infinitise the subject that is otherwise pent in its finitude:

> The Two, which is inaugurated by the encounter and whose truth results from love, does not remain closed in upon itself. Rather, it is a passage, a pivotal point, *the first numericality*. This Two constitutes a passage, or authorises the pass, from the One of solipsism (which is the first datum) to the infinity of beings and of experience. The Two of love is a hazardous and chance-laden meditation for alterity in general. It elicits a rupture or a severance of the *cogito*'s One; by virtue of this very fact, however, it can hardly stand on its own, opening instead onto the limitless multiple of Being. (Badiou 2003a: 28)

Badiou makes of the event a kind of epiphany, an opening that makes way for something else. The event opens on to the undetermined nature of things, constituting a break in the chain of determinations. The event exposes the subject to the privation of being un- or underdetermined – confronted by the '*il y a*', with only that to go on. For Badiou, events are both rare and exemplary, and thus at least potentially consequential: they extend, propagate, ramify. But events in Beckett are neither rare nor consequential. Every new moment renews, without deepening, exposure to finitude. Beckett's finitude is radical in this sense; it casts no shadow, inaugurates no series. Finitude has no syntax; it is perseverance without project. This accounts for the power of repetition, the awareness of 'that again', the epiphany that shows and gives rise to nothing, and yet recurs, paratactic, a privation deprived of improvement. It is this which makes it a 'finite thinking' in Nancy's sense. More than just thinking that keeps finitude in mind, as a precaution or memento, it is a thinking that is itself finite. Nancy's work helps us to characterise Beckett's finitude, provided we recognise that the latter does not provide itself with principles in this way: that it does not allow itself to persist indefinitely in the finite condition of not being able to make an end. It refuses the infinitising tendency – and consolation – of Nancy's finite thinking; it does not allow the certainty of there being an end, to everything, inevitably, to sediment into an abstract, and therefore end-averting certification.

This means that Beckett's work should be held back from philosophy, should be allowed to fall short of philosophy, to come up short before it, precisely because of its desire not to infinitise finitude. When Bem and Bom in *What Where* report the failure of their attempts to extort confessions, V. says 'It is a lie'. I want to hear in that the echo of King Lear's cry 'They told me I was everything. 'Tis a lie. I am not ague-proof' (*King Lear*, 4.6, 104). If we want Beckett to be everything, we are on our own. My point is that, in delivering Beckett up to the infinitude from which he shrank, whether in construing his work as an Aladdin's cave of hermeneutical opportunity, and a source for henceforth unconstrained performative reappropriations, or as a work wholly unconstrained by season or territory, a work without borders, we do a violence to what may be the most difficult and distinct provocation of his work.

Radical finitude, I have said. By this, I do not mean rigorous, programmatic or totalising infinitude, the root-and-branch, eradicating whole-hoggery that always seems to come in the train of what is called 'radical thought'. Beckett's finitude is both a predicament and a choice, the choice of a predicament ('in search of the difficulty rather than in its clutch' [Beckett 1983: 139]). It is a finitude that is never used up, or said and done; a finitude never to be fully accounted for, abbreviated or economised on, because there will always be, what there only ever is, more of the here and now. A finitude that, seemingly without let or cease, itself remains finite. This surely might be an addition to company, if only up to a point.

References

Anon n.d. 'Roger Godeau'. *Mémoire du cyclisme*. http://www.memoire-du-cyclisme. net/palmares/godeau_roger.php [Accessed 18 June 2005].

Anon n.d. 'Sartre's Existentialism in Samuel Beckett's *Waiting for Godot*'. http:// www.123helpme.com/preview.asp?id=20926 [Accessed 19 November 2011].

Anon 1835. 'The Royal Irish Academy', *Dublin Penny Journal* 4 (24 October): 120–1.

Anon 1992. 'Samuel Beckett Festival and Symposium, April 1992, The Hague, The Netherlands'. http://www.samuelbeckett.nl/festival.htm [Accessed 15 August 2007].

Anon 2006. 'Beckett Embraced by Native Land', *CBS News* (13 April). http://www. cbsnews.com/stories/2006/04/13/entertainment/main1497010_page2.shtml [Accessed 15 August 2007].

Abbott, H. Porter 1996. *Beckett Writing Beckett: The Author in the Autograph*. Ithaca: Cornell University Press.

Ackerley, C. J., and S. E. Gontarski, 2004. *The Grove Companion to Samuel Beckett*. New York: Grove Press.

Ackroyd, Peter 1984. *T. S. Eliot*. London: Hamish Hamilton.

Agamben, Giorgio 2004. *The Open: Man and Animal*, trans. Kevin Attell. Stanford: Stanford University Press.

Albright, Daniel 2003. *Beckett and Aesthetics*. Cambridge: Cambridge University Press.

Allison, J. Reginald 1924. 'The Care of Accumulators', *Weather and Wireless Magazine* 2: 42–3.

Anderdon, Mary 1662. *A Word to the World*. London: no publisher.

Aristotle 1910. *Historia Animalium*, trans. D'Arcy Wentworth Thompson. Oxford: Clarendon.

Armstrong, David 2006. 'The Silent Speaker', *Forbes Magazine* 4 (October). http://www.forbes.com/free_forbes/2006/0410/084.html?partner=yahoomag [Accessed 24 May 2014].

Athanasopoulou-Kypriou, Spyridoula 2000. 'Samuel Beckett Beyond the Problem of God', *Literature and Theology* 14: 34–51.

Auden, W. H. 1976. *Collected Poems*, ed. Edward Mendelson. New York: Random House.

Augustine, Saint, of Hippo 1912. *St. Augustine's Confessions. With an English Translation by William Watts*. 2 Vols. London: William Heinemann/New York: Macmillan.

Bachelard, Gaston 1948. *La Terre et les rêveries de la volonté*. Paris: José Corti.

Badiou, Alain 2003a. *On Beckett*, eds. Alberto Toscano and Nina Power, trans. Bruno Bosteels, Nina Power and Alberto Toscano. London: Clinamen.

2003b. *Saint Paul: The Foundation of Universalism*, trans. Ray Brassier. Stanford: Stanford University Press.

2007. *Being and Event*, trans. Oliver Feltham. London: Continuum.

2010. *Theoretical Writings*, eds. and trans. Ray Brassier and Alberto Toscano. London: Continuum.

Bair, Deidre 1978. *Samuel Beckett: A Biography*. London: Jonathan Cape.

Baldwin, Hélène L. 1981. *Samuel Beckett's Real Silence*. University Park and London: Pennsylvania State University Press.

Banfield, Ann 2003. 'Beckett's Tattered Syntax', *Representations* 6: 6–29.

Bataille, Georges 1988. *Inner Experience*, trans. Leslie Anne Boldt. Albany: SUNY Press.

Baudry, Jean-Louis 1985. 'Ideological Effects of the Basic Cinematographic Apparatus', in *Movies and Methods: An Anthology: Vol. 2*, ed. Bill Nichols. Berkeley: University of California Press, pp. 531–42.

Beck, Alan 2002 *The Death of Radio? An Essay in Radio Philosophy for the Digital Age*. http://www.savoyhill.co.uk/deathofradio/ [Accessed 25 July 2013].

Beckett, Samuel 1970a. *Das letzte Band: Regiebuch der Berliner Inszenierung*, ed. Volker Canaris. Frankfurt: Suhrkamp.

1970b. *More Pricks Than Kicks*. London: Calder and Boyars.

1970c. *Proust and Three Dialogues With Georges Duthuit*. London: John Calder.

1972. *Watt*. London: Calder and Boyars.

1973. *Molloy. Malone Dies. The Unnamable*. London: Calder and Boyars.

1974. Draft of *That Time*. Reading University Library MS 1477.

1976. *Pour finir encore et autres foirades*. Paris: Minuit.

1977a. *La dernière bande, suivi de Cendres*. Paris: Minuit.

1977b. *How It Is*. London: John Calder.

1978a. *Pas, suivi de quatre esquisses*. Paris: Editions de Minuit.

1978b. *Happy Days/Oh les beaux jours*, ed. James Knowlson. London: Faber.

1982. Unpublished Letter, 7 February 1982 to Steven Connor.

1983. *Disjecta: Miscellaneous Writings and a Dramatic Fragment*, ed. Ruby Cohn. London: John Calder.

1984. *Collected Shorter Prose 1945–1980*. London: John Calder.

1986. *Complete Dramatic Works*. London: Faber and Faber.

1989. *Nohow On: Company. Ill Seen Ill Said. Worstward Ho*. London: John Calder.

1991. *Cap au pire*, trans. Edith Fournier. Paris: Minuit.

1992. *The Theatrical Notebooks of Samuel Beckett. Vol III: Krapp's Last Tape*, ed. James Knowlson. London: Faber and Faber.

2003. *Murphy*. London: Calder Publications.

2009. *The Letters of Samuel Beckett: Volume 1: 1929–1940*, eds. Martha Dow Fehsenfeld, Lois More Overbeck, George Craig and Dan Gunn. Cambridge: Cambridge University Press.

2011. *The Letters of Samuel Beckett: Volume 2, 1941–1956*, eds. George Craig, Martha Dow Fehsenfeld, Dan Gunn and Lois More Overbeck. Cambridge: Cambridge University Press.

2012. *The Collected Poems of Samuel Beckett: A Critical Edition*, eds. Seán Lawlor and James Pilling. London: Faber and Faber.

Benstock, Bernard 1988. 'The Gnomonics of Dubliners', *Modern Fiction Studies* 34: 519–39.

Bierce, Ambrose 2000. *The Unabridged Devil's Dictionary*, ed. David E. Schultz. Athens, GA, and London: University of Georgia Press.

Bion, Wilfred R. 1993. 'Attacks on Linking' in *Second Thoughts: Selected Papers on Psycho-Analysis*. London: Karnac, pp. 93–109.

Bryden, Mary 1997. *Samuel Beckett and the Idea of God*. London: Macmillan.

Bulhof, Ilse N., and Laurens ten Kate, 2000. *Flight of the Gods: Philosophical Perspectives on Negative Theology*. New York: Fordham University Press.

Buning, Marius 1990. 'Samuel Beckett's Negative Way: Intimations of the Via Negativa in His Late Plays', in *European Literature and Theology in the Twentieth Century: Ends of Time*, eds. David Jasper and Colin Crowder. London: Macmillan, pp. 129–42.

Burnyeat, M. F. 1997. 'Postscript on Silent Reading', *Classical Quarterly* 47: 74–6.

Burroughs, William S. 1968. *The Ticket That Exploded*. London: Calder and Boyars.

and Daniel Odier 1969. *The Job: Interview With William Burroughs*. London: Jonathan Cape.

Butler, Lance St. John 1984. *Samuel Beckett and the Meaning of Being: A Study in Ontological Parable*. London: Macmillan.

1992. '"A Mythology With Which I Am Perfectly Familiar": Samuel Beckett and the Absence of God', in *Irish Writers and Religion*, ed. Robert Welsh. Gerrards Cross: Colin Smythe, pp. 169–84.

Campbell, Charles 1989. 'Samuel Beckett: Playwright, Winner of Nobel Prize', *Boston Globe* (27 December): 67.

Caputo, John D. 1997. *The Prayers and Tears of Jacques Derrida: Religion Without Religion*. Bloomington and Indianapolis: Indiana University Press.

Carroll, Lewis 1976. *The Annotated Alice: Alice's Adventures in Wonderland and Alice Through the Looking Glass*, ed. Martin Gardner. Harmondsworth: Penguin.

Carson, Ciaran 1996. *Opera et Cetera*. Oldcastle: Gallery Press.

Clément, Bruno 2006. 'What the Philosophers Do With Samuel Beckett', trans. Anthony Uhlmann, in *Beckett After Beckett*, eds. S. E. Gontarski and Anthony Uhlmann. Gainesville: University Press of Florida, pp. 116–37.

Coe, Richard N. 1964. *Beckett*. Edinburgh and London: Oliver and Boyd/New York: Grove Press.

Cohen, Leonard 1992. 'The Future', *The Future*. Columbia Records.

Cohn, Ruby 2001. *A Beckett Canon*. Ann Arbor: University of Michigan Press.

Conner, Kim 1997. 'Beckett and Radio: The Radioactive Voice', *Samuel Beckett Today/Aujourd'hui* 6: 303–12.

Connor, Steven 1988. *Samuel Beckett: Repetition, Theory and Text.* Oxford: Blackwell.
  2000. *Dumbstruck: A Cultural History of Ventriloquism.* Oxford: Oxford
    University Press.
  2003. *The Book of Skin.* London: Reaktion.
  2006a. 'Beckett's Atmospheres', in *Beckett After Beckett,* eds. S. E. Gontarski and
    Anthony Uhlmann. Gainesville: University of Florida Press, pp. 52–65.
  2006b. *Fly.* London: Reaktion.
  2008. 'Beckett and Bion', *Journal of Beckett Studies* 17: 9–34.
  2009. 'Michel Serres: The Hard and the Soft'. http://www.stevenconnor.com/
    hardsoft [Accessed 24 May 2014].
  2010. *The Matter of Air: Science and Art of the Ethereal.* London: Reaktion.
  2011a. *Paraphernalia: The Curious Lives of Magical Things.* London: Profile.
  2011b. *A Philosophy of Sport.* London: Reaktion.
Cordingley, Anthony 2012. 'Beckett's "Masters": Pedagogical Sadism, Foreign
    Language Primers, Self-Translation', *Modern Philology* 109: 510–43.
Coward, Harold, and Toby Foshay (eds.) 1992. *Derrida and Negative Theology.*
    Albany: State University of New York Press.
Critchley, Simon 1997. *Very Little . . . Almost Nothing: Death, Philosophy, Literature.*
    London: Routledge.
Cronin, Anthony 1997. *Samuel Beckett: The Last Modernist.* London: Flamingo.
Curr, John 1797. *The Coal Viewer, and Engine Builder's Practical Companion.*
    Sheffield: John Northall.
Deleuze, Gilles, and Félix Guattari 1983. *Anti-Oedipus: Capitalism and Schizophrenia,*
    trans. Robert Hurley, Mark Seem and Helen R. Lane. Minneapolis: University
    of Minnesota Press.
  1987. *A Thousand Plateaus: Capitalism and Schizophrenia,* trans. Brian Massumi.
    Minneapolis: University of Minnesota Press.
Dennett, Daniel C. 1993. *Consciousness Explained.* Harmondsworth: Penguin.
Department of Defense, U.S. 2002. 'DoD News Briefing – Secretary Rumsfeld and
    General Myers', 12 February 2002. http://www.defense.gov/transcripts/tran-
    script.aspx?transcriptid=2636 [Accessed 24 May 2014].
Derrida, Jacques 1976. *Writing and Difference,* trans. Alan Bass. London: Routledge
    and Kegan Paul.
  1982. *Margins of Philosophy,* trans. Alan Bass. Brighton: Harvester Press.
  1989. 'How to Avoid Speaking: Denegations', trans. Ken Frieden, in *Languages
    of the Unsayable: The Play of Negativity in Literature and Literary Theory,* eds.
    Sanford Budick and Wolfgang Iser. New York: Columbia University Press,
    pp. 3–70.
  1995. *On the Name,* ed. Thomas Dutoit, trans. David Wood et al. Stanford:
    Stanford University Press.
  2008. *The Animal That Therefore I Am,* ed. Marie-Louise Mallet, trans.
    David Wills. New York: Fordham University Press.
Dobbin, Beci 2014. *Granular Modernism.* Oxford: Oxford University Press.
Duckworth, Colin 2000. 'Beckett and the Missing Sharer', *Samuel Beckett Today/
    Samuel Beckett Aujourd'hui* 9: 133–43.

Eliot, T. S. 1958. *Selected Essays*. 3rd edn. London: Faber and Faber.

Ellmann, Richard 1982. *James Joyce*. 2nd edn. New York, Toronto and Oxford: Oxford University Press.

Esslin, Martin 1982. 'Samuel Beckett and the Art of Broadcasting', in *Mediations: Essays on Brecht, Beckett and the Media*. New York: Grove Press, pp. 125–54.

Feldman, Matthew 2006. *Beckett's Books: A Cultural History of Samuel Beckett's 'Interwar Notes'*. London: Continuum.

Fenton, James 2006. 'Read My Lips', *Guardian* (29 July). http://www.guardian.co.uk/books/2006/jul/29/featuresreviews.guardianreview27 [Accessed 24 May 2014].

Fischer, Stephen Roger 2003. *A History of Reading*. London: Reaktion.

Fish, Stanley 1994. *There's No Such Thing As Free Speech, And It's a Good Thing Too*. Oxford: Oxford University Press.

Forster, E. M. 2005. *A Passage to India*, ed. Oliver Stallybrass. London: Penguin.

Fox, Douglas 2009. 'Timewarp: How Your Brain Creates the Fourth Dimension', *New Scientist* 2731 (21 October): 32–7.

Fox, George 1660. *A Word to the People of the World: Who Hates the Light, to Be Witnessed by the Light in Them All*. London: Thomas Simmons.

Freud, Sigmund 1955. 'Beyond the Pleasure Principle', in *The Standard Edition of the Complete Psychological Works of Sigmund Freud, Volume XVIII (1920–1922): Beyond the Pleasure Principle, Group Psychology and Other Works*, trans. James Strachey et al. London: Hogarth Press, pp. 1–64.

1961a. 'Negation', in *The Standard Edition of the Complete Psychological Works of Sigmund Freud, Volume XIX (1923–1925): The Ego and the Id and Other Works*, trans. James Strachey et al. London: Hogarth, pp. 233–9.

1961b. 'A Note Upon the "Mystic Writing-Pad"', in *The Standard Edition of the Complete Psychological Works of Sigmund Freud, Volume XIX (1923–1925): The Ego and the Id and Other Works*, trans. James Strachey et al. London: Hogarth, pp. 227–34.

Frost, Everett C. 1999. 'Mediatating on Beckett, Embers and Radio Theory', in *Samuel Beckett and the Arts: Music, Visual Arts, and Non-Print Media*, ed. Lois Oppenheim. New York: Garland, pp. 311–31.

Gadamer, Hans-Georg 2006. *A Century of Philosophy: Hans-Georg Gadamer in Conversation With Ricardo Dottori*, trans. Rod Coltman and Sigrid Koepke. London and New York: Continuum.

Garner, Stanton B. 1993. '"Still Living Flesh": Beckett, Merleau-Ponty, and the Phenomenological Body', *Theatre Journal* 45: 443–60.

Gavrilov, A. K. 1997. 'Reading Techniques in Classical Antiquity', *Classical Quarterly* 47: 56–73.

Gibson, Andrew 2006. *Beckett and Badiou: The Pathos of Intermittency*. Oxford: Oxford University Press.

Gluck, Barbara 1979. *Beckett and Joyce*. London: Associated University Presses.

Gontarski, S. E. 1977. 'Crapp's First Tapes: Beckett's Manuscript Revisions of Krapp's Last Tape', *Journal of Modern Literature* 6: 61–68.

and Anthony Uhlmann 2006. *Beckett After Beckett*. Gainesville: University of Florida Press.

Goodman, Nelson 1978. *Ways of Worldmaking*. Indianapolis, IN: Hackett.

Habermas, Jürgen 1996. *Between Facts and Norms: Contributions to a Discourse Theory of Law and Democracy*, trans. William Rehg. Cambridge, MA: MIT Press.

Hall, Michael 2006. 'More Kicks Than You Might Think', *Guardian* (13 April). http://arts.guardian.co.uk/beckett/story/0,,1751741,00.html [Accessed 15 August 2007].

Harmon, Maurice, ed. 1998. *No Author Better Served: The Correspondence of Samuel Beckett and Alan Schneider*. Cambridge, MA and London: Harvard University Press.

Harvey, Lawrence E 1970. *Samuel Beckett: Poet and Critic*. Princeton: Princeton University Press.

Hawthorne, Nathaniel 1991. *The House of The Seven Gables*, ed. Michael Davitt Bell. Oxford and New York: Oxford University Press.

Hayles, N. Katherine 1999. *How We Became Posthuman: Virtual Bodies in Cybernetics, Literature and Informatics*. Chicago: University of Chicago Press.

Heidegger, Martin 1975. *Poetry, Language, Thought*, trans. Albert Hofstadter. New York: Harper and Row.

1985. *Being and Time*, trans. John Macquarrie and Edward Robinson. Oxford: Basil Blackwell.

1995. *The Fundamental Concepts of Metaphysics: World, Finitude, Solitude*, trans. William McNeill and Nicholas Walker. Bloomington: Indiana University Press.

Hill, Jonathan 1978. *The Cat's Whisker: 50 Years of Radio Design*. London: Oresko Books.

Jajdelska, Elspeth 2007. *Silent Reading and the Birth of the Narrator*. Toronto: University of Toronto Press.

James, Henry 1961. 'Preface', *Roderick Hudson*. New York: Charles Scribner's Sons, pp. v–xx.

James, William 1981. *The Principles of Psychology*. Cambridge, MA: Harvard University Press.

Johnson, William A. 2000. 'Toward A Sociology of Reading in Classical Antiquity', *American Journal of Philology* 121: 593–627.

Joyce, James 1975. *Finnegans Wake*. London: Faber and Faber.

1986. *Ulysses: The Corrected Text*, ed. Hans Walter Gabler. Harmondsworth: Penguin.

Kamber, R. 1983, 'Sartre's Nauseas', *Modern Language Notes*: 1279–85.

Kattsoff, Louis O. 1955. 'Psychopathology of the Academic World', *Journal of Higher Education* 26: 311–18.

Kenner, Hugh 1961. *Samuel Beckett: A Critical Study*. New York: Grove Press.

Kern, Edith 1970. *Existential Thought and Fictional Technique: Kierkegaard, Sartre, Beckett*. New Haven and London: Yale University Press.

Kiberd, Declan 1985. 'Samuel Beckett and the Protestant Ethic', in *The Genius of Irish Prose*, ed. Augustine Martin. Dublin and Cork: Mercier Press, pp. 121–30.

Knowles, Sebastian D. G. 2003. 'Death By Gramophone', *Journal of Modern Literature* 27: 1–13.

Knowlson, James (ed.) 1985. *Happy Days: Samuel Beckett's Production Notebook*. London: Faber.

1996. *Damned to Fame: The Life of Samuel Beckett*. London: Bloomsbury.

Knox, B. M. W. 1968. 'Silent Reading in Antiquity'. *Greek, Roman and Byzantine Studies* 9: 421–35.

Kristeva, Julia 1984. *Revolution in Poetic Language*, trans. Margaret Waller. New York: Columbia University Press.

Kroll, J. L. 1977. 'The Surd as Inadmissible Evidence: The Case of Attorney-General v. Henry McCabe', *Journal of Beckett Studies* 2: 47–58. http://www.english.fsu.edu/jobs/num02/Num2JeriKroll.htm [Accessed 24 May 2014].

Lamont, R. C. 1959. 'The Metaphysical Farce: Beckett and Ionesco', *French Review* 32: 319–28.

Larkin, Philip 1988. *Collected Poems*, ed. Anthony Thwaite. London: Marvell Press and Faber and Faber.

Lyotard, Jean-François 1990. *The Inhuman: Conversations on Time*, trans. Geoffrey Bennington and Rachel Bowlby. Cambridge: Polity Press.

Maines, Rachel P. 1999. *The Technology of Orgasm: "Hysteria," the Vibrator, and Women's Sexual Satisfaction*. Baltimore: Johns Hopkins University Press.

Mandell, Laura 2007. 'What Is the Matter? Or, What Literary History Neither Hears Nor Sees', *New Literary History* 38: 755–76

Mandle, W. F. 1987. *The Gaelic Athletic Association and Irish Nationalist Politics 1994–1924*. London: Christopher Helm/Dublin: Gill and Macmillan.

Manguel, Alberto 1996. *A History of Reading*. London: HarperCollins.

Marinetti, F. T. and Pino Masnata 1992. 'La Radia', in *Wireless Imagination: Sound, Radio, and the Avant-Garde*, eds. Douglas Kahn and Gregory Whitehead. Cambridge, MA and London: MIT Press, pp. 266–8.

Martial (Marcus Valerius Martialis) 1993. *Epigrams*, ed. and trans. D. R. Shackleton Bailey. Cambridge, MA and London: Harvard University Press.

Marvell, Andrew 1971. *The Poems and Letters of Andrew Marvell*. 2 Vols. 3rd edn., eds. H. M. Margoliouth, Pierre Legouis and E. E. Duncan-Jones. Oxford: Clarendon.

Merleau-Ponty, Maurice 1968. *The Visible and the Invisible: Followed By Working Notes*, ed. Claude Lefort, trans. Alphonso Lingis. Evanston: Northwestern University Press.

1996. *Phenomenology of Perception*, trans. Colin Smith. London and New York: Routledge.

Millard, A. J. 2005. *America on Record: A History of Recorded Sound*. 2nd edn. New York: Cambridge University Press.

Monroe, B. S. 1910. 'An English Academy', *Modern Philology* 8: 107–22.

Mooney, Sinéad 2000. '"Integrity in a Surplice": Samuel Beckett's (Post-) Protestant Politics', *Samuel Beckett Today/Samuel Beckett Aujourd'hui* 9: 223–37.

Mortley, G. E. 1924. 'Crystal Rectification', *Weather and Wireless Magazine* 2: 13–14.

Morton, David L. 2004. *Sound Recording: The Life Story of a Technology*. Baltimore: Johns Hopkins University Press.

Müller-Doohm, Stefan 2005. *Adorno: A Biography*. Cambridge: Polity.

Nancy, Jean-Luc 2003. *A Finite Thinking*, ed. Simon Sparks. Stanford; Stanford University Press.

Nead, Lynda 2007. *The Haunted Gallery: Painting, Photography, Film c. 1900*. New Haven and London: Yale University Press.

Ong, Walter J. 1967. *The Presence of the Word: Some Prolegomena for Religious and Cultural History*. New Haven: Yale University Press.

Onimus, Jean 1968. *Beckett (Les Ecrivains Devant Dieu)*. Bruges: Desclée de Brouwer.

Ovid (Publius Ovidius Naso) 1567. *The XV. Bookes of P. Ouidius Naso, Entytuled Metamorphosis, Translated Oute of Latin into English Meeter, by Arthur Golding Gentleman...* London: William Seres.

   1987. *Amores: Text, Prolegomena and Commentary*, ed. J. C. McKeown. 4 Vols. Liverpool: Francis Cairns.

Oxenhandler, Neil 1970. 'Toward the New Aesthetic', *Contemporary Literature* 11: 169–91.

Pascal, Blaise 1962. *Pensées*. Paris: Editions du Seuil.

   1995. *Pensées*, trans. A. J. Krailsheimer. London: Penguin.

Phillips, Helen 2009. 'Déjà Vu: Where Fact Meets Fantasy', *New Scientist* 2701 (25 March): 28–31.

Pilling, John 1976. *Samuel Beckett*. London: Routledge and Kegan Paul.

Pinter, Harold. 1991. *Plays: One*. London: Faber and Faber.

Pound, Ezra 1971. *Selected Letters, 1907–1941*, ed. D. D. Paige. New York: New Directions.

Prigogine, Ilya, and R. Lefever 1968. 'Symmetry Breaking Instabilities in Dissipative Systems. II', *Journal of Chemical Physics* 48: 1695–1700.

Rayment-Pickard, Hugh 2003. *Impossible God: Derrida's Theology*. Aldershot and Burlington VT: Ashgate.

Richards, I. A. 2001. *Principles of Literary Criticism*. London and New York: Routledge.

Richardson, Stanley, and Jane Alison Hale 1999. 'Working Wireless: Beckett's Radio Writing', in *Samuel Beckett and the Arts: Music, Visual Arts, and Non-Print Media*, ed. Lois Oppenheim. New York: Garland, pp. 269–94.

Riley, Denise 2004. '"A Voice Without a Mouth": Inner Speech', *Qui Parle* 14: 57–104.

Rilke, Rainer Maria 2001. 'Primal Sound', in *The Book of Music and Nature: An Anthology of Sounds, Words, Thoughts*, eds. David Rothenberg and Marta Ulvaeus. Middletown: Wesleyan UP, pp. 21–24.

Saenger, Paul 1997. *Space Between Words: The Origins of Silent Reading*. Stanford: Stanford University Press.

Sartre, Jean-Paul 1948. *Existentialism and Humanism*, trans. Philip Mairet. London: Methuen.

   1976. *Nausea*, trans. Robert Baldick. Harmondsworth: Penguin.

   1984. *Being and Nothingness: An Essay on Phenomenological Ontology*, trans. Hazel E. Barnes. London: Methuen.

Schiller, Johann Christoph Friedrich von 1967. *On the Aesthetic Education of Man.* eds. and trans. Elizabeth W. Wilkinson and L. A. Willoughby. Oxford: Clarendon Press.

Schuchard, Ronald 1974. 'T S Eliot as an Extension Lecturer 1916–1919', *Review of English Studies* 25: 163–73, 292–304.

Seaton, Matt 2004. Rev. of *One More Kilometre and We're in the Showers: Memoirs of a Cyclist* by Tim Hilton. *Guardian* (10 July). http://books.guardian.co.uk/reviews/sportandleisure/0,6121,1257824,00.html

Segel, Harold B. 1998. *Body Ascendant: Modernism and the Physical Imperative.* Baltimore and London: Johns Hopkins University Press.

Serres, Michel 1982. *The Parasite*, trans. Lawrence R. Schehr. Baltimore: Johns Hopkins University Press.

   1997. *The Troubadour of Knowledge*, trans. Sheila Faria Glaser and William Paulson. Ann Arbor: University of Michigan Press.

   2001. *Hominescence*. Paris: Le Pommier.

   2006. *Récits d'Humanisme: Essais*. Paris: Le Pommier.

   2008. *The Five Senses: A Philosophy of Mingled Bodies (I)*, trans. Margaret Sankey and Peter Cowley. London: Continuum.

   2009a. *Ecrivains, savants et philosophes font le tour du monde*. Paris: Le Pommier.

   2009b. *Temps des crises*. Paris: Le Pommier.

Sharlemann, Robert P. (ed.) 1992. *Negation and Theology*. Charlottesville: University Press of Virginia.

Sloterdijk, Peter 2004. *Schäume: Sphären, Vol. 3: Plurale Sphärologie*. Frankfurt: Suhrkamp.

Steiner, George 1967. *Language and Silence: Essays 1958–1966*. London: Faber and Faber.

Suits, Bernard 1973. 'The Elements of Sport', in *The Philosophy of Sport: A Collection of Original Essays*, ed. Robert G. Osterhoudt. Springfield, IL: Charles C. Thomas, pp. 48–64.

Tertullian (Quintus Septimius Florens Tertullianus) 1956. *Q. Septimii Florentis Tertulliani De Carne Christi Liber: Tertullian's Treatise on the Incarnation*, ed. Ernest Evans. London: S.P.C.K.

Tiffany, Daniel 1995. *Radio Corpse: Imagism and the Cryptaesthetic of Ezra Pound.* Cambridge, MA and London: Harvard University Press.

Trower, Shelley 2012. *Senses of Vibration: A History of the Pleasure and Pain of Sound*. New and London: Continuum.

Uexküll, Jakob von, and George Kriszat 1992. 'A Stroll Through the Worlds of Animals and Men: A Picture Book of Invisible Worlds', trans. Claire M. Schiller, *Semiotica* 8: 319–91.

Vries, Hent de 2005. *Minimal Theologies: Critiques of Secular Reason in Adorno and Levinas*, trans. Geoffrey Hale. Baltimore and London: Johns Hopkins University Press.

Watt, Douglas F. 1990. 'Higher Cortical Functions and the Ego: Explorations of the Boundary Between', *Psychoanalytic Psychology* 7: 487–527.

Wolosky, Shira 1995. *Language Mysticism: The Negative Way of Language in Eliot, Beckett and Celan*. Stanford: Stanford University Press.

Wood, David 1990. *Philosophy at the Limit*. London, Boston, Sydney and Wellington: Unwin Hyman.

Wood, James 1999. *The Broken Estate: On Literature and Belief*. London: Jonathan Cape.

Woodward, R. S. 1905. 'Academic Ideals', *Science* NS 21.424 (January 13): 41–6.

Woolf, Virginia 1925. 'Modern Fiction', in *The Common Reader. First Series*. London: Hogarth, 184–95.

Wurtzler, Steve J. 2007. *Electric Sounds: Technological Change and the Rise of Corporate Mass Media*. New York: Columbia University Press.

Zeifman, Hersh 1975. 'Religious Imagery in the Plays of Samuel Beckett', in *Samuel Beckett: A Collection of Criticism*, ed. Ruby Cohn. New York: McGraw-Hill, pp. 85–94.

Zilliacus, Clas 1976. *Beckett and Broadcasting: A Study of the Works of Samuel Beckett for and in Radio and Television*. Åbo: Åbo Akademi.

Žižek, Slavoj 2003. *The Puppet and the Dwarf: The Perverse Core of Christianity*. Cambridge, MA and London: MIT Press.

Index